THE HALAKHAH AT QUMRAN

STUDIES IN JUDAISM IN LATE ANTIQUITY

EDITED BY

JACOB NEUSNER

VOLUME SIXTEEN

LAWRENCE H. SCHIFFMAN

THE HALAKHAH AT QUMRAN

LEIDEN
E.J. BRILL
1975

THE HALAKHAH AT QUMRAN

BY

LAWRENCE H. SCHIFFMAN
Assistant Professor of Hebrew, New York University

TUTA SUB AEGIDE PALLAS · EJB ·

LEIDEN
E. J. BRILL
1975

ISBN 90 04 04348 9

PRINTED IN THE NETHERLANDS

To my wife

פיה פתחה בחכמה ותורת חסד על לשונה

(*Prov. 31:26*)

TABLE OF CONTENTS

Acknowledgements IX
List of Abbreviations XI

Introduction 1
1. The Study of Qumran *Halakhah* 1
2. The Sources of Qumran *Halakhah* 4
A. *The Zadokite Fragments* 4
B. *Megillat Ha-Serakhim* 5
C. *The War Scroll* 7
D. *The Temple Scroll* 8
3. Comparative Sources 9
A. Bible 9
B. Apocrypha and Pseudepigrapha 10
C. Philo Judaeus 11
D. Josephus 12
E. Rabbinic Literature 13
F. Other Jewish Sects. 17
4. Qumran and the History of Jewish Law 19

I. Halakhic Terminology at Qumran 22
1. *Nigleh* and *Nistar* 22
2. *Meduqdaq*, *Nimṣa'*, *Perush*. 32
3. *Mishpaṭ*, *Miṣwah* 42
4. *Yissurim* 49
5. *Drš*, *Midrash* 54
6. *Serekh* 60
7. *Moshab Ha-Rabbim* 68
Summary: The Derivation of *Halakhah* at Qumran . . . 75

II. Introduction to the Qumran Sabbath Code 77
1. The Sabbath in Qumran Literature 77
2. A Form-critical Note on the Sabbath Code 80

III. The Qumran Sabbath Code: Text and Commentary . . . 84
1. The *Tosefet Melakhah* 84
2. Discussion of Business. 87
3. Walking in the Field 90
4. A One Thousand Cubit Sabbath Limit 91

5. Preparation of Food before the Sabbath 98
6. Eating and Drinking within the Camp. 101
7. Drinking and Washing on a Journey 102
8. Performance of Sabbath Work by a Non-Jew 104
9. The Cleanliness of Sabbath Garments 106
10. Entering a Partnership. 109
11. Pasturing Animals 111
12. Carrying from Domain to Domain 113
13. Opening a Sealed Vessel. 115
14. Wearing of Perfume Bottles. 116
15. Handling Rocks and Earth. 117
16. Carrying Infants. 119
17. Encouraging a Servant to Labor. 120
18. Caring for Domesticated Animals. 121
19. Spending the Sabbath among Gentiles. 123
20. Violation of the Sabbath for the Sake of Wealth. . . . 124
21. Saving ot Life 125
22. Sacrifices. 128
Summary: Qumran Sabbath Law. 131

Conclusion: *Halakhah* and the Identity of the Sect 134

Bibliography 137

Index of Citations 149

1. Hebrew Scriptures 149
2. Qumran Literature 152
3. Apocrypha and Pseudepigrapha 154
4. Philo and Josephus 154
5. New Testament 155
6. Rabbinic Literature.. 155
A. Mishnah 155
B. Tosefta 156
C. Palestinian Talmud. 157
D. Babylonian Talmud 157
E. Minor Tractates 158
F. Targumim 158
G. Midrashim 159

Index of Hebrew and Aramaic Terms Explained 160

General Index 163

ACKNOWLEDGEMENTS

This volume represents the major part of my Brandeis University dissertation *The Halakhah at Qumran* (February, 1974). I owe my training in biblical and Jewish studies to the efforts of the three scholars who constituted my dissertation committee. Professors A. A. Altmann and N. M. Sarna, both of Brandeis University, and Professor B. A. Levine of New York University. The present work is, in fact, a crystalization of that training. Professors Sarna and Altmann undertook to read each chapter as it was completed. Their comments and suggestions are everywhere evident. Professor Sarna was kind enough to reread the entire work before the final typing. The responsibility for any errors is, of course, mine. Professor Levine also read the completed manuscript and was of great help in preparing the work for publication. He was also a constant source of encouragement.

Professor S. Talmon of the Hebrew University discussed the project with me at its inception. Likewise, I gained substantially from discussions and correspondence with Professor J. Neusner of Brown University. I am most grateful to him for undertaking to publish my work in this series and for the support of the Max Richter Foundation toward its publication. A contribution for which I am most grateful has also been made by the Center for Near Eastern Studies of New York University, Dean R. Bayly Winder, Director. Professor P. Chelkowski of New York University assisted me in regard to the Persian derivation of the term *serekh*.

Finally, I wish to thank my wife for reading and typing the work several times, preparing the bibliography and indexes, and for her many excellent suggestions, and, most of all, for her unfailing encouragement of my research.

New York University
June 26, 1974

L.H.S.

LIST OF ABBREVIATIONS

For short title references or fuller bibliographic description see the Bibliography

ADRN	*Aboth de Rabbi Nathan*, ed. S. Schechter.
AJSLL	*American Journal of Semitic Languages and Literatures.*
ANET	J. Pritchard, ed., *Ancient Near Eastern Texts.*
APOT	R. H. Charles, ed., *Apocrypha and Pseudepigrapha of the Old Testament.*
B.	Babylonian Talmud.
BA	*Biblical Archaeologist.*
BASOR	*Bulletin of the American Schools of Oriental Research.*
BDB	F. Brown, S.R. Driver, C. Briggs, *Hebrew and English Lexicon of the Old Testament.*
BJRL	*Bulletin of the John Rylands Library.*
CBQ	*Catholic Biblical Quarterly.*
CDC	Cairo Damascus Covenant (*Zadokite Fragments* or *Damascus Document*).
DJD	D. Barthélemy, J.T. Milik, *et al.*, eds., *Discoveries In the Judean Desert* I; M. Baillet, J.T. Milik, R. de Vaux, *Discoveries in the Judean Desert* III.
DS	R. Rabbinovicz, *Diqduqe Soferim.*
DSD	Dead Sea Discipline (*Manual of Discipline* or *Rule Scroll*).
DSH	Dead Sea Habakkuk Commentary (*Pesher*).
DST	Dead Sea Thanksgiving Scroll (*Hodayot*).
DSW	Dead Sea War Scroll (*Scroll of the War of the Sons of Light against the Sons of Darkness*).
EJ	*Encyclopaedia Judaica* (1971-2).
Enc. Bib.	*Encyclopaedia Biblica* (*Miqra'it*).
Enc. Tal.	*Encyclopedia Talmudit.*
Ges.	E. Kautzsch, ed., *Gesenius' Hebrew Grammar*, trans. A.E. Cowley.
HTR	*Harvard Theological Review.*
HUCA	*Hebrew Union College Annual.*
"*HWT*"	"*Hashlamot We-Tosafot*," in *Mishnah*, ed. Ch. Albeck.
IDB	*Interpreter's Dictionary of the Bible.*
IEJ	*Israel Exploration Journal.*
JAOS	*Journal of the American Oriental Society.*
JBL	*Journal of Biblical Literature.*
JE	*Jewish Encyclopedia.*
JJS	*Journal of Jewish Studies.*
JNES	*Journal of Near Eastern Studies.*
(new) JPS	New translation, *The Torah*, and *The Book of Isaiah*, by the Jewish Publication Society.
JQR	*Jewish Quarterly Review* (O.S.= original series, N.S.= new series).
JSK	N. Wieder, *The Judean Scrolls and Karaism.*
JSS	*Journal of Semitic Studies.*
JTS	*Journal of Theological Studies.*
Lex. Bib.	*Lexicon Biblicum.*
LXX	Septuagint.
M.	Mishnah.
MD	P. Wernberg-Møller, *The Manual of Discipline.*
MGWJ	*Monatschrift für Geschichte und Wissenschaft des Judentums.*
MH	J. Licht, *Megillat Ha-Serakhim.*

MMY	H. Yalon, *Megillot Midbar Yehudah.*
MT	Massoretic Text.
M.T.	Maimonides, *Mishneh Torah.*
P.	Palestinian Talmud.
PAAJR	*Proceedings of the American Academy for Jewish Research.*
QS	C. Rabin, *Qumran Studies.*
RB	*Revue biblique.*
REJ	*Revue des études juives.*
RQ	*Revue de Qumran.*
RSV	Revised Standard Version.
T.	Tosefta.
Tan. B.	*Midrash Tanḥuma*ʾ, ed. S. Buber.
TK	S. Lieberman, *Toseftaʾ Ki-Fshuto.*
VT	*Vetus Testamentum.*
ZAW	*Zeitschrift für die Alttestamentliche Wissenschaft.*

INTRODUCTION

1. *The Study of Qumran Halakhah*

After the discovery by Solomon Schechter of the "Fragments of a Zadokite Work," the scholarly world was plunged into a long debate about the dating of this text. Schechter had dated the *Zakodite Fragments* to Second Temple times, suggesting affinities with the Dositheän sect of the Samaritans.[1] Because of many similarities of language, content, and form to Karaite literature, Büchler argued for Karaite origins.[2] S. Zeitlin has supported this theory of Karaite provenance, and at the same time he has made the text available in photographic format.[3]

Soon after Schechter's discovery, L. Ginzberg, in his work *Eine unbekannte jüdische Sekte*,[4] posited the existence in the Second Commonwealth of an hitherto undiscovered sect. Forty years later, Ginzberg's foresighted theory was to be proven by the discovery of the Dead Sea Scrolls.

The additional texts simply raised anew all the questions pertaining to the *Zadokite Fragments*. But this time, based on carbon dating of the cloth wrappings, paleographic evidence, and the types of pottery in which the scrolls were found, the vast majority of scholars decided in favor of Second Commonwealth dating.[5]

There was still no agreement on the nature of the sect. It was identified with Essenes,[6] early Pharisees,[7] an early Christian baptismal

---

[1] *Documents of Jewish Sectaries* (1910) I, XXI-XXVI.

[2] "Schechter's 'Jewish Sectaries,'" *JQR* N.S. 3 (1912/3), 429-85. Cf. A. Marmorstein, "*Eine unbekannte jüdische Sekte*," *Theologisch tijdschrift* 52 (1918), 92-122 and the survey in J. A. Fitzmyer, "Prolegomenon," in the 1970 reprint of Schechter, 14.

[3] *The Zadokite Fragments*, *JQR* Monograph Series 1 (1952), and (Review of R. T. Hereford, *The Pharisees*,) *JQR* N.S. 16 (1925/6), 385f.

[4] First published in *MGWJ* 55 (1911), 222-98, 56 (1912), 33-48, 285-307, 417-48, 546-66, 664-89, 57 (1913), 153-67, 284-308, 394-418, 666-96, 58 (1914), 16-48, 143-77, 395-429, and then in its entirety in 1922. This work is expected to appear shortly in an English translation (*An Unknown Jewish Sect*) which will include three previously unpublished chapters as well as some notes by H. L. Ginsberg and S. Lieberman.

[5] Most recently, see F. F. Bruce, "Dead Sea Scrolls, Description," *EJ* 5 (1971), 1398.

[6] This is the prevailing view (Fitzmyer, 15). Cf. W. H. Brownlee, "A Comparison of the Covenanters of the Dead Sea Scrolls with Pre-Christian Jewish Sects," *BA* 13 (1950), 50-72.

[7] C. Rabin, *Qumran Studies* (1957), especially vii-ix.

sect,[8] Zadokites,[9] and Zealots;[10] some persisted in considering even the new documents of Karaitic authorship.[11] To identify the Qumran sect, scholars have considered the *halakhot* and the peculiar contemporizing exegesis found in these texts. *Halakhah* and exegesis are necessarily interrelated, since in Judaism the *halakhah* is primarily derived through or anchored to Scriptural interpretation or hermeneutics.

In Rabbinic Judaism there is an added feature, the oral Law. Strangely, with all the comparisons that have been made between the Qumran and Rabbinic legal systems, there has been little inquiry into the basic question: Did the sect have an oral Law? If not, how did the sect supplement biblical law, at best an incomplete system?

In seeking to identify the sect, scholars have studied Qumran *halakhah* with a reverse methodology. They began with preconceived views on the nature of the sect and proceeded to demonstrate these by selecting specific laws through which the desired affinity could be shown. L. Ginzberg attempted to study all the laws in the *Zadokite Fragments* as a body, and to reserve judgment until he completed this work. Unfortunately, Ginzberg did not have the benefit of the Qumran scrolls.

In light of the new evidence now available, the *halakhah* of the sect demands a reexamination. It is necessary to reserve judgment on the question of the identity of the sect until its *halakhah* has been thoroughly investigated. Second, it is not justifiable to select only a few laws for study. One must review entire subjects and study all relevant material. Only then will a general picture emerge. Third, the comparative method must be applied for exegetical and perhaps historical purposes.

This volume is meant to be a beginning of such a comprehensive investigation. What has been done here is to inquire into the general principles of Qumran *halakhah* and the question of oral Law. A study

---

[8] J. L. Teicher, "The Dead Sea Scrolls: Documents of a Jewish Christian Sect of Ebionites," *JJS* 2 (1951), 67-99.

[9] In the title of Rabin's edition (Fitzmyer 14, 36 n. 8a).

[10] G. R. Driver, *The Judean Scrolls: The Problem and a Solution* (1964), and C. Roth *The Historical Background of the Dead Sea Scrolls* (1958). But see Fitzmyer, 37 n. 15 for criticism of this theory.

[11] S. Zeitlin, "History, Historians and the Dead Sea Scrolls," *JQR* N.S. 55 (1964/5), 97-116, and earlier, "The Essenes and Messianic Expectations," *JQR* N.S. 45 (1954/5), 83-119, and "The Pharisees," *JQR* N.S. 52 (1961/2), 97-129.

of legal terms in the Dead Sea Scrolls is undertaken in chapter 1 to see how the law is derived. Terms for law or legal institutions are examined one by one. All passages which elucidate these expressions are assembled, provided with philological notes, and discussed. For each term a definition emerges which helps to clarify the method by which the sect derived its law. The terms are not studied out of context, but rather they are discussed with other expressions to which they are connected.

This study, in attempting to develop a method for the analysis of a body of *halakhot*, has taken the Sabbath laws as a paradigm. It must be remembered, however, that the selection of one area of the Qumran law limits somewhat the conclusions that may be drawn. Only after a study of all legal material from Qumran will further observations about its general character be possible.

Chapter 2 contains a discussion of non-legal references to the Sabbath in Dead Sea literature which form the background for the Sabbath code. Then the literary features of the laws are examined in light of recent form-critical studies of biblical and Rabbinic literature.

The Sabbath laws themselves are dealt with in chapter 3 which provides the text with philological notes and detailed commentary. One of the conclusions which emerges from chapter 1 is extremely helpful in studying the Sabbath *halakhot*. The term *perush* implies an exegesis based only on the analysis of the text in question, without recourse to other passages from Scripture. *Midrash*, on the other hand, is an exegesis in which a corroborative passage in Scripture plays a part. Two passages may be harmonized, or one explained in light of the other. In studying the Sabbath laws of the sect we may classify each law as a *perush* or *midrash*. This is a first step toward understanding the hermeneutical system of the Qumran sect.

In preparing the commentary, texts were assembled from all systems of *halakhah* in an effort to elucidate the laws of Qumran. These comparisons may eventually result in historical conclusions.

Comparative material presents a problem, however. The value of the conclusions drawn is dependent on the relationship, chronological and historical, of the traditions surveyed. Thus, it is important to determine the provenance and textual history of the materials. Such an understanding is a *sine qua non* for a study of this type. Although there are many advantages to the comparative method, we must recognize the limitations of the sources before us.

2. *Sources of Qumran Halakhah*

A. *The Zadokite Fragments*

The *Zadokite Fragments*, found in the Cairo *genizah* in two fragmentary manuscripts, were first published by S. Schechter.[12] Schechter's reading of the manuscripts was somewhat inaccurate,[13] and he insisted that Cambridge University not give anyone access to the original for five years. The result was that the commentaries of R. H. Charles,[14] L. Ginzberg, M. H. Segal[15] and others were made on the basis of Schechter's edition. All the emendations they proposed were based on speculation. Access to the manuscripts would have clarified many of these questions. Writing after the discovery of the Qumran scrolls, C. Rabin reedited the text under the title *The Zadokite Documents*. His commentary makes ample reference to the new material from the Judean desert. The methodology of the edition is problematical, however. Where MSS. A and B overlap, they are combined so that an eclectic text results. But it seems more likely that these are two recensions, and adding them together only obscures the meaning of the text. Second, Rabin lists all the readings suggested by his predecessors, without regard to whether they are possible readings of the manuscript or emendations made during the initial five years. For these reasons it is necessary to study the photographic plates published by S. Zeitlin.[16]

In 1952 cave 4 was discovered. In it were found seven or eight fragments of this text (4QD$^{a\text{-}g\,(h)}$). These are still not completely published.[17] Additional fragments were found in caves 5 and 6.[18] It is therefore legitimate to consider the Cairo text part of Qumran literature.

The objection might be raised that perhaps the sect only read this work but did not adhere to its laws. Yet the linguistic and conceptual affinities between this and other sectarian texts establish the origin of the *Zadokite Fragments* at Qumran.

---

12 *Documents* I.

13 See the list of corrections in Fitzmyer, 20-24.

14 *Apocrypha and Pseudepigrapha of the Old Testament* (1913) II, 785-834.

15 "*Sefer Berit Dameseq*," *Ha-Shiloaḥ* 26 (1912), 390-406, 483-506.

16 Unfortunately, the quality of these reproductions is not very good. Better copies can be obtained from Cambridge University Library.

17 See Fitzmyer, 37 n. 13 for bibliography.

18 See M. Baillet, J. T. Milik, R. de Vaux, *DJD* III, 128-131, 181 and Fitzmyer, n. 14.

Rabin has divided the work into two sections, the admonition and the laws. The admonition is a Deuteronomy-like speech designed to encourage adherence to the teachings and *halakhot* of the sect. It expresses the attitudes of the sect to its laws. The laws deal with oaths and vows, communal organization, Sabbath and purity. Milik, who is to publish the new fragments, has indicated that the order of the text must be modified somewhat in light of his new material.[19] Further, the unpublished manuscripts throw light on new areas of *halakhah*: cultic purity of priests and sacrifices, diseases, fluxes of men and women, laws of marriage, agriculture and tithes, relations with pagans and between the sexes, a prohibition of magic, etc. A bibliography on the *Zadokite Fragments* has been prepared by J. Fitzmyer.[20]

B. *Megillat Ha-Serakhim*

The *Megillat Ha-Serakhim*, also called *Rule Scroll*, was among the first group of complete texts found. This scroll is so named because it contains collections of regulations, each collection called a *serekh*. The scroll is comprised of three independent compositions. For this reason the scribe left the concluding column of the first two sections blank.[21] The first and largest text is the *Serekh Ha-Yaḥad*, the *Manual of Discipline*. This text prescribes the sectarian way of life and system of beliefs for the present. Halakhic material in this document covers the initiation of new members, the organization of the sect, the penal system (regarding sectarian offenses) and the sectarian legislative and judicial assembly, the *moshab ha-rabbim*. There is also much material revealing the sectarian attitude to the law. Many subjects treated in the *Zadokite Fragments* are not discussed in the *Manual of Discipline*. It is probable that the *Manual of Discipline* assumes the existence of a full code, either in a more complete recension of the *Zadokite Fragments* than is presently known or in another work. It must be emphasized that the halakhic material in the *Manual of Discipline* pertains only to the internal organization of the sect. The text is a collection of short codes, probably composed individually and then redacted.[22]

The *Serekh Ha-ʿEdah*, or *Rule of the Community*, is concerned with eschatological *halakhah*. It pertains to Israel and the sect after the war

---

19 Fitzmyer, 17-19.
20 Pp. 25-34.
21 J. Licht, *Megillat Ha-Serakhim* (1965), 3-5.
22 *Ibid.*, 18-24.

described in the *War Scroll.* The first part of this short text outlines a ceremony at which the people of Israel come to the sect to be instructed in the Law. The second deals with the obligations and rights of a citizen (*'ezraḥ*) and with the organization of the community of the future. The third section discusses the banquet which is led by the Messiahs of Aaron and Israel.[23]

The *Serekh Ha-Berakhot*, or *Rule of Benedictions*, is in fragmented condition. It contains three blessings to be uttered by the *maskil* [24] for those who revere God (the sect), the Zadokite priests, and the prince (*nasi'*). This text is also eschatological.[25]

The importance of these last two texts in terms of *halakhah* lies in their presentation of idealized views of the future. Such ideals are often the development of tendencies already visible in the present. Thus these texts sometimes help to clarify questions relating to the sect's law. Further, all of these materials share a common terminology.

While the *Manual of Discipline* is well-preserved, the *Rule of the Community* and the *Rule of Benedictions* are fragmentary. The *Manual of Discipline* was already published with photographic plates in 1951.[26] It was not until 1955 that the other texts appeared, likewise in transcription and photographic plates.[27] Additional texts of the *Manual of Discipline* were found in cave 4 (4QS^{a-j}).[28] Although these do not constitute an entire scroll, they allow the comparison of readings for many parts of the text. Many of these readings contradict previously proposed emendations. Unfortunately, no variants have been found for the other two texts.

The *Manual of Discipline* has been edited several times. W. H. Brownlee was the first to publish a commentary.[29] Notable is the work of P. Wernberg-Møller who provided this document with textual notes, translation and commentary.[30] J. Licht has published

---

[23] *Ibid.*, 242-5.

[24] On this term see chap. 1, n. 24.

[25] Licht, *MH*, 273-5.

[26] M. Burrows, J. Trever, W. H. Brownlee, *The Dead Sea Scrolls of St. Mark's Monastery, Vol. II, Fascicle 2*; *Plates and Transcription of the Manual of Discipline* (1951).

[27] D. Barthélemy, J. T. Milik, *et al. DJD* I, 107-130, plates xxii-xxix.

[28] J. T. Milik, "*Texte des variantes des dix manuscripts de la Règle de la Communauté trouvés dans la grotte 4*," *RB* 67 (1960), 411-16.

[29] *The Dead Sea Manual of Discipline*, *BASOR* Supplementary Studies, 10-12 (1951).

[30] *The Manual of Discipline* (1957).

an excellent edition of all three *serakhim* with introduction, textual apparatus and commentary.[31] The importance of this edition also lies in its consideration of the previously divided scroll as a whole. Licht also includes fragments from "parallel compositions"[32] found in cave 5.

C. *The War Scroll*

The War of the Sons of Light against the Sons of Darkness conforms in style, language and ideas to the bulk of the Qumran literature. The purpose of this scroll is to describe the plans and regulations for the final battle of the sect against its enemies. This war, which must be fought in accord with the laws of Moses, is to usher in the eschaton. The scroll specifies in detail the laws of the Torah relating to military tactics and organization. It also includes a liturgy to be recited in connection with the battles. It must be remembered that the purpose of this text was to supply information which the Qumranites expected to need in the near future. They thought they were living on the verge of the end of days. The scroll deals in detail, among other things, with the laws of conscription, purity of the camp, sacrificial cult, prayers and thanksgivings.[33] All of these are subjects which must be part of the discussion of Qumran *halakhah*.

The text was first published by E. L. Sukenik,[34] and additional fragments were published by C. H. Hunzinger.[35] Y. Yadin has published two editions, the first of which is in Hebrew.[36] In the preface to the English translation of this edition, Yadin writes that he has made changes and additions.[37] For most purposes, then, the English edition is the most thorough and up-to-date. It includes an introduction dealing with the plan of the war, military organization, equipment, rites, theology of the sect, etc. Text, translation and commentary follow. This transcription diverges in only minor details from that prepared by Sukenik.

---

[31] *Megillat Ha-Serakhim* (1965).

[32] Pp. 304-6.

[33] Y. Yadin, *The Scroll of the War of the Sons of Light against the Sons of Darkness* (1962), 3-17.

[34] *Megillot Genuzot*, 2 vols. (1948, 50), republished and expanded in *'Oṣar Ha-Megillot Ha-Genuzot* (1956).

[35] "*Fragmente einer älteren Fassung des Buches Milḥamā aus Höhle 4 von Qumrān*," *ZAW* 69 (1957), 131-51. Cf. *DJD* 1, 135f.

[36] *Megillat Milḥemet Bene 'Or Bi-Bene Ḥoshekh* (1955).

[37] *War Scroll*, vii-ix.

D. *The Temple Scroll*

When the *Temple Scroll* is published, it should provide a wealth of material on Qumran *halakhah*. The content of the scroll, according to Y. Yadin, concerns four major areas: (1) a collection of *halakhot* on various subjects, including ritual purity, (2) enumeration of sacrifices and offerings for the various festivals, (3) description of the building of the Temple, and (4) statutes of the king and the army. The author wanted his work to appear to be a divine revelation to Moses. Rules are stated by God in the first person singular. The author groups laws by subject and supplies many laws not found in the Torah or later legal traditions. The scroll is unusually strict in matters of ritual purity, and there is a special section pertaining to burial and the dead. Many of these laws can be compared with their Mishnaic counterparts.

Detailed laws of festivals and their offerings are provided. Mention is made of two festivals previously unknown. A solar calendar like that of the other Dead Sea documents and Jubilees is followed throughout. According to the scroll, the omer period began on the first Sunday after the first day of Passover.

The most important subject of this text is the Temple. Its dimensions and layout are not in agreement with those of Herod's sanctuary. There is a description of the celebration of Tabernacles in relation to which ritual purity is discussed.

Then follow rules about the king and his army, which do not agree with those of the *War Scroll*. While the *War Scroll* describes offensive warfare, the *Temple Scroll* deals with defensive operations.[38]

From the information given by Yadin, not only are there new areas of *halakhah* to be explored, but this text may yield information on how the law was derived at Qumran. In chapter one we deal with halakhic exegesis as a method for derivation of the law. Most of the laws in the *Zadokite Fragments* are obliquely derived—the sources are not stated. The *Temple Scroll* seems to link its *halakhot* with Scripture. This text should allow more detailed study of the methods by which sectarian law was determined.

It stands to reason that in the absence of this text, many of the conclusions of this study must remain tentative in nature, for it is certain that publication of the scroll will necessitate modifications in the interpretation of individual problems and texts.

[38] Y. Yadin, "The Temple Scroll," *New Directions in Biblical Archaeology*, ed. D. N. Friedman, J. Greenfield (1971), 156-166.

From these sources, the following emerge as the main areas of Qumran *halakhah*: (1) organization of the sect, (2) Sabbath, (3) calendar, (4) ritual purity, (5) oaths and vows, (6) courts and testimony, (7) cult and ritual, (8) war, and (9) the eschatological ritual. There is one other area of *halakhah* which has recently been shown to be fertile ground for study—the scribal practice.[39] This area differs in that the implied *halakhot* which guided the scribes of Qumran must be extracted from the study of their manuscripts. While all these areas are of importance for an understanding of the sect, the study to follow will concentrate on the Sabbath as a paradigm for further research. It is hoped that the method applied here will be used for the remaining areas of law as well.

3. *Comparative Sources*

A. *Bible*

It stands to reason that no study of the Dead Sea sect, steeped as it was in the study and copying of the Bible, can proceed without close attention to biblical material. First, it is necessary to investigate all legal terms against their biblical background. Not only will such a study provide an idea as to how the term was used in earlier Hebrew, but it may provide an important clue to Qumran usage. The meaning of a term or expression in Qumran literature may be a reflex of a usage encountered in the sect's studies. The term or phrase may be used in a way peculiar to the sect due to a sectarian exegesis of the pertinent biblical material.

Second, the study of each area of Qumran *halakhah* must be preceded by a study of relevant biblical texts. This is especially true if we assume that Qumran law represents a certain understanding of Scripture. Unless the student of the sect approaches the Bible without preconceptions, he may fail to see how a certain exegesis has conditioned the law of the sect.

Third, both legal codes and narrative accounts must be considered. From narratives it is possible to learn how people lived, from codes, how they were supposed to live. In other words, it is not sufficient to look only at the legal codes of the Pentateuch. All relevant material must be examined.

---

[39] J. P. Siegel, *The Scribes of Qumran, Studies in the Early History of Jewish Scribal Customs, with Special Reference to the Qumran Biblical Scrolls and to the Tannaitic Traditions of MASSEKHETH SOFERIM*, Brandeis Univ. Doctoral Dissertation, 1972. Cf. his "The Employment of Palaeo-Hebrew Characters for the Divine Names at Qumran in the light of Tannaitic Sources," *HUCA* 42 (1971), 159-172.

Fourth, the sect considered itself as continuing the traditions of biblical Israel. It is necessary to look at biblical traditions historically and to ask whether the sect's views do not often derive from the period of the return. This point has been emphasized by S. Talmon. There can be no doubt that many practices of the sect can be traced to this period.

B. *Apocrypha and Pseudepigrapha*

The Apocrypha and pseudepigrapha are works dating primarily from the Second Commonwealth period.[40] A number of these texts, as well as writings of this genre previously unknown, were unearthed at Qumran.[41] Thus the relevance of the Apocrypha and pseudepigrapha for the study of Qumran literature is established. It is certain that the legal traditions of Jubilees, Enoch, Tobit, etc. were known to the sect. The existence of some common legal traditions, like that of the solar calendar, does not prove that the Qumran sect authored any of these works. It is more likely that they originated in related sects and represented part of the library at Qumran. Noteworthy for their halakhic content are Jubilees, Susanna, Tobit and Judith.[42]

Since a large part of the study to follow concerns the Sabbath, it is important to discuss the book of Jubilees which contains much of value on this subject. L. Finkelstein[43] points out that the book of Jubilees must be considered in light of Rabbinic sources since it was "doubtless written in Hebrew, contains numerous laws and allusions to Aggadic statements, and presents generally the appearance of a targum or midrash."[44] Nevertheless, the book did not originate with either the Pharisees or the Sadducees. Schechter[45] has shown that it cannot be Pharisaic as the lunar calendar was of prime importance to the Pharisees, and Jubilees espouses a solar calendar. It cannot be of Sadducean origin because the author accepts the immortality of the soul and differs considerably with the Sadducean calendar. Finkelstein

---

40 For a survey see J. Licht, "*Sefarim Ḥiṣonim U-Genuzim*," *Enc. Bib.* 5, 1103-1121.

41 F. M. Cross, *The Ancient Library of Qumran* (1961), 44, *DJD* I, 82-107.

42 See Ch. Tchernowitz, *Toledot Ha-Halakhah* IV (1950), 343-410.

43 "The Book of Jubilees and the Rabbinic Halaka," *HTR* 16 (1923), 39-61. Cf. A. Epstein, "*Le Livre des Jubilés*," *REJ* 22 (1891), 16-20, H. Bietenhardt, "*Sabbatvorschriften von Qumrān im Lichte des rabbinischen Rechts und der Evangelien*," *Qumran Probleme* (1963), ed. H. Bardke, 54f. who sees Jubilees as a Qumran text (See below n. 50).

44 P. 39.

45 I do not know to which of Schechter's works Finkelstein is referring. Perhaps it is the introduction to *Documents* I.

concludes that the book must emanate from some sectarian group (he wrote in 1923) and cautions, most wisely, against rejecting the possibility of sects whose existence is not yet known.[46] C. Tchernowitz[47] observes that in Jub. 45:16 the Torah was still in the hands of the priests rather than the scribes, pointing to composition during the Hasmonean period. The *Zadokite Fragments* indicate that the sect quoted Jubilees.[48] Indeed, texts of Jubilees were found at Qumran.[49] A further caution must be added to Finkelstein's. When dealing with sects, one need not find exact correspondence, only a common religious climate. When such a climate can be demonstrated, one group can shed light on the other. This is the case with the author of Jubilees and the Dead Sea sect.[50]

C. *Philo Judaeus*

Those works of Philo of primary value for the study of the *halakhah* are the ones which deal with the explanation of the Torah as a legal code, particularly the *Life of Moses*, *On the Decalogue*, and *On the Special Laws*. This last composition was the first attempt to subsume all the commands of the Torah under the Ten Commandments. In the course of these works Philo discusses his interpretation of the laws, often reflecting differences with the tannaitic law.

In approaching his *halakhah* it is necessary to ask what his sources were. Some studies have simply assumed that Philo drew on the Palestinian *halakhah* and that, accordingly, all his *halakhot* can be understood by reference to Rabbinic texts. This method was followed by B. Ritter,[51] but has two disadvantages. First, it neglects the fact that the Rabbinic collections are much later and contain material from as much as six hundred years after Philo. Second, this technique ignores the possibility that some of Philo's legal teachings may have derived from Hellenistic sources. Whenever available, Hellenistic

---

46 See also Tchernowitz IV, 345.

47 IV, 353f. J. N. Epstein, *Mebo'ot Le-Sifrut Ha-Tannaim* (1957), 227 dates the book to the second century B.C.E.

48 See below, 40 and the material in 85, n. 6, as well as S. Zeitlin, *Zadokite Fragments*, 15-18.

49 See below, 40, n. 118.

50 J. Grintz, "Jubilees, Book of," *EJ* 10 (1971), 325 and Bietenhardt in n. 43 take the view that Jubilees was a text authored by the Qumran sect. This is not possible for the material published in *DJD* I, 82-84, plate xvi, is sufficient to show that the Qumran Jubilees material is not in Qumran Hebrew but in a dialect similar to that of the MT.

51 *Philo und die Halacha* (1879).

sources must be taken into account to determine whether such influence may exist. Using such a method, I. Heinemann[52] has concluded that Philo is completely independent of Palestinian *halakhah* but draws on Greek and Roman sources. He denies Philo any acquaintance with the Palestinian "oral Law."

E. R. Goodenough[53] sees the basis of Philo's law in the decisions of the Jewish courts in Alexandria. Those laws having no Hellenistic parallel, he sees as having Jewish origin. S. Belkin[54] has shown that many of Philo's laws are best understood by reference to the Palestinian legal system. He accepts the view that the Jewish courts in Egypt also had a hand in these matters. He does not claim exclusive influence for Palestine, but steers a middle course. His purpose, though, is to investigate those laws to which the Palestinian *halakhah* is relevant. He demonstrates this connection unquestionably.

It is necessary to caution against the assumption that certain areas of law need not be considered in light of the Hellenistic tradition. One may think that Greek and Roman sources are of little value in understanding Philo's Sabbath law, yet S. Lieberman has shown how these traditions affected even laws of the cult.[55]

There are several ways in which Philo's *halakhah* may compare with that of the tannaim. There are numerous examples in which it deviates from the main part of a Rabbinic *halakhah* while agreeing in some details. Often Philo regards extra-biblical ordinances as authoritative interpretation of Scripture. Most important, he frequently agrees with an older *halakhah* of which remnants are found in tannaitic literature. Often Philo agrees with a view raised as a possibility in the Talmud and then rejected. Lauterbach cautions, however, against assuming that all Philonic deviations from Palestinian law represent older *halakhot*. Many are apparently traditions derived from Alexandrian courts and may never have been known in Palestine.[56]

D. *Josephus*

Josephus (c. 38 to after 100 C.E.) was a priest born in Jerusalem. According to his account, he was, as a youth, consulted in matters of *halakhah*. He also experimented with sectarian life. Especially im-

[52] *Philons griechische und jüdische Bildung* (1931-2, rep. 1962), methodological introduction, 5-15.

[53] Especially *The Jurisprudence of the Jewish Courts in Egypt* (1929).

[54] *Philo and the Oral Law* (1940). For a review of previous approaches, see viii-x.

[55] *Hellenism in Jewish Palestine* (1962), 115-179.

[56] "Philo Judaeus, his Relation to the Halakhah," *JE* 10, 15-18.

portant is the account of the Jewish sects given by Josephus. His *Jewish Antiquities* was written to acquaint the Greek-speaking world with the history of the Jews, and its purpose was polemical. In Book 4 Josephus discusses many *halakhot*, some of which embody traditions otherwise unknown. In his *Against Apion* Josephus lashes out against anti-Semitism. In the second part, he relates much information about the Jewish observances of his time.[57]

Ch. Albeck[58] has cautioned against the unconditional use of Philo and Josephus in studying the history of *halakhah*. He states that Philo is motivated by a Jewish feeling more than by Jewish teachings, while Josephus is writing for a non-Jewish audience and wants to amalgamate Judaism with Greek points of view. Both often derive their statements from Scriptural exegesis of their own, and may not represent the normative *halakhah* of their day.[59]

E. *Rabbinic Literature*

Rabbinic literature is a wide term for materials covering at least five centuries. We will see how important it is to distinguish the layers of material that make up this literature. An introductory word on its relevance and use in Qumran studies is necessary. Recently, J. P. Siegel has investigated the scribal practices and inherent *halakhah* of the scribes of Qumran.[60] He has made extensive use of Rabbinic literature, particularly of the tannaitic traditions in the post-Talmudic tractate Soferim. (It must be noted that almost all these traditions were verified by him as tannaitic by comparison with other Rabbinic texts.) His work shows how important Rabbinic literature can be for an understanding of the *halakhah* of the Dead Sea sect. There is no way of knowing what historical connections actually existed. What is important is that Judaism, even in this early period, was halakho-centric.

Tannaitic Judaism emerged out of the milieu which produced the Qumran scrolls. The processes of thought and legal derivation in the two systems can be mutually instructive in the same way that Babylonian *halakhah* can be understood with the help of Mesopotamian legal materials.[61] The comparative method is really the only

---

57 A. Schalit, "Josephus Flavius," *EJ* 10 (1971), 251-263 and bibliography, 265.

58 *Das Buch der Jubiläen und die Halacha* (1930), 3.

59 Cf. *ibid.*, 54 n. 188, 57f. n. 218.

60 See *Scribes of Qumran*, 8-11, 13-18.

61 Cf. B. Levine, "*Mulūgu/Melûg*: The Origins of a Talmudic Legal Institution," *JAOS* 88 (1968), 271-285. He convincingly demonstrates the influence of Mesopotamian law on Palestinian institutions.

way in which the complex legal texts from Qumran can be unraveled. However, this method must be applied critically. When similarities are found, one has to avoid jumping to unwarranted conclusions. But cautiously used, Rabbinic traditions can be of substantial help in studying the Dead Sea Scrolls.

There is one difference between the method employed here and that of J. P. Siegel. While he relies on the tractate Soferim as a source for tannaitic traditions, our method is to cite the tannaim from the earliest possible source. This insures that *baraitot* can be seen in the unexpanded form. It cannot be repeated too often that the date of a Rabbinic statement cannot alone be determined by the date of the collection in which it is found. Many traditions were passed down orally for hundreds of years before being redacted in collections. Each statement must be individually dated.

J. Neusner has recently studied the Rabbinic traditions relating to the pre-70 Pharisees.[62] Unfortunately, his method excludes all anonymous statements[63] (thought to be ancient by many scholars[64]) yet it has much value for our study. Neusner has suggested that the only way to verify the dates of traditions is to find them quoted or referred to in their present form by later authorities. Only in such cases is it possible to establish a firm *terminus ante quem*.[65] While we do not go so far as to assume that traditions not verified must not be early, there is no question that this technique of verification can be of great help in fixing the dates of Rabbinic traditions.

The Tosefta is extremely important for the study of Qumran *halakhah*. The Mishnah only embodies "normative" traditions. S. Lieberman has shown that the Tosefta may even contain references to the Dead Sea sect.[66] At the very least it contains many older *halakhot* and divergent views which may shed light on the laws of the sect. Likewise, many such traditions will be found in the tannaitic Midrashim.

The discussions of the Mishnah which took place in the academies of the amoraim were redacted in two collections, the Palestinian and

---

[62] *The Rabbinic Traditions about the Pharisees before 70*, 3 vols. (1971).

[63] See III, 281, 301 and below, 21 n. 81.

[64] See Urbach, "Mishnah," *EJ* 12 (1971), 94f., Ch. Albeck, *Mabo' La-Mishnah* (1959), 76, A. Guttmann, "The Problem of the Anonymous Mishnah," *HUCA* 16 (1941), 145. This is especially true of the descriptions of the Herodian Temple and its ritual.

[65] *Rabbinic Traditions* III, 180-185, *From Politics to Piety* (1973), 92-5.

[66] "Light on the Cave Scrolls from Rabbinic Sources," *PAAJR* 20 (1951), 395-404.

Babylonian Talmudim. These works are composites of tannaitic and amoraic material on all subjects. If used critically and historically, they can be valuable tools for research. The material in the Talmudim is of several kinds.

First, there is material which occurs in the various tannaitic collections already discussed. Here we follow the method of citing a tradition from its earliest source. It must be emphasized that the earliest version of a Rabbinic tradition is sometimes contained in a later compilation. The textual (or oral) history of the passage is often to a large extent independent of the collection in which it is found. Statements cited from tannaitic collections are usually in an earlier form than the often expanded quotations in the Talmudim. Even where the tannaitic source preserves a better text, it is often helpful to see how the material was interpreted by the amoraim. Here the student must beware. One cannot assume that the Talmudic understanding of a tannaitic tradition is necessarily correct.

The second type is of tannaitic traditions, *baraitot*, not found in any of the other known collections. Since these materials occur in an amoraic context, additional care is necessary. Further, there may even be fictitious *baraitot* in the Talmudim.[67] The tannaitic traditions are indicated by the redactors of the Talmudim by means of certain formulae preceding their citation. These statements are often quoted by the amoraim precisely because they contradict the Mishnah. These contradictions are often resolved by the Rabbis. For historical purposes, though, it is necessary to look at the unresolved and uninterpreted sources to see if they contain variant halakhic traditions. The *baraitot* of the Talmudim have been collected by M. Higger.[68]

A third stratum is that of the amoraic traditions. These are quite a bit later than the period of Qumran and therefore of considerably less relevance to the study of Qumran legal traditions. The amoraic traditions have two important aspects, however. They often provide explanations for *baraitot* which are not otherwise understandable, and they also raise exegetical possibilities. Since we conclude that Qumran law is based on halakhic exegesis, it is important to determine how the sect interpreted the Torah. The amoraic method involves the raising of as many possibilities as can be imagined, providing helpful suggestions of how one might interpret the Law. Often

[67] See L. Jacobs, "Are there Fictitious Baraitot in the Babylonian Talmud?" *HUCA* 42 (1971), 185-196, B. De Vries, "Baraita, Beraitot," *EJ* 4 (1971), 189-193.

[68] *ʾOṣar Ha-Baraitot* (1930-50).

these views lead to an understanding of the sect's *halakhah*. Speculation on historical lines of continuity is beyond the scope of this work.

Lest this methodology appear overly skeptical, it is necessary to point out that what is advocated here is not a disbelief or disrespect for the sources. Rather, each source is weighed as to its integrity and logical plausibility. When interpretations of the amoraim do not seem to reflect the plain meaning of tannaitic traditions, they are abandoned—but never before. It is always assumed that the amoraim were closer than we to the source of the material and may have been in contact with correct exegetical traditions.

The Palestinian Talmud[69] is especially important for the history of the *halakhah* because it often contains traditions not known from other sources. Sometimes it cites otherwise unattested *baraitot*. Since Palestinian and Babylonian law often differed, it is important to consider the material in the Palestinian Talmud as well as that in the Babylonian.

Because of the long and complicated history of the Talmudic traditions, Talmudic texts must be verified. The scholar must adopt a methodology to insure that he has a correct text. In this study, all passages were checked in the appropriate collations of variants and compared with parallel passages in other Rabbinic works (some of which are available in scientfic editions). Checking these texts is worthwhile, for on a number of occasions this safeguard helped avoid conclusions that would have been based on spurious texts. It must also be acknowledged that a thorough check of the manuscripts for every passage cited might have detected a few more errors. Such an effort, however, was beyond the scope of this project. It can only be hoped that critical editions of the remaining Rabbinic texts will appear in the near future.

A word must be said about traditional Talmudic commentaries. There is a tendency among some scientific investigators to assume that the works of their medieval predecessors deserve little attention. Sometimes we find Talmudic material cited and interpreted in a manner at variance with the entire exegetical tradition without even a footnote. The commentaries of the medieval scholars, particularly of the periods of the Geonim and *rishonim*,[70] are valuable for three reasons:

[69] See L. I. Rabinowitz, "Talmud, Jerusalem," *EJ* 15 (1971), 997-9.

[70] The *rishonim* are those scholars in the period between the close of the Geonic period (death of Hai Gaon) and the renewal of ordination by Meir ben Baruch Ha-Levi. The period in question extends from the middle of the eleventh century to the middle of the fifteenth. See I. M. Ta-Shma, "Rishonim," *EJ* 14 (1971), 192f.

First, they provide in-context, running commentaries which explain what the particular teacher means by his view. Second, the *rishonim* excelled in finding (and reconciling) contradictions between Talmudic materials. While we may often reject their harmonizations, the questions they raise and the material they collect are most helpful. Many times a possibility raised by these scholars can provide a key to understanding a Qumran *halakhah*. Third, these commentators often deal with textual problems and may testify to readings not available in any of the extant manuscripts. Further, they may explain the ramifications of the variant readings.[71] Thus traditional commentaries must be used, but critically.

In discussing the Sabbath Code (chapter 3), the derivation of a *halakhah* given in Rabbinic texts is often compared with that of Qumran. But do the Rabbinic derivations reflect the actual origins of the law, or later attempts to give support to already existing practices? This matter has long been disputed among scholars of Rabbinic Judaism. We can only say that comparison of the exegetical processes of the sectarians and the Rabbis is made with full knowledge that the Rabbinic derivations may be contrived. While beyond the scope of this study, we should say that Rabbinic traditions show evidence of the simultaneous operation of both processes. Some laws are actually the result of Scriptural interpretation. In other cases, exegesis provides support (called *'asmakhta'* by the amoraim) for previously known laws.

F. *Other Jewish Sects*

Samaritans.—Affinities in regard to language and biblical recension with the Qumran sect make comparison of the *halakhah* of the Samaritans to that of Qumran imperative. The only early Samaritan source is the exegetical *Memar Marqa'* (fourth century). The Middle Arabic halakhic texts are probably of medieval origin. To some extent the medieval Samaritan traditions were influenced by Karaism (to be discussed presently) and Islam. Samaritan materials, then, can be of real value only in suggesting avenues of thought and legal derivation. After all, the Samaritans are a literalist sect. Even if a large number of affinities between the *halakhah* of the Dead Sea sect and the Samaritans were found, the most that could be concluded would be the influence of the Dead Sea group on the Samaritans. There is no way of knowing what the Samaritan law was like in the pre-Christian period. Some

---

71 Cf. E. E. Urbach, *Ba'ale Ha-Tosafot* (1968), 523-574.

idea of Samaritan life can be gained from traditions about the Samaritans contained in works the dating of which is unquestionable. We will have occasion to cite such material from Rabbinic texts and Josephus. It must be remembered that these sources are biased against the Samaritans.

The Karaites.—Originated in the eighth century by Anan ben David and his followers (Ananites), Karaism represents the amalgamation of various heterodox trends in Babylonian-Persian Jewry.[72] Karaism absorbed the remnants of some previous sects possibly including the Sadducees and Boethusians. Some scholars have tried to date the Dead Sea Scrolls to the Middle Ages and to attribute their authorship to the Karaites.[73] Not only is archaeological evidence against this dating, but only a small number of exact correspondences can be found. What do exist are many correspondences in trend of thought, exegesis and terminology. It is here that comparative study of the two groups is important since many old schismatic traditions must have been part of the sectarian heritage of Karaism. Some of these may even go back to the Sadducean teachings of the Second Commonwealth.

The later history of Karaism involves the acceptance of many Rabbinite doctrines. For this reason, all later halakhic texts from this sect must be used with extreme caution. It is also important for this study that the Karaites reject the oral Law concept, yet derive a full *halakhah* through Scriptural exegesis. Most often used is the method of analogy (*heqesh*) which played an important part in the early *midrash halakhah* of Ezra.

The most important Karaite works for our study are Anan's *Sefer Ha-Miṣwot* and J. Hadassi's *'Eshkol Ha-Kofer* (of which legal material is only a small part). Much early material has been collected by S. Pinsker in his *Liqqute Qadmoniot* II. Especially important are the comparative studies of N. Wieder[74] and N. Golb.[75]

---

[72] See S. Baron, *A Social and Religious History of the Jews* V (1957), 209-285.

[73] See above 1f., nn. 2 and 11.

[74] *The Judean Scrolls and Karaism* (1962), "The Dead Sea Type of Biblical Exegesis among the Karaites," *Between East and West*, ed. A. Altmann (1958), 75-106, "The Qumran Sectaries and the Karaites," *JQR* N.S. 48 (1956/7), 97-113, 269-92, "Sanctuary as a Metaphor for Scripture," *JJS* 8 (1957), 165-175, "The Idea of a Second Coming of Moses," *JQR* N.S. 46 (1955/6), 356-64 "The Law-Interpreter of the Sect of the Dead Sea Scrolls: A Second Moses," *JJS* 4 (1953), 158-75, etc.

[75] "The Dietary Laws of the Damascus Covenant in Relation to those of the Karaites," *JJS* 8 (1957), 51-69, "Literary and Doctrinal Aspects of the Damascus Covenant in Relation to those of the Karaites," *JQR* N.S. 47 (1957), 354-74, etc.

Falashas.—The Falashas are an ethnic group in Ethiopia claiming Jewish descent. Their history and origin are still shrouded in mystery. Their sacred texts include the Bible, some Apocryphal and pseudepigraphal works and the *Te'ezaza Sanbat*, a treatise on the Sabbath containing many *halakhot*. M. Wurmbrand has shown that the *halakhot* in this text derive from the book of Jubilees.[76] In the event that they stem from the same circles that produced Jubilees, the Falashas would have some affinities with the Dead Sea sect. It must be remembered that there are elements in the Falasha tradition original to them and of medieval origin. For this reason, extreme care must be exercised in drawing conclusions about Qumran from the literature or practices of this sect. Texts of the Falashas have been assembled by W. Leslau in *The Falasha Anthology*.

4. *Qumran and the History of Jewish Law*

How will this research relate to the various questions regarding the history of Jewish law? Are the legal traditions of the Dead Sea community typical of Second Temple Judaism, and what can be learned from them about the development of the *halakhah* in this period?

We can state with certainty (chapter 1) that the Qumran legal traditions are derived exclusively through exegesis. It has been shown by Y. Kaufmann that exegesis for the derivation of law (*midrash halakhah*) was already in use in the period of the return.[77] This early *midrash halakhah* involved the analysis of relevant "biblical" material, the harmonization of conflicting sources, and the use of several passages to derive one law. Indeed, the nature of *midrash* as an exegetical method is that it involves the understanding of one passage in Scripture in light of another. For this technique, the examples cited by Kaufmann are the earliest we have. Even if the books of Ezra and Nehemiah are to be dated somewhat later than the period they describe, it would not change the fact that halakhic exegesis of this type was already in existence before the Qumran documents were written. S. Talmon has argued that, indeed, other Qumran traditions can also be traced back to this period.[78] No doubt the early years of the Second Common-

---

[76] "*Hilekhot Shabbat 'eṣel Ha-Falashim*," *Sefer Urbach*, ed. A. Biram (1955), 236-43.

[77] *Toledot Ha-'Emunah Ha-Yisraelit* IV, 327-9, 331-8, 346-51.

[78] "The New Covenanters of Qumran," *Scientific American* 225, no. 5 (Nov., 1971), 80.

wealth were formative for what was to become post-biblical Judaism. According to Talmon, the Dead Sea sectarians saw themselves as continuing the biblical tradition. So they may have imitated what they found in the later books of the Bible.

It can be asked, then, whether the Qumran system of legal derivation does not, in fact, date from the period of the return. Unfortunately, there is a gap of several hundred years between the sources, and we cannot be sure if Qumran exegesis represents a living tradition of the early Second Commonwealth. Furthermore, we still do not know if what is found at Qumran is evidence for the state of the law among other Jewish groups or is peculiar to the Qumran sect alone. Therefore, it is uncertain to what extent the conclusions of the study here presented can be used to reconstruct the history of what later became the Rabbinic tradition.

It is definite that the sectarians had no compunctions about putting their legal traditions into writing. This practice is in marked contrast to the later Rabbinic dicta discouraging or prohibiting the writing of *halakhot*. In Rabbinic tradition, the prohibition of the use of written halakhic texts was designed to reinforce the doctrines of oral Law and oral transmission. The concept of oral Law meant that there were laws which were not linked to any Scriptural derivation. Instead, these laws were believed to have been given orally on Sinai and passed down from Moses through the generations. Other laws were linked to Scripture by means of hermeneutical devices themselves believed to have been given orally on Sinai. The oral transmission doctrine and oral Law concept are entirely absent from Qumran.

It has recently been argued by J. Neusner[79] that these principles were introduced into Judaism in the Yavnean period. He is certainly right in stating that there is no evidence for oral transmission before Yavneh, except the legendary account regarding Hillel.[80] If so, it comes as no surprise that the Qumran sectarians wrote their laws. The bias against writing legal traditions only grew out of the oral Law concept, and that concept had not yet been introduced into Judaism.

---

[79] "Rabbinic Traditions about the Pharisees before A.D. 70: The Problem of Oral Transmission," *JJS* 22 (1971), 3f. Cf. *Rabbinic Traditions* (1971) III, 164.

[80] B. Shabbat 31a (tannaitic). Cf. *ADRN*, ed. Schechter, 31 a-b (both versions) and W. Bacher, "*Die Ausdrücke, mit denen die Tradition bezeichnet wird,*" *JQR* O.S. 20 (1908), 595, n. 1.

But can one argue that the absence of an oral Law at Qumran lends support to Neusner's thesis of its later origin? Neusner is primarily concerned with the Pharisaic-rabbinic tradition, and, until we can show that the Dead Sea sectarians are typical of the Judaism of their time, we cannot use them to prove anything about other groups. It is hoped that the study of further areas of Qumran *halakhah* can help to clarify the position of the Qumran sect within the Judaism of the Second Commonwealth. When this has been done, it may be possible to draw conclusions relevant to the history of Rabbinic *halakhah*.[81]

---

[81] On p. 14 we referred to Neusner's work on the Rabbinic traditions relating to the pre-70 Pharisees. Since going to press, Neusner's *A History of the Mishnaic Law of Purities* has begun to appear. Neusner has established "*prima facie* reliability of the attributions" of named traditions to Yavneh and Usha and went further to show that unattested or unassigned traditions "in principle and in detailed articulation are closely tied to an attributed law, or are diametrically opposed to a tradition assigned to a specific person and so may with confidence be located in the same division as the contrary law," *i.e.* at Yavneh or Usha. It is through close exegesis of the text that Neusner determines the close ties between assigned and unassigned traditions. Only a very small number of the anonymous traditions he studied cannot be dated with any degree of certainty. Neusner concludes that there is no evidence that the unnamed traditions originated earlier than the named ones. In other words, the anonymous traditions he investigated also derive from the Yavnean and Ushan periods (Neusner, *Purities* III (1974), 237-249).

CHAPTER ONE

HALAKHIC TERMINOLOGY AT QUMRAN

1. *Nigleh and Nistar*

The key to determining whether the Qumran sectarians had a doctrine of oral Law or not is the interpretation of the technical terms *nigleh* and *nistar*.[1]

DSD 5:7-12 mentions the *niglot* as the opposite of the *nistarot*.

כול הבא לעצת היחד יבוא בברית אל לעיני כול המתנדבים ויקם על נפשו בשבועת אסר לשוב אל תורת מושה ככול אשר צוה בכול לב ובכול נפש לכול הנגלה ממנה לבני צדוק הכוהנים שומרי הברית ודורשי רצונו ולרוב אנשי בריתם המתנדבים יחד לאמתו ולהתלך ברצונו ואשר יקים בברית על נפשו להבדיל מכול אנשי העול ההולכים בדרך הרשעה כיא לוא התשבו בבריתו כיא לוא בקשו ולוא דרשהו בתוקיהו לדעת הנסתרות אשר תעו בם לאששמה [2] והנגלות עשו ביד רמה לעלות אף למשפט ...

> Everyone who comes to the council of the community [3] shall enter the covenant of God in the presence of all the volunteers, and shall take upon himself through a binding oath [4] to return to the Law of Moses, according to everything which He commanded, with all (his) heart and all (his) soul, in respect of everything which has been revealed (*nigleh*) from [5] it to the Sons of Zadok, the priests who guard His covenant and seek His will, and to the majority of the men of their covenant who volunteer together for His truth and to live by His will. And he shall [6] establish by a covenant upon himself to separate (himself) from all men of iniquity who walk in the path of evil, for they have not been reckoned [7] in His covenant for they did not search and

---

[1] Cf. Deut. 29:28 and Ps. 19:13.

[2] Read *l'šmh* (*le-'ashmah*).

[3] On *yḥd* as a name for the "community" see S. Talmon, "The Sectarian *yḥd*—a Biblical Noun," *VT* 3 (1953), 133-140.

[4] Cf. Num. 30:11.

[5] Wernberg-Møller, *MD*, 95 explains that the use of the Torah as a source for *halakhah* requires the translation "from it."

[6] For the meaning of *we-'asher* in this context, see J. Licht, *MH*, 36f.

[7] Brownlee, *Manual*, *ad loc.*, points out that the *hofʿal* of this root is otherwise unknown. This may be a *hitpaʿel* from which the *taw* has fallen out. For this phenomenon see Licht, *MH*, 46 and H. Yalon, "*Asimilizaṣiah shel Taw Be-ʿIbrit U-Be-'Aramit*," *Tarbiz* 3 (1931/2), 99-106. Considering the initial *ḥet*, this would assume virtual doubling. The *hitpaʿel* of *ḥšb* occurs in Num. 23:9.

> did not study His laws [8] to know the secrets (*nistarot*) [9] in which they erred incurring guilt,[10] and the revealed (*niglot*) they did (violate) defiantly...

In this passage, W. H. Brownlee [11] translated *nistarot* "unconscious sins" and *niglot* "conscious sins." He did not explain, however, how the "men of iniquity" could be condemned for their transgressions if they did not even know they were violating the law. Nor does his explanation make clear the connection between knowledge and the "unconscious sins." In short, he fails to grasp the legal character of these terms.

P. Wernberg-Møller [12] translated "hidden" and "revealed things." He rightly observed that the "revealed things" referred to "the particular interpretations 'revealed' to the members of the community by study ...." [13]

Licht [14] realized that the first use of *nigleh* in this passage is slightly different from the second. The first refers to that revealed to the sect, while the second is known to the entire people of Israel. The *nistar* is understood by him to refer to the correct legal interpretations known only to the sect.

N. Wieder [15] concluded that the terms *nigleh* and *nistar* distinguish two kinds of precepts in the Torah. The *niglot* are those stated in clear terms about which there is no doubt as to meaning and manner of implementation. It stands to reason that there is no dissension concerning these. The *nistarot* are commandments worded in general or vague terms lacking detailed instructions as to how to carry out the law. The meaning and scope of these prescriptions is "hidden." Israel is divided about the meaning and interpretation of these com-

---

[8] This passage has presented problems for the commentators. They have seen *biqshu* as somehow governing the objective suffix of *ḥuqehu*. In fact, *bqš* here is in combination with the preposition *b* (as it is in Jer. 5:1) and should be translated by "search." The suffix on *derashuhu* should be taken as anticipating the object. All of this is conditioned by Zeph. 1:6. On the suffixes see Licht, *MH*, 44f.

[9] See Wernberg-Møller, *ad loc.* He opposes Brownlee's view that *nistarot* and *niglot* refer to transgressions committed in private and public.

[10] Cf. Lev. 4:3, 5:26, and new JPS, *ad loc.* See also H. Orlinsky, ed., *Notes on the New Translation of the Torah* (1969), 209f.

[11] *Manual*, *ad loc.*

[12] Translation, *ad loc.*

[13] P. 95, n. 36. Cf. his comments to DSD 1:9.

[14] *MH*, *ad loc.*

[15] *JSK*, 53-62.

mandments. Wieder points to the Sabbath law as a prime example of the *nistarot*.[16]

The sect attacked its opponents for not searching in the Law. The intensive search of the Torah (*midrash ha-torah*) was the only way of ascertaining the meaning of the *nistarot*. Wieder compares this doctrine to the Karaite view that the Torah is self-sufficient and self-explanatory; all meanings could be discovered through exegesis. Piety, however, was a prerequisite for discovering the meaning of the Law. Al-Qumīsī uses the same terms for these two classes of commandments, except that while the Qumran literature used *nif ʿal* participles, the Karaite used the *qal* passive.[17]

In this passage the knowledge of the sect is referred to as *nigleh*, "revealed," to the Sons of Zadok.[18] In other words, that which is *nistar*, hidden or secret, to the outside community may be described as *nigleh*, revealed, to the sect.[19] The text then goes on to say that the "men of iniquity" (enemies of the sect) did not study the law to learn of its secrets (*nistarot*).

The study of the law leads to knowledge of the *nistar*. Finally, the *nigleh* is known to the "men of iniquity" as otherwise it would be impossible for them to violate its prescriptions defiantly. This would seem to indicate that *nigleh* consists of God's revealed Law, the Torah.

The *nistarot* are also mentioned in CDC 3:12-16:

ובמחזיקים במצות אל אשר נותרו מהם הקים אל את בריתו לישראל עד עולם לגלות להם נסתרות אשר תעו בם כל ישראל שבתות קדשו ומועדי כבודו עדות צדקו ודרכי אמתו וחפצי רצונו אשר יעשה האדם וחיה בהם פתח לפניהם

> And with those who hold fast to the commandment(s) of God, who remained of them, God established His covenant with Israel eternally: to reveal to them secrets (*nistarot*) in which all Israel erred. His holy Sabbaths,[20] His glorious festivals, His righteous testimonies,[21] His truthful ways, and the desires of His will, which man shall observe that he may live,[22] He opened before them.[23]

---

[16] Cf. M. Ḥagigah 1:8.

[17] Wieder, *JSK*, 60f. An earlier but less accurate transcription of Al-Qumīsī's text appeared in L. Ginzberg, *Ginze Schechter* (1928-9) II, 473f.

[18] On the role of the Sons of Zadok, see below 72-5.

[19] Cf. the phrase *le-gallot nistarot* in CDC 3:13f. quoted below.

[20] For this phrase, see Neh. 9:14.

[21] Vocalizing *ʿedot*, as all the other phrases are pl. Cf. Ps. 119:138. It is also possible to vocalize *ʿedut*. Cf. Ps. 119:144.

[22] An adaptation of Lev. 18:5, which new JPS translates, "by the pursuit of which man shall live," and Neh. 9:29. Targum Jon. understands this to refer to "eternal life."

[23] Ginzberg, *MGWJ* 55 (1911), 682 connects this phrase with the following in CDC, citing Is. 41:18.

Laws concerning which God has made known to the sect the correct interpretation are referred to as *nistarot*. Other Jews are regarded as ignorant of this interpretation.

In DSD 9:13-14, a list of requirements for the *maskil*,[24] we read:

לעשות את רצון אל ככול הנגלה לעת בעת ולמוד את כול השכל הנמצא לפי העתים ואת חוק העת

> To do the will of God according to everything that is revealed from time to time [25] and to learn [26] all the knowledge (*sekhel*) which is derived [27] according to the times, and the law of the time.

Here the first clause refers to the *nigleh* and the second to sectarian knowledge, called *sekhel*, but, no doubt, equivalent to *nistar*. The law apparently changes with the times. [28] To the sect its present law was tailored to meet the prevailing stage of pre-Messianism. This progression or evolution of the law with the stages of history affected both the revealed and the secret. Only in the end of days would this progressive revelation be completed.[29]

---

[24] *Maskil* is a technical term denoting not only a wise man, but one who teaches wisdom (*sekhel*). See Wernberg-Møller, *MD*, 66 and Wieder, *JSK*, 104-120. Cf. Dan. 11:33, 12:3 in which the verb *yabinu* is applied to the activity of the *maskilim*. This verb must be taken in the sense of giving instruction, as in Neh. 8:7. It is interesting that the rècipient of this instruction in Dan. 11:33 is the *rabbim*. I have chosen to leave *maskil* untranslated because of the secondary implication of "wise men" which would be obscured by the translation "instructors." Against this interpretation of "instructors," cf. *melumede ḥoq* parallel to *maskile binah* in DSW 10:10. See now H. Kosmala, "Maskil," *The Journal of the Ancient Near Eastern Society of Columbia University* 5 (1973, The Gaster Festschrift), 235-241, especially 240.

[25] On the progressive revelation of the law, see Wieder, *JSK*, 67-70 and Rabin to CDC 6:14. For the *b* cf. the phrases *shanah be-shanah* and *paʿam be-faʿam* (Wernberg-Møller to DSD 8:15). The sequence *k*. . .*b*. . . occurs in 1 Sam. 18:10, Num. 24:1, Jud. 16:20, 20:30f., 1 Sam. 3:10, 20:25. I cannot locate an example of *l*. . .*b*. . . .

[26] Taking *lamod* as an inf. of *lmd*. Cf. *habdel* in l. 20. Habermann saw it as an inf. of *mdd* (Licht). Wernberg-Møller, *ad loc*., comments that "the phrase presupposes that the bulk of revelations was put down in writing and contained in a particular book," a view interesting in light of the thesis to be developed in this study. According to him (*MD*, 123) these revelations were contained in the *Sefer He-Hagu*.

[27] This term will be discussed below, 33-6.

[28] A number of fragments of DSD have been found. These in general exhibit minor variations from the text of 1QS. There is, however, one fragment which contains a shortened version of page 5 (Licht, *MH*, 6f.). I would doubt, however, that the versions of DSD reflect the changes of the law described here. Possibly, DSD and CDC reflect varying stages of development in certain areas of *halakhah*.

[29] Wieder, *JSK*, 69f.

Another passage contains the combination of *nigleh* and the root *skl* (DSD 9:18-20):

להשכילם ··· להלך תמים איש את רעהו בכול הנגלה להם היאה עת פנות הדרך למדבר ולהשכילם כול הנמצא לעשות בעת הזואת

The *maskil* is told:

> To teach them... to live [30] perfectly each man with his neighbor according to all which is revealed (*nigleh*) to them, *i.e.* (in) the time of clearing the path to the desert,[31] and to teach them (*le-haskilam*) all which is derived (*nimṣa'*) [32] (for them) to do [33] at this time.

This same idea of progressive change is found in DSD 8:15-16 in reference to the *nigleh*:

היאה מדרש התורה [אשר] צוה ביד מושה לעשות ככול הנגלה עת בעת וכאשר גלו הנביאים ברוח קודשו

> This is the interpretation of the Torah [34] [which] He commanded through Moses [35] to observe, according to [36] everything that is revealed (*nigleh*) from time to time,[37] and as the prophets have revealed by His holy spirit.[38]

This passage also informs us that the prophets are included in the *nigleh*; [39] the sect felt no compunctions about deriving law from the prophetic literature.

---

[30] Literally "walk." The phrase is based on Ps. 15:2.

[31] The sect regarded its return to the desert as preparation for the realization of its eschatological hopes. See S. Talmon. "The 'Desert Motif' in the Bible and in Qumran Literature," *Biblical Motifs*, ed. A. Altmann (1966), 55-63. The phrase is taken from Is. 40:3. Notice the connection of *ba-midbar* with the phrase following it. This is the opposite of the Masoretic accentuation, yet yields a parallelism. This same interpretation has been adopted in new JPS. Probably under the influence of Is. 40:3, MS. d reads *ba-midbar*. MS. e agrees with 1QS.

[32] MS. d reads *be-khol ha-nimṣa'*, probably an exegetical addition. MS. e reads *u-le-hamshilam be-khol*, "to rule them by all. . . ." Cf. Dan. 11:39, Ps. 8:7, and Job 25:2 for the *hifʿil* of *mšl*. The *hifʿil* in B. Sotah 36b is conditioned by Ps. 8:7.

[33] Alternately, "derived to be done," assuming a *nifʿal* infinitive from which the *h* has been assimilated.

[34] The term *midrash* (*ha-torah*) will be discussed below, 54-60.

[35] "Through Moses," so new JPS to Num. 4:37 and Wernberg-Møller, *ad loc*. MS. e omits the rest of this passage.

[36] "According to" is omitted in MS. d.

[37] See note 25.

[38] This term, *ruaḥ ha-qodesh*, is used regularly in Rabbinic literature for the gift of prophecy. See I. Heinemann, "*Die Lehre vom heiligen Geist im Judentum und in den Evangelien*," *MGWJ* 66 (1922), 173ff. Cf. Bacher, *ʿErkhe Midrash* (1922/3) I, 122f., II, 290-294.

[39] Note the use of *glh* for delivering a prophecy. Cf. DSD 1:3, CDC 5:21-6:1 (on this passage, see Y. Yadin, "Three Notes on the Dead Sea Scrolls," *IEJ* 6 (1956), 158-62, and Wernberg-Møller, *MD*, 130).

In a list of requirements for those joining the sect in DSD 1:9 the following difficult passage appears:

להתהלך לפניו תמים כול הנגלות למועדי תעודותם

> To walk before Him perfect in all that has been revealed (*niglot*)[40] for their appointed times.[41]

One might be tempted to take this as a reference to loyalty to the sectarian calendar, but the above passages ought to make clear that *le-moʿade teʿudotam* refers to the changing of the law in accord with the stages of history.

Further, the sectarian law—the *nistar*—must be kept secret by the sect. The *maskil* is required (DSD 9:17):

ולסתר את עצת התורה בתוך אנשי העול

> To keep secret (*le-satter*)[42] the counsel of the Torah [43] from [44] among the men of inquity.[45]

---

[40] Taking *temim kol ha-niglot* as a construct chain, as suggested by Licht (second interpretation), *ad loc.* See Ges. rules 128a, x.

[41] On this phrase see Wernberg-Møller, *ad loc.* The syntax here involves the linking in construct of a noun, *moʿadim*, "times," with another noun, *teʿudot*, connoting that which is appointed to happen by divine decree (so Licht, *ad loc*). The second noun serves as a modifier for the first. Cf. Ges. rule 128p. *Ruaḥ ha-qodesh* would be an example of the same syntax. H. Yalon, *Megillot Midbar Yehudah* (1967), 85f., takes *teʿudah* as a "convenant." This would require the translation "at the times of their covenants."

[42] The *piʿel* of *str* is a *hapax legomenon* (Is. 16:3). (Its passive (*puʿal*) occurs once in Pr. 27:5.) It is also used in DST 5:11. It is quite widespread in medieval Hebrew poetry (Even-Shoshan, *s. v.*). It cannot be determined, however, if this usage was an ancient survival, or, more likely, a poetic innovation based on the biblical usage. It is possible that this is a *qal* (*li-setor*), but this is less likely since the scrolls usually write *waw* for *ō* vowels (Licht, *MH*, 47).

[43] So also MS. e. MS. d reads *ʿaṣato*.

[44] Wernberg-Møller's proposed emendation of *be-tokh* to *mi-tokh* ("Textual Notes," *ad loc.*) is unnecessary in light of the demonstrated interchangeability of *b* and *m* as prepositions in biblical Hebrew. See N. M. Sarna, "The Interchange of the Prepositions *Beth* and *Min* in Biblical Hebrew," *JBL* 78 (1959), 310-316, C. H. Gordon, *Ugaritic Textbook* (1965), 92f., and M. Dahood, *Ugaritic-Hebrew Philology* (1965), 26f. For Phoenician cf. Z. Harris, *A Grammar of the Phoenician Language* (1936), 29f. (He wrote before Ugaritic and so did not understand the phenomenon.), J. Friedrich, W. Röllig, *Phönizisch-Punische Grammatik* (1970), rule 251 (and note), and W. F. Albright, "The Phoenician Inscriptions of the Tenth Century B. C. from Byblus," *JAOS* 67 (1947), 158, n. 42. More recently, see W. Chomsky, "The Ambiguity of the Prefixed Prepositions *bet*, *lamed*, *mem* in the Bible," *JQR* N. S. 61 (1970), 87-89. For the post-biblical period, see S. Greenberg, "*Le-Berurah shel Mishnah*," *Sinai* 10 (1941/2), 158f. We can assume that this interchange, like many other archaisms, survived in the Hebrew of the sect. Note, *e. g.*, the parallelism of *be-maʿayan* and *mi-maqor* in DSD 3:19. We will

(Note 45 p.t.o.)

Finally, DSD 8:1-16 clarifies the relationship between *nigleh* and *nistar*. In 8:1-2 we are told that when there are:

בעצת היחד שנים עשר איש וכוהנים שלושה תמימים בכול הנגלה מכול התורה ···

> In the counsel of the community twelve men and three priests [46] perfect in all which is revealed (*nigleh*) from [47] the entire Torah...,

after two years they should form a community (8:11f.):

וכול דבר הנסתר מישראל ונמצאו לאיש הדורש אל יסתרהו מאלה מיראת רוח נסוגה

> And anything which is hidden (*nistar*) from Israel and is derived [48] by the man who is expounding,[49] let him not keep it secret from these for fear of a backsliding spirit.

To begin a community [50] it is necessary for the 15 members to have perfect knowledge of the *nigleh*. After two years they form their community, and the expounder need never worry about keeping secret from them the *nistar*, known only to the sect, as they are all qualified members.

---

call attention to further examples throughout this study. I hope to collect them in an article sometime. For possible examples of this interchange in post-biblical Hebrew cf. the reading *mi-marom* for *ba-marom* in the grace after meals (S. Baer, *Siddur ʿAbodat Yisrael*, 560) and *mi-maʾor* for *be-ʾor* in the final blessing of the *ʿAmidah* (L. Finkelstein, "The Development of the Amidah," *Contributions to the Scientific Study of Jewish Liturgy*, ed. J. Petuchowski (1970), 176).

[45] The words to be kept secret in 2 (4) Esdras 14:6 are not to be taken as referring to an oral legal tradition but rather to apocalyptic teachings (Charles, *APOT* II, 621). Contrast the view of L. Ginzberg, "Tamid, the Oldest Treatise of the Mishnah," *Journal of Jewish Lore and Philosophy* 1 (1919), 34-37, who has taken the end of this chapter to refer to the entire corpus of tannaitic literature. Cf. *Legends of the Jews* (1968) IV, 357f., VI, 445f., n. 50. He is followed by Epstein, *Tannaim*, 15f. Note the statement in *Sifre* Deut. 87 (ed. Finkelstein, 151) on the need to say (transmit) the oral Law in secret (*be-seter*) (Licht). G. Allon, *Meḥqarim Be-Toledot Yisrael* (1970) I, 177-181 has shown that 4 Ezra cannot refer to the tannaitic literature. See also S. Belkin, *The Alexandrian Halakhah in Apologetic Literature of the First Century C. E.* (1936), 28f., and S. Brown, "The Secret of the Kingdom of God' (Mark 4:11)," *JBL* 92 (1973), 60-74.

[46] Note the chiasm: 12 ╳ men
priests ╳ 3

[47] See p. 22 n. 5.

[48] Both Licht, *ad loc.* and Wernberg-Møller to DSD 6:25 compare the form *wnʿnsw* in DSD 6:25 suggesting that in both cases the final *waw* may be considered extra. Licht is no doubt correct in rejecting the reading *wnmṣʾ* in MS. d (according to the critical apparatus, in the notes he has MS. e) because of the rule of *lectio difficilior*. Wernberg-Møller (to 6:25) suggests that the *waw* may be an accusative ending conditioned by a *nifʿal* + *ʾet* construction. See Ges. rule 121b.

[49] The *ʾish ha-doresh*, the "man who is expounding," will be discussed below, 32f., 57f.

[50] See Licht, *MH*, 110. Cf. Wernberg-Møller, *MD*, 122f.

A similar idea is expressed in CDC 15:10-13:

אל יודיעהו איש את המשפטים עד עמדו לפני המבקר שמה יתפתה בו בדרשו אתו
וכאשר יקים אותו עליו לשוב אל תורת משה בכל לב ובכל נפש [נפר]עים א[נו] ממנו
אם ימ[ע]ל

> Let no man make known to him the regulations (*mishpaṭim*) until he stand before the examiner [51] lest he behave like a fool upon examination.[52] But when he takes it upon himself to return to the Law of Moses with all (his) heart and with all (his) soul we [exact] (punishment) from him if he transgress.

Apparently, the new recruit was not informed of the sect's rules [53] until after his examination. Henceforth, he becomes liable for punishment if he violates them. The purpose of this procedure was to guarantee that the *nistar*, known only to the sect, would not be transmitted to outsiders by rejected applicants for membership in the community.

Based on the foregoing discussion of *nigleh*, it is possible to venture a tentative explanation for a passage which up until now has been

---

[51] The parallel usage of this term in Rabbinic literature seems to have gone unnoticed in the editions, although mentioned in addenda (Vol. 9, *s. v. bqr*) to Kohut's *ʿArukh Ha-Shalem*. On the *mebaqqere mumin*, officials of the Jerusalem Temple who examined potential sacrificial victims for blemishes, see B. Ketubot 106a, P. Sheqalim 4:2 (ed. Krot, 4:3 (48a), in Vilna ed. of Babli, 10b), *Shir Ha-Shirim Rabbah* 3, to 3:7. In view of this Rabbinic usage we have chosen to translate "examiner." On this office at Qumran, see R. Marcus, "*Mebaqqer* and *Rabbim* in the Manual of Discipline VI, 11-13," *JBL* 75 (1956), 398-402 and J. F. Priest, "*Mebaqqer*, *Paqid* and the Messiah," *JBL* 81 (1962), 55-61. This official must have had ancient antecedents. Ugaritic text 1056:7 mentions a *pqr·yḥd*. Gordon, Glossary, 2091, calls attention to the parallel between this and the Qumran official. He translates the Ug., "overseer of the (religious) community." Mowinckel compares an official of the cult termed *mubaqqir* (one who examines omens), known from Nabatean. Cf. Ps. 27:4 which Mowinckel accordingly understood as, "to examine the omens in His Temple" (*The Psalms in Israel's Worship* I, 6, 238 (where he translates "inquires"), II, 54). Mowinckel compares the Qumran *mebaqqer* in II, 54 n. 5.

[52] Rabin's note on this passage must be corrected. Speaking of the verb *pth* he states that "the verb means 'to behave like a fool' in a 1st-cent. passage" in B. ʿErubin 65a. In fact, the verb in that passage means "to be persuaded or assuaged," as it is interpreted by Rashi and Ritbaʾ. The passage refers to the man who is assuaged through wine and cannot refer to acting like a fool, as the Rabbis liken this action to God's quick acceptance of Noah's sacrifice (and appeasement by it. Cf. Maharshaʾ, *ad loc.*). In our passage, the *hitpaʿel* indicates making, showing, or conducting oneself in a particular way, hence, to act like a fool. See Ges. rule 54d. Rabin's derivation from *pth* is acceptable, but the citation of B. ʿErubin 65a is irrelevant.

[53] We will return to the discussion of *mishpaṭim* below, 42-47.

assumed to be corrupt and in need of emendation. CDC 5:1-5 reads:

ועל הנשיא כתוב לא ירבה לו נשים ודויד לא קרא בספר התורה החתום אשר היה בארון כי לא [54] נפתח בישראל מיום מות אלעזר ויהושע ויושׁע [55] והזקנים אשר עבדו את העשתרת ויטמון נגלה עד עמוד צדוק

It has previously been assumed that the object of *lo' niftaḥ* was the Torah. It would appear more likely that this phrase refers to the ark of the covenant in which, according to tradition, a copy of the *sefer torah* was placed as an act of official publication. This scroll could always be consulted to confirm the law, as was the custom in antiquity.[56] In the latter portion of the passage, *nigleh* has been emended to *we-lo' nigleh*.[57] Rejecting this emendation we translate as follows:

> And regarding the Prince it is written (Deut. 17:17): "He shall not have many wives,"[58] but David had not read the sealed Book of the Law,[59] which was in the ark, which (*viz.* the ark) had not been opened in Israel from the day of the death of Eleazar and Joshua and the elders. Since they (Israel)[60] worshipped Ashtoret, the *nigleh* (*i.e.* the Torah) was hidden [61] until the arising of Zadok.

---

[54] Here follows a word (probably *nfth*) through which the scribe has drawn a line to indicate erasure. We therefore omit it from the transcription and translation.

[55] Rabin, *ad loc.*, suggests that a later scribe added the usual spelling of the name for clarity but retained the old Palestinian form which he found in his text. Schechter, *ad loc.*, considers this a dittography.

[56] *Hellenism*, 85f., 200-202.

[57] Rabin and Schechter, *ad loc.* Schechter also suggests the possibility of emending to *megillah*, the scroll, *i. e.*, the Torah. Our interpretation will yield the same meaning without resorting to emendation. The rule of *lectio difficilior* would caution against correcting a passage like this. See Ginzberg, *MGWJ* 55 (1911), 693f.

[58] So new JPS to Deut. 17:17.

[59] The roots *ḥtm* and *glh* are opposites in Jer. 32:11. Cf. the Rabbinic phrase *torah ḥatumah*, a complete Law (so Rashi to B. Giṭṭin 60b). This phrase is used in the discussion of whether the Torah was given in a series of *megillot* or as one complete document. Despite the similarity of phrasing, however, this Rabbinic usage does not throw light on the Qumran text under discussion.

[60] Schechter, *ad loc.*, refers to Jud. 2:13. Ginzberg (*MGWJ* 55 (1911), 691f.) correctly notes that this passage (Jud. 2:7-13) indicates that the foreign worship began *after* the death of Joshua. Accordingly, the antecedent of *'asher* must be sought in *be-Yisrael.* Qumran Hebrew does not require that the antecedent immediately precede the pronoun. Ginzberg also compares 2 K. 23:22 and Neh. 8:17 but it is hard to see the influence of these verses on our passage in CDC.

[61] For *wa-yatmun*, Schechter (*ad loc.*) reads *wa-yitamen*. If this reading is accepted, it can be assumed that the *waw* represents an original *yod*, which functioned as a *mater lectionis*. The difficulty in distinguishing *yod* from *waw* in Qumranic manuscripts is well-known. If the *Zadokite Fragments* did originate at Qumran, or in similar circles, its early MSS. were, no doubt, similar to those found at Qumran. Cf. Y. Ratzaby, "Remarks Concerning the Distinction between *Waw* and *Yodh*

Zadok is probably Hilkiah the Zadokite who discovered the Book of the Law in the time of Josiah.[62] The sect believed that in undertaking the *bedeq ha-bayit*, Hilkiah opened the *'aron* which had been hidden during the time of Manasseh and his Assyrian worship,[63] and for the first time read the authentic copy of the Torah which had been deposited there as part of its official publication.

The term *nigleh* also serves as the basis of an interesting piece of sectarian "aggadic" [64] exegesis on Amos 5:26-27. In CDC 7:14-16 we read:

כאשר אמר והגליתי את סכות מלככם ואת כיון צלמיכם מאהלי דמשק ספרי התורה הם סכות המלך כאשר אמר והקימותי את סוכת דויד הנפלת ...

> As He said (cf. Amos 5:26-27 [65]), "And I exiled the *sikkut* of your king and the image of your idols from the tents of Damascus." The books of the Law are the *sikkut* of the king, as He said (Amos 9:11), "And I will raise up the fallen tent (*sukkat*) of David."[66]

The play on words was common in Rabbinic exegesis and seems to have been used by the sect.[67] Here the root *glh* suggests not exile, as is the literal meaning of the verse, but revelation. The verse from

---

in the Habakkuk Scroll," *JQR* N.S. 41 (1950/1), 155-7, P. Wernberg-Møller, "*Waw* and *Yod* in the 'Rule of the Community,'" *RQ* 2 (1959-60), 223-36, D. M. Beegel, "Ligatures with Waw and Yodh in the Dead Sea Scrolls," *BASOR* 129 (1953), 11-14, A. Kimron, "*Ha-Habḥanah ben Waw Le-Yod Bi-Teʿudot Midbar Yehudah*," *Bet Miqra'* 52 (1972/3), 102-112, S. Kaufman, "The Job Targum from Qumran," *JAOS* 93 (1973), 323 n. 26. Rabin (*ad loc.*), however, points to several examples in CDC and DSD of the substitution of the active for the passive. Ginzberg (*ibid.*) emends to *we-ha-tamun nigleh ʿet ʿamod ṣadoq*. We accept his interpretation but see no need for emendation.

[62] So Rabin and Ginzberg, *ad loc.* Cf. 2 K. 22:8 and 2 Chron. 34:14 according to which Hilkiah found the book. Ginzberg notes that 1 Chron. 5:38f. records that Hilkiah was the grandson of Zadok. For this reason he may have been called *ben ṣadoq*. Ginzberg suggests that the text may originally have read accordingly.

[63] On the hiding of the ark, cf. Ginzberg, *Legends* VI, 377f., n. 118.

[64] For want of a better label for this *Gattung*, I borrow a term from Rabbinic usage.

[65] Ginzberg (*MGWJ* 56 (1912), 46f. and 58 (1914), 46f.) notes that this is not a misquotation. The verse has been purposely adapted for exegetical reasons. But cf. S. Talmon, "Aspects of the Textual Transmission of the Bible in Light of Qumran Manuscripts," *Textus* 4 (1964), 126-132.

[66] On this verse see most recently H. N. Richardson, "*Skt* (Amos 9:11): 'Booth' or 'Succoth'?" *JBL* 92 (1973), 375-381.

[67] *E. g.* P. Shebuʿot 1:5 (ed. Krot. 1:8, 33b). See W. H. Brownlee, "Biblical Interpretation among the Sectaries of the Dead Sea Scrolls," *BA* 14 (1951), 56. Ginzberg (*MGWJ* 56 (1912), 47) notes that a pun may be based on the root *skt* (Deut. 27:9). *Sikkut* would then be "that to which the people should listen," or the Torah.

Amos is now read as follows: "I will reveal the *sikkut* of your King," *i.e.* God. Based on this reading of Amos, the *sikkut* must be that revealed by God, the Torah.[68] Amos 9:11 is quoted to provide a proof-text to the effect that *sikkut* can refer to the Torah.[69] This proof assumes a pun and sectarian interpretation of the second verse also. The Qumranites must have seen this second text as referring to God's promise to reestablish ("raise up") the Torah which had been abandoned ("fallen"), for which purpose He had chosen the sect.

The *nigleh*, then, is nothing more than Scripture, while the *nistar* is sectarian interpretation of it. Although it is tempting to view the *nistar* as the equivalent of the Rabbinic oral Law, this view cannot be maintained,[70] for the oral Torah is characterized by the inclusion of laws *not* found in the Bible, while *nistar* is derived only through divinely-inspired biblical exegesis. It would appear that, like the Sadducees and the later Karaites, the Qumran sect relied exclusively on interpretation of the Bible for the derivation of its *halakhah*.

2. *Meduqdaq*, *Nimṣa'*, *Perush*

DSD 8:11f. has been cited [71] mentioning the expounder of the Law (*'ish ha-doresh*). If ten members of the sect formed a community, it was required that there be perpetual study of the Law. This is the import of DSD 6:6-8:

ואל ימש במקום אשר יהיו שם העשרה איש דורש בתורה יומם ולילה תמיד עליפות איש לרעהו והרבים ישקודו ביחד את שלישית כול לילות השנה לקרוא בספר ולדרוש משפט ולברך ביחד

> In [72] a place in which there are ten, there shall not be absent a man expounding the Law day and night, always alternating [73] each with

[68] Cf. Ibn Ezra to Ps. 73:7.

[69] On the use of the tabernacle (*sukkah*) as a symbol of the Law in Philo, see Wolfson, *Philo* I, 149.

[70] Cf. J. M. Baumgarten, "The Unwritten Law in the Pre-Rabbinic Period," *Journal for the Study of Judaism* 3 (1972), 12 n. 1.

[71] P. 28.

[72] The emendation to *mi-maqom*, proposed by Wernberg-Møller, *ad loc.*, is unnecessary in light of DSD 6:3-4, below, 71.

[73] Heb. *'alifot*. This is an example of the interchange of *'ayin* and *ḥet* in Qumran Hebrew. For other examples, see Licht, *MH*, 47 and the studies of H. Yalon, *MMY*, 54f., 72 (originally published as "*Megillat Sirkhe Ha-Yaḥad*," *Qiryat Sefer* 28 (1951/2), 65-74), S. Talmon, "A Note on the Dead Sea Manual of Discipline (1QS) VI, 11-13," *JJS* 8 (1957), 113-115, P. Wernberg-Møller, "Observations on the Interchange of ' and *ḥ* in the Manual of Discipline (DSD)," *VT* 3 (1953), 104-5, M. H. Goshen-Gottstein, "Linguistic Structure etc.," in *Aspects of the Dead Sea Scrolls* (1958), 107ff. S. Lieberman has pointed out that in the Tosefta Makkot 5 (4):15, MS. Erfurt, there occurs the form *mit'alefin*, while MS. Vienna and the

his neighbor. And the assembly shall be assiduous [74] to read the Bible [75] as a community one-third of each [76] night of the year, and to expound the Law and recite benedictions as a community.

The last part of the passage shows that study of the Bible was the activity of all members of the sect for at least four hours a day. The purpose of this study was to expound the law, *li-derosh mishpaṭ*.

The idea that all necessary guidance in matters of *halakhah* comes from biblical exegesis is echoed in CDC 16:1f.:

על כן יקום איש על נפשך לשוב אל תורת משה כי בה הכל מדוקדק

Therefore everyone take upon yourself [77] to return to the Law of Moses for in it everything is specified (*meduqdaq*).[78]

Schechter translated *meduqdaq* as "exactly explained." Rabin translated "can be learnt," taking *meduqdaq* as a passive participle rather than as an adjective. But these scholars did not notice that *meduqdaq* also implies discovery by the sect's exegesis, as can be seen from a parallel in CDC 15:9-10. There the word *nimṣa'*, a technical term for the sect's exegetical deductions, is substituted for *meduqdaq*:

ל[שוב א]ל תורת משה בכל לב [ובכל] נפש אל הנמצא לעשות בכ[ל ק]ץ [הרשע]

To [return t]o the Law of Moses, with all (his) heart [and with all] (his) soul, to that which has been derived (*nimṣa'*) (for them) to do [79] in al[l of the per]iod of (evil).

editio princeps read *mitḥalefin* (ed. Zuckermandel, 445, cf. textual notes). Lieberman's suggestion is reported by I. Sonne, "Remarks on the 'Manual of Discipline' (1QS) Column VI, 6-7," *VT* 7 (1957), 405-8. Lieberman has also cited more tannaitic examples. See his *TK* III, 274, 366f., *Greek in Jewish Palestine*, 135 n. 151, and J. N. Epstein, *Mabo' Le-Nusaḥ Ha-Mishnah* (1964) I, 10. Cf. also *'Arukh Ha-Shalem* 9, 196, *s. v. ḥrp* (8) and B. Beṣah 32a. A most interesting problem is the reading of 2 Chron. 33:13 cited in B. Sanhedrin 103a (cf. the note at the right margin). The parallels cited by A. L. Jellin, *Yefeh 'Enayim*, *ad loc.*, preserve the correct reading. Cf. *DS*, *ad loc.*, note *resh*, M. Abulafia, *Yad Ramah*, *ad loc.* (who cites Micah 1:11, *'emdato*, to which see Mandelkern's note *s. v. 'md*). See also 1 Sam. 17:7 (and Masoretic note) and 2 Sam. 21:19, as well as 2 K. 20:13 and Is. 39:2, J. Friedrich, W. Röllig, *Phönizisch-Punische Grammatik*, rule 36, and Z. Frankel, *Mebo' Ha-Yerushalmi* (1869/70), 76.

[74] Translating with M. 'Abot 2:14 (Licht). On the form, see Yalon, *MMY*, 23f., 72. Cf. Rabin, *QS*, 44.

[75] On *sefer* as a term for a book of the Bible see, Dan. 9:2, and the sources cited in N. M. Sarna, "Bible, the Canon, Text," *EJ* 4 (1971), 816. For the Rabbinic sources see W. Bacher, *'Erkhe Midrash*, 92, 247.

[76] So Licht, Wernberg-Møller, *ad loc.*

[77] Ginzberg (*MGWJ* 56 (1912), 676) reads *nafsho*, comparing l. 4.

[78] Cf. the use of *meduqdaq* for "explicitly recorded in a book" (not orally transmitted) in CDC 16:3.

[79] See DSD 9:18-20 (above, 26) and note 33.

Schechter failed to notice the legal and exegetical significance of the term *nimṣa'* as well. Rabin notes that "to find" "refers to the knowledge of the laws." [80] He suggests that it denotes the uncovering of the law.

The origin of the term *nimṣa'* however, must lie in biblical usage. In Jud. 14:18 the verb means "to solve" a riddle. It must be remembered that the solution of a riddle involves the interpretation of orally transmitted material. The verb is used, beginning with the story of the discovery of the book in the time of Josiah, for the locating of a book or document in a library or archives. This usage occurs eight times in connection with the narrative of 2 K. 22, 23 and 2 Chron. 34. In the period of the return this same verb served to indicate that certain genealogical documents could not be located in the archives (Ezra 2:62, Neh. 7:5, 64).

It would appear that in Second Temple times there was a technical usage of *mṣ' katub ba-sefer* to refer to locating material in a document or text. Neh. 7:5 uses the root in regard to genealogies. In Neh. 8:14 it refers to the Torah. The *sefer mosheh* with which *mṣ'* is used in Neh. 13:1 is, no doubt, the same text. In Est. 6:2 the reference is to finding something written in the chronicles of the king of Persia. In Dan. 12:1 mention is made of some book, but it cannot be determined if it refers to the book of Daniel or some other work. All of the references in which the root *mṣ'* in late Hebrew means "to find" in a book include the word *sefer*.

These last two usages were continued in Rabbinic parlance. P. Ta'anit 4:2 (68a) refers to a tradition that a genealogical document was found in Jerusalem tracing Hillel's Davidic descent. The phraseology of this statement is in accord with what has been found in the Bible. As to the meaning of locating a reference within a text, S. Lieberman has called attention to the tannaitic passage regarding the three Torah scrolls of the Temple Court.[81] Here the phrase *maṣ'u katub* (preceded by *sefer*) has the same meaning it had in Scripture. Lieberman further notes, though, that in these traditions the phrase has become a technical term equivalent to εὕρομεν γεγραμένον

---

[80] *QS*, 100.

[81] *Hellenism*, 21f. See *Sifre* Deut. 366, ed. Finkelstein, 423, *'Abot De-Rabbi Natan*, version II, ch. 46, ed. Schechter, 65a, P. Ta'anit 4:2 (68a), Soferim 6:4, ed. Higger 169f. (cf. his note), *Midrash Tannaim*, p. 222 (to Deut. 33:27), *Bereshit Rabbah* 9:5, ed. Theodor-Albeck, 70 (and parallels in note). Cf. S. Talmon, "The Three Scrolls of the Law that Were Found in the Temple Court," *Textus* 2 (1962), 14-27.

used by the scholiasts on Homer. It must also be noted that this passage contains the other usage of *mṣ'* in the sense of locating a text in a library or archives. It is apparent that both of these usages went hand in hand.

The sect has taken this terminology one step further, emphasizing the relationship between close reading of a text and its exegesis. The sect took the verb *mṣ'* to include not only that found explicitly in the text, but also that which was derived through its study.[82] Here the Qumranites may have been influenced by the fact that in several biblical passages [83] *mṣ'* is used to denote the successful result of the action of the verb *drš*. Certainly, the literal meaning of the phrases in question is that of finding what one is looking for. Yet the exegetical meaning of *drš* at Qumran may have influenced the understanding of these verses and, hence, of the verb *mṣ'*.

The verb *mṣ'* serves as a technical term for the sectarian process of deriving law by the method of biblical exegesis. The result of this activity is termed the *nimṣa'*, or "derived." The verb *skl* can be used in the sense of "to teach the *nimṣa'* " [84] or, in the nominal form *sekhel*, as a synonym for the "derived" law. In DSD 8:11 [85] the verb *mṣ'* is used specifically for the discovery or derivation of the *nistar* by the *'ish ha-doresh*, the "expounder" or "seeker." In CDC 15:9-10 *nimṣa'* appears as a synonym for *meduqdaq* (CDC 16:1-2). Finally, in a list of requirements for those entering the sect, CDC 6:18-20 demands:

ולשמור את יום השבת כפרושה ואת המועדות ואת יום התענית כמצאת באי הברית החדשה בארץ דמשק להרים את הקדשים כפירושיהם ...

> And to observe the Sabbath day according to its specification(s) (*perush*) [86] and the festivals and the day of the fast according to that derived (*muṣ'et*) by[87] the members of the new covenant in the land

[82] The expression *yaga'ti...(we-lo') maṣa'ti* found in relation to the Torah in B. Megillah 6b is not to be taken in a technical sense. It simply refers to the expending of effort and to the achievement or lack of achievement of the desired result. This is clear from comparison with B. Berakhot 58a and P. Berakhot 9:2 (13c) (cf. T. Berakhot 6:2) as well as the mention of business in B. Megillah 6b. The origin of this phrase is in Jer. 45:3.

[83] Is. 55:6, Ezek. 22:30, Ps. 10:15, 1 Chron. 28:9, 2 Chron. 15:2.

[84] For the combination of *mṣ'* and *skl*, see Prov. 3:4 and DSD 9:13f., 19f., quoted above, 26.

[85] Above, 28.

[86] Translating according to tannaitic usage. Cf. Bacher, *'Erkhe Midrash* I, 107 and Rabin to CDC 6:14.

[87] Schechter read *miṣwat*. We follow Rabin in taking this as a *pu'al*, fem. s., participle of *mṣ'*. Indeed, Mishnaic Hebrew shows many forms in which the initial *mem* of the *pu'al* participle has fallen off. This must have been the case especially

of Damascus, to set aside the holy offerings [88] according to their specification(s) (*perush*).

In this passage the *muṣ'et* is the sectarian law derived through biblical exegesis. There is no reason, then, to be surprised at the use of *perush* as a synonym for *muṣ'et*. *Perush*, in the language of the covenanters, is another term for the law derived from Scripture by interpretation. From the evidence published so far it appears that the use of *perush* was restricted to the *Zadokite Fragments*.

I. Heinemann has studied the history of the root *prš* as an exegetical term.[89] He says that in Hebrew and Assyrian the root means "to divide" or "decide." The basic meaning in the Semitic languages is "to separate." The abstract meaning ("decide") developed later.[90] He notes the phrase *parashat ha-kesef* (Est. 4:7)[91] and explains that money is separated as it is counted.[92] In Lev. 24:12 and Num. 15:34 the root means "to render a legal decision." He acknowledges that the root has been taken in a philological sense in Ezra 4:18 and Neh. 8:8. Yet he insists that the real meaning in this context is "careful reading" necessary to understand the text. He concludes that this root is never used in an exegetical sense in the Bible.

Heinemann refers to the use of *perush* in the *Zadokite Fragments* citing the phrases *perush ma'asehem*, and *perush shemotam*. He says these terms mean "the exact description of their actions," and "the exact description of their names." *Perush ha-torah* specifies only what the Torah clearly decrees.

In tannaitic usage the term has several definitions. It can refer to (1) a legal decision,[93] (2) the expression or pronunciation of words

---

with initial *mem* roots. See Segal, *Diqduq*, rule 203. This phenomenon is already observed in the Bible (Ges. rule 52s). This also explains the defective spelling in our text. This *pu'al*, however, is elsewhere unattested. If *muṣ'et* were taken as a *hof'al* of *yṣ'* this would be a confusion of initial *yod* and *mem* verbs similar to that of *ysr* and *msr* to be discussed below. We take *muṣ'et ba'e ha-berit* as a construct chain. Cf. note 40. Taking *ba'e ha-berit* as the *nomen rectum* we may assume that it denotes agency and, hence, add "by" in the translation. Rabin (*QS*, 100) translates "the finding of."

88 So Rabin, *ad loc.*

89 "*Hitpatḥut Ha-Munaḥim Ha-Miqṣo'iyim Le-Ferush Ha-Miqra'*," *Leshonenu* 15 (1946/7), 108-115.

90 Perhaps without influence of Assyrian. Heinemann compares *gzr*, *ḥtk*, and *psq*.

91 Cf. Est. 10:2. New JPS to Est. 4:7 translates "all about the money."

92 Heinemann notes Gen. 21:28f. which deals with sheep, however.

93 B. Ketubot 60a according to reading of *She'eltot* (Heinemann).

in their exact form,[94] a usage close to that of Ezra and Nehemiah, (3) the clarification of details, either (a) in the Bible itself, or (b) by the later scholars (tannaim). In the second case (b) the root refers to giving specific details, making distinctions, fixing a measure or amount (minima and maxima), giving the Scriptural source for a statement of the Sages or fixing the meaning of something. While this last group of meanings comes closest to the later uses, it is still not philological. M. Parah 1:1 is the only place where the tannaim use this root in regard to explaining the text of a law. Only in the time of the amoraim does this root acquire the sense of philological explanation.[95]

Can Heinemann's analysis be accepted? It seems that Heinemann has failed to make an important distinction between "exegetical" and "philological." A careful reading and explanation of the text go hand in hand. All the meanings which Heinemann sees in the tannaitic usage, while not referring to philological exegesis, are exegetical in character. One who reads a text carefully must specify its ramifications and significance. While this may not be a philological explanation, it may provide comments on the text, adding details and clarifying the exact meaning of the material. This is the meaning of the root as a legal term at Qumran. It refers to the specific details of the commandments deduced by their careful reading. This is not philology, but it certainly is exegesis. The same would apply to Neh. 8:8. The careful reading of the Torah involved the explanation of the text. Finally, Heinemann has to explain away the use of the root in M. Parah 1:1. Instead, this should be seen as an example of how a root usually signifying careful reading and explanation can be used in a philological sense. After all, no one can deny that the problem in this *mishnah* is one of philology.

To return to Qumran, Schechter took the *perush ha-torah* to be the "interpretation of the Law" (Torah).[96] In other cases he took *perush* as "explanation," [97] Rabin translates *perush ha-torah* as "the exact statement of the Law." He comments that this is "the detailed manner in which a general prescription is to be applied." He rightly points out that the meaning "commentary" is medieval.[98]

---

[94] M. Sanhedrin 7:5.

[95] Cf. *Pesiqta' Rabbati* 14, ed. Friedmann, 6lb.

[96] CDC 4:8, 6:14.

[97] See especially 4:4-6.

[98] To CDC 6:14. He cites the tannaitic use of *perush* as opposed to *'iqqar* in B. Sanhedrin 87a.

Delcor[99] accepts the explanation given by Lagrange[100] for *perush* in the *Zadokite Fragments*. "*Perush* seems to me to signify the orthodox explanation of the Law, its true sense." This *perush* was not an innovation but was an attempt to recover through revelation (divinely-inspired exegesis) the original meaning of the Mosaic institutions in order to conform to them. These observations are acceptable but only begin to describe the full significance of the term *perush* at Qumran.

A broken passage in CDC 14:17-19 furnishes proof of the sectarian implications of this technical term:

וזה פרוש מושב ה[ק]הל וזה פרוש המשפטים אשר [יתהלכו בהם בקץ הרשעה]

> And this is the specification (*perush*) of the session of the [. . .[101] con-] gregation and this is the specification of the regulations (*mishpaṭim*) by which [they shall live[102] in the period of evil.]

Perush, here, is connected with the "period of evil," a clearly sectarian concept. It will be demonstrated further on[103] that *mishpaṭim* also is a technical term associated with sectarian law. CDC 6:13-15 also contains a specialized use of *perush*:

ולא תאירו מזבחי חנם אם לא ישמרו לעשות כפרוש התורה לקץ הרשע

> For you shall not kindle fire upon my altar[104] in vain, unless they (the priests) are careful to do according to the specification(s) (*perush*) of the Torah for the period of evil.

The sect enjoined its members from participation in the Jerusalem cult because of disagreement with the administration of the Temple on matters of ritual. These disagreements stemmed, no doubt, from the sectarian methods of exegesis (*perush*).

Talking about the Sons of Zadok, CDC 4:7-10 states:

וכל הבאים אחריהם לעשות כפרוש התורה אשר התוסרו בו הראשנים עד שלים הקץ
השנים האלה כברית אשר הקים אל לראשנים לכפר על עונותיהם כן יכפר אל בעדם

> As to all who come after them to do according to the specification(s)

---

[99] "*Contribution à l'étude de la législation des sectaries de Damas et de Qumran*," *RB* 62 (1955), 71.

[100] "*La secte juive de la Nouvelle Alliance au pays de Damas*," *RB* 9 (1912), 220 n. 1. The translation is mine. Delcor (71) also refers to Lieberman, *Hellenism*, 200, n. 5 but it seems that Delcor has confused *prs* and *prš*, two independent roots.

[101] It is possible that the break after the *h* should be restored with "*rabbim*. . . ." *Moshab ha-rabbim* is a term for the sect's assembly.

[102] Lit. "walk."

[103] Below, 42-47.

[104] Translating with RSV to Mal. 1:10.

> (*perush*) of the Torah in which the previous generations [105] were instructed [106] until the end [107] of the [108] period of these years, according to the covenant which God established for the previous generations to make atonement for their transgressions, so may God make atonement for them.

Here it is assumed that the sectarian interpretation of the Torah has ancient roots. The sect regards itself as being the only group to carry on the covenant which God made with Israel. All others have strayed from the correct interpretation, once known to all of Israel.

In a case involving a plague (*nega*ʿ), when the priest is not expert in the law, CDC 13:4-7 commands:

ואם משפט לתורת נגע יהיה באיש ובא הכהן ועמד במחנה והבינו המבקר בפרוש התורה ואם פתי הוא הוא יסגירנו כי להם המשפט

> And if there shall be a case of the law of "(If) there be a plague on a man,"[109] then the priest shall come and stand in the camp and the examiner [110] shall instruct him in the specification(s) (*perush*) of the Torah, for (even) if he be a fool,[111] *he* shall quarantine him, for judgment is theirs.

---

105 So new JPS to Deut. 19:14.

106 So Schechter.

107 It is possible to take *šlym* as a *plene* spelling of *shalem*, a *pi*ʿ*el* infinitive absolute which would follow the prep. ʿ*ad*. It would appear that the use of *yod* as a *mater lectionis* in our MSS. of CDC is more common than in the material found at Qumran (on which see Yalon, *MMY* 51f. (first pub. as "*Megillat Yesha*ʿ*yahu A*," *Qiryat Sefer* 27 (1950/1), 163-72) and 72 (see note 73 for original pub.). Neither is it possible to contradict this suggestion by referring to the form *šlm* in CDC 1:10 as the latter is an adjective, hence, equivalent to the part. of the stative verb. In other words, it differs in vocalization. A second possibility, although somewhat unlikely, is that we are dealing here with an Aramaism in which the adj. *shelim* (Targ. Onk. and Jon. to Gen. 17:1 and Ex. 12:5, and Targ. Onk. to Gen. 33:18) is serving as a substantive. On Aramaisms in the Qumran scrolls, see Yalon, *MMY*, 55-57, Licht, *MH*, 44, and E. Y. Kutscher, *Ha-Lashon We-Ha-Reqa*ʿ *Ha-Leshoni shel Megillat Yisha*ʿ*yahu Ha-Shelemah Mi-Megillot Yam Ha-Melaḥ* (1957), 19-22, 141-163, 380-385. I would shy away from the emendation proposed by Schechter and Rabin because of the recurrence of *šlym* in CDC 4:10.

108 Ginzberg, *MGWJ* 55 (1911), 685, notes the irregular occurrence of the definite article in the phrase *ha-qeṣ ha-shanim*. He may be correct in deleting the first article. See, however, Ges. rules 127f-i where similar examples are cited from the Bible.

109 A reference to either Lev. 13:9 or 29. The term *torah* is used at the conclusion of this same chapter in Leviticus (v. 29).

110 See 29 note 51.

111 Schechter almost admits that his emendation (to *pashah*, "increased") is unconvincing in light of an identical Rabbinic prescription found in *Sifra*ʾ Tazriaʿ 1:9 and M. Negaʿim 3:1. The *Sifra*ʾ, however, uses *shoṭeh* rather than *peti*. The normal definition of *shoṭeh* is "madman" or "insane" (Jastrow, *s. v.*), yet definitions for *peti* are "easily persuaded," "simple" or "fool" (Jastrow, *s. v.*). Perhaps we must take *shoṭeh* in *Sifra*ʾ in the same sense as in the phrase *ḥasid shoṭeh*, "a foolish

It is to be assumed that here, as in many other cases involving ritual purity, the sect differed with the Jerusalem priesthood. The *perush* in which the examiner is expected to instruct the priest was based upon the specific sectarian interpretation of the law.

The passage to be cited next indicates that the *perush* is integrally connected to a text. These sectarian interpretations are *not* oral Law. Oral Law in its technical sense is material purportedly transmitted to Moses by God at Sinai, not laws adduced only from creative or original interpretation of the biblical text. CDC 16:2-4 [112] states:

ופרוש קציהם לעורון ישראל מכל אלה הנה הוא מדוקדק על ספר מחלקות העתים ליובליהם ובשבועותיהם

> And the specification (*perush*) of their epochs,[113] of the blindness of Israel from all of these,[114] behold it is calculated [115] in the *Book* [116] *of the Divisions of the Times into their Jubilees and Sabbatical Cycles.*

This book has been identified by many scholars [117] with the book of Jubilees, copies of which were found at Qumran [118] and which was, no doubt, part of the sect's library. It is even possible that this pseudepigraphal work was part of a sectarian canon.

This use of *perush* must be seen in light of the evidence to be discussed in connection with *serekh* [119] which indicates that *perush* can

---

saint" (M. Sotah 3:4, cf. B. Sotah 21b, P. Sotah 3:4 (ed. Krot. 3:3, 19a), M. T. ʿArakhin We-Ḥaramin 8:13). This "foolish saint" is not an imbecile, but rather one who acts foolishly or incompetently in a given circumstance. For a comparison of this regulation in CDC with the Rabbinic law see Albeck, "*HWT*" to Negaʿim 3:1 (p. 552).

[112] Ginzberg (*MGWJ* 56 (1912), 676) considers this passage secondary. He thinks that it was inserted to contradict the line before which states that all is specified in the Torah. The author of this passage would then be someone for whom the book of Jubilees held special importance. In view of what we now know about the place of Jubilees in the sect, there is no reason to see this passage as secondary. See note 118. It must also be remembered that the calendar of the sect was that of Jubilees.

[113] Cf. Yalon, *MMY*, 77 who renders *qeṣ* as equivalent to Heb. *parashah*.

[114] *Sc.* the exact sectarian observance of the law. Cf. CDC 8:2 (Rabin).

[115] Schechter: "exactly explained." We translate in accordance with the Aramaic non-duplicated cognate *dwq* which is used by Targum Jonathan in the *paʿel* to translate *we-ḥishab* (Targ. Jon. to Lev. 25:27, 50, 52, 27:18 and 23).

[116] The idiom *katub ʿal* (Jer. also *ʾel) sefer* is regular in biblical literature. Here *katub* has been replaced by *meduqdaq*.

[117] *E.g.* Schechter and Rabin, *ad loc.*

[118] Published in *DJD* I, 82-84, III, 77-79; and in J. T. Milik, "*Fragment d'une source du Psautier* (4Qps 89) *et fragments des Jubilés, du document du Damas*, etc.," *RB* 73 (1966), 94-106.

[119] Below, 65-7.

denote a "list." What is found in the book mentioned here is a listing of periods, calculated and specified. At first glance, it may appear from this passage that the *perush* is found in the book and is not something external. Indeed, such a view is held by the sect which equates a text with its correct interpretation. In other words, the interpretation is intrinsic, not extrinsic. In actuality, the *perush* is not part of the text. To the sect, however, the *perush* of the Law is found in it. It needs only to be discovered by one who has the necessary inspiration. Thus, *perush* must arise directly from a written text in which the *perush* is "specified" (*meduqdaq*) or "found" (*nimṣa'*). Once again, the *perush* is not the product of an oral process, but of the study of a written text. The same may be said of *nistar*, *sekhel*, and *nimṣa'* and of the remaining terms to be discussed.

In view of the problems regarding the canon at Qumran, it would be interesting to know if the term *perush*, applied to a text, was used only for canonical works. If so, this passage would prove that Jubilees had achieved canonicity at Qumran. Unfortunately, this is the only passage in which *perush* appears relating to a book other than those of the Hebrew Scriptures. There is, then, no way to answer this question. Perhaps the continuing publication of texts from the area will supply more data.

Of the difference between *pesher* and *perush* it is sheer oversimplification to say that *pesher* is an Aramaic equivalent of Hebrew *perush* and to cite other evidences of Aramaisms in the Dead Sea Scrolls.[120] *Pesher* is a term used to denote "aggadic" interpretation while *perush* denotes interpretation for the purpose of discovering the details of the *halakhah*. It is probable that these two terms, *perush* and *pesher*, imply the same exegetical method in that neither requires the use of further evidence from biblical literature.[121]

All groups of Jews realized that the Torah could not be lived by if taken literally. The Rabbis were freed from the yoke of literalism by the oral Law concept. Within the context of oral Law, the sages enacted laws which had no basis in Scripture but which made the biblical system livable. At Qumran the exegetical method of *perush* played the same role. Through this technique, laws could be derived from verses without the use of proof-texts. In other words, *perush* afforded the Qumran sect the same escape from the literal word that the dual-Torah concept gave the Rabbinic Jews.

---

[120] Cf. Delcor, "*Contribution*," 71.

[121] See below, 59f.

3. *Mishpaṭ*, *Miṣwah*

Two of the passages containing *perush* also contain the term *mishpaṭ* (CDC 13:4-7, 14:17-19). *Mishpaṭ* is used in two basic ways. The first usage, with which we will not be concerned here, is the meaning "custom, manner, or case," which is met regularly in biblical literature.[122] The second usage, also with roots in biblical literature, is that of "laws," or "regulations." [123] It is with this meaning that *mishpaṭ* occurs as a sectarian technical term, apparently somewhat similar in connotation to *perush*. The particularly sectarian nature of the term as well as its connections with *perush* and *midrash* were already realized by Schechter.[124] Wernberg-Møller noted the connection of *mishpaṭ* with the exegetical activity of the sect and defined it as "rule, Law, Right." [125]

M. Delcor [126] has also treated this sectarian legal term. Its origin is as a term for customary law, the sentence of a judge. At Qumran it designates the divine law, or, more usually, the community's regulations. Delcor did not realize that even where the term applied to God's law, it is God's law as interpreted by the sect. He did not understand the important links between *mishpaṭ*, *perush*, and *miṣwah*.

CDC 20 provides a clear picture of the use of *mishpaṭ* by the sect. Lines 27-30 read:

וכל המחזיקים במשפטים האלה ל[צ]את [ו]לבוא על פי התורה וישמעו לקול מורה ויתודו ...

> But all who hold fast to these regulations (*mishpaṭim*) to [g]o out [and] to come in according to the Torah, and who obey the voice of [the] teacher and who confess...

It is clear that the *mishpaṭim* are those laws determined by the exegesis of the teacher, the sect's leader.[127] Lines 31f. continue:

---

[122] For biblical usage see S. Loewenstamm, "*Mishpaṭ*, *Mishpaṭ Ha-Miqra'*," *Enc. Bib.* 5, 614f., Orlinsky, *Notes*, 177. For this first usage see CDC 9:15, 12:3, 15, 13:5, 7, 14:12, 16:12, 19:19, 20:1, 9, 10, DSD 2:15, 3:17, 4:18, 20, 5:12, 8:19, 9:5. Cf. the poetic usages, apparently based on the sectarian connotations, in DSD 4:2, 4.

[123] For the LXX translations of this term, see S. Blank, "The LXX Rendering of Old Testament Terms for Law," *HUCA* 7 (1930), 270-274. Cf. J. van der Ploeg, "Studies in Hebrew Law," *CBQ* 12 (1950), 248-250.

[124] *Documents* I, LIX (Ktav reprint, 91).

[125] Translation and commentary to DSD 8:24.

[126] "*Contribution*," *RB* 61 (1954), 541, cf. 535, 539.

[127] See F. F. Bruce, *The Teacher of Righteousness in the Qumran Texts* (1957), C. Rabin, "The 'Teacher of Righteousness' in the Testament of the Twelve Patriarchs?" *JJS* 3 (1952), 127f., H. H. Rowley, "The Teacher of Righteousness in

והתיסרו במשפטים הראשונים אשר נשפטו בם אנשי היחיד [128] והאזינו לקול מורה צדק

> And they who have been [129] instructed in the original [130] regulations (*mishpaṭim*) by which the men of the community were judged [131] and who have listened to the voice of the righteous teacher...

CDC 4:7-10 has been discussed above.[132] There it is the *perush ha-torah* which is the object of instruction (*ysr*). The almost parallel terminology suggests that *mishpaṭim* might be used interchangeably with *perush ha-torah*, and, hence, that *mishpaṭim* are the regulations derived through sectarian exegesis. Further evidence is found in CDC 14:17-19 also cited above [133] where the phrase *perush ha-mishpaṭim* appears. This is an example of the familiar Qumran usage of two synonyms in construct with one another, apparently for explanation or emphasis.[134]

The sectarian nature of the *mishpaṭim* is again confirmed in CDC 12:19-20:

סרך מושב ערי ישראל על המשפטים האלה להבדיל בין הטמא לטהור ולהודיע בין הקודש לחול ואלה החקים למשכיל להתהלך בם עם כל חי למשפט עת ועת וכמשפט הזה יתהלכו זרע ישראל ולא יוארו

> The order [135] of the session of the cities of Israel according to these regulations (*mishpaṭim*): to distinguish between the impure and the pure and to discriminate [136] between the holy and the profane. And these are the laws for the *maskil* [137] to live by with every living thing, according to the regulation (*mishpaṭ*) of each time,[138] and according to this regulation (*mishpaṭ*), shall the offspring of Israel live and not be cursed.

---

the Dead Sea Scrolls," *BJRL* 40 (1957), 114-146, O. R. Sellers. "A Possible Old Testament Reference to the Teacher of Righteousness," *IEJ* 5 (1955), 93 ff., J. Weingreen, "The Title Moreh Sedek," *JSS* 6 (1961), 162-74.

[128] Read *hyḥd*.

[129] CDC 20:27-33 is a list of qualifications for achieving a reward described in 33b and 34. The verbs in the list are all in the imperfect tense except the two in this passage. We therefore must assume that there is an attempt here to indicate by the switch to the perfect that the events herein described occurred in time anterior to those described by the imperfect verbs. Otherwise, why the change in tense?

[130] For the use of *rishon*, see below, 51f.

[131] Cf. the similar wording in DSD 9:10f.

[132] P. 38f.

[133] P. 38.

[134] See Licht, *MH*, 32.

[135] The term *serekh* will be discussed below, 60-68.

[136] BDB, *s. v. ydᶜ*. *Le-hodiaᶜ* also implies making known the distinction.

[137] See note 24.

[138] See note 25.

The association of *mishpaṭim* with laws of purity makes the case even stronger for the term's sectarian implications. The sect's stringency in these matters is well-known. The connection with the *maskil* and the notion of progressive change of the law (*ʿet ba-ʿet*), also mentioned here with *mishpaṭ*, further confirms the sectarian nature of the *mishpaṭim*. Finally, the singular and plural forms (*mishpaṭ* and *mishpaṭim*) are both subject to this connotation.

It is in line with this sectarian usage that one must understand the legislation of CDC 14:6-8:

והכהן אשר יפקד אש[139] הרבים מבן שלושים שנה עד בן ששים מבונן בספר [ההגו][140]
ובכל משפטי התורה לדברם כמשפטם

> And the priest who shall muster the assembly[141] (shall be) from thirty to sixty years old, learned[142] in the *Sefer* [*He-Hagu*] and in all of the regulations (*mishpeṭe*) of the Torah, to pronounce them[143] according to their regulation.

It has been established that *Sefer He-Hagu* is a synonym for the Torah.[144] The *paqid*[145] must be learned in the Torah (*nigleh*) as well as in the sectarian regulations (*mishpeṭe ha-torah*).

Mentioned above[146] was CDC 15:10-13 in which the members of the sect are prohibited from making known the *mishpaṭim* of the

---

139 Read *ʾet* (Schechter). Rabin's restoration to *brʾs*, based on DSD 6:14, is no more convincing, and, as he indicates, "excludes the otherwise attractive rendering 'who musters.' " *ʾEt* is used regularly in CDC. Cf. Kutscher, 316. See most recently G. W. Nebe, "*Der Gebrauch der sogenannten nota accusativi ʾet in Damaskusschrift XV, 5.9 und 12*," *RQ* 8 (1973), 257-264.

140 Restoring with CDC 1:6 and 13:2 (Rabin and Schechter).

141 The process of mustering is described several lines above on this same page. Apparently, the members were arranged in order and their names listed. On these lists, see below, 66f. For the connection of this sectarian organization with military tactics, see Yadin, *War Scroll*, 60f.

142 *Mebonan* is a *polal* participle (passive in meaning) of the root *byn*. See Ges. rule 72m and paradigm M. Cf. Deut. 32:10.

143 Schechter suggests taking this as "to lead them" in the sense in which *dbr* occurs in biblical *hifʿil*, Syriac and Rabbinic usage. The noun *dabbar* ("leader") must be based on a *piʿel* with the meaning of "lead."

144 See Wieder, *JSK*, 215-251, M. Goshen-Gottstein, " 'Sefer-Hagu'—The End of a Puzzle," *VT* 8 (1958), 286-8, I. Rabinowitz, "The Qumran Author's *spr hhgw/y*," *JNES* 20 (1961), 109-14, Rabin to CDC 10:6 and Licht, *MH*, 255f. A. M. Honeyman, "Note on a Teacher and a Book," *JJS* 4 (1953), 131f. translates, "book of exposition, study, interpretation," following Ginzberg, *MGWJ* 56 (1912), 306f., 417. Cf. Baumgarten, "Unwritten Law," 10 n. 2.

145 On this official, see J. Priest, "*Mebaqqer*, *Paqid* and the Messiah," *JBL* 81 (1962), 55-61, G. R. Driver, *Aramaic Documents of the Fifth Century B. C.* (1957), 15-17.

146 P. 29.

group to an applicant until he has passed an examination. Clearly this was to keep the sectarian regulations the secret (*nistar*) of the sect.[147]

In the *Zadokite Fragments*, *mishpaṭ* is used as part of a heading preceding a law or group of laws of clear sectarian character. This format is followed in the Sabbath laws (CDC 10:14) and those of freewill offerings (CDC 16:12 and 13). A similar formula occurs twice in the *Manual of Discipline*. The phrase *we-ʿeleh ha-mishpaṭim* in DSD 6:24 and 8:20 precedes a long list of penalties for violation of sectarian *halakhah*.

DSD 8:24f. states:

ואם בשגגה יעשה והובדל מן הטהרה ומן העצה ודרשו המשפט אשר לוא ישפוט איש ולוא ישאל על כול עצה שנתים ימים

> And if he does (it)[148] in error, then he shall be separated from the purity[149] and from counsel[150] and they shall exact punishment (*mishpaṭ*),[151] that he not judge a(ny) man and that he not be asked for any counsel for two years.

Here the phrase *we-darshu ha-mishpaṭ* refers to the exacting of punishment. In discussing DSD 6:6-8, the phrase *li-derosh mishpaṭ* was differently interpreted.[152] This combination of verb and object was equivocal and could refer to either of two processes, the discovery of the law through exegesis or the fixing and exacting of a penalty. Alternately, one could accept the reading of MS. d to DSD 8:24, *u-min ha-mishpaṭ*, in place of *we-darshu ha-mishpaṭ* in the St. Mark's MS. This would leave only the interpretation proposed above for this phrase, that of determining the law by sectarian exegesis, and would mean that as a punishment the violator was deprived of his privilege to participate in the progressive discovery of the law.[153]

---

147 *Mishpaṭ(im)* is used in the same context in DSD 6:15, 22f. Cf. Rabin, *QS*, 6.

148 Heb. *yaʿaseh*, active, parallel to "who shall violate a word of the Law of Moses" (1.22).

149 A reference to the sect's victuals which had to be prepared and eaten in a state of absolute Levitical purity. See Licht, *MH*, 147f. and compare his survey of tannaitic purity laws, 294-303.

150 He is deprived of his right to participate in the community's legislative assembly, the *moshab ha-rabbim* (Licht, to 8:18).

151 Licht's interpretation is undoubtedly influenced by the reading of MS. d *u-min ha-mishpaṭ*.

152 P. 33.

153 It seems that the following sentence supports the variant reading in that it promises that he may return to *moshab*, *midrash*, and *ʿeṣah*. *Midrash*, however, can only refer to the aspect of study or interpretation; it cannot be used to connote the exacting of punishment.

CDC 7:1-3 commands the sectarian:

להזיר מן הזונות כמשפט להוכיח איש את אחיהו כמצוה ולא לנטור מיום ליום ולהבדל מכל הטמאות כמשפטם

> To [154] abstain from fornication [155] according to the regulation (*mishpaṭ*), to admonish each man his neighbor according to the commandment [156] and not to bear a grudge from one day to the next,[157] and to separate oneself [158] from all impure things according to their regulation (*mishpaṭ*).

Here the regulation, *mishpaṭ*, clearly refers to the peculiar sectarian laws regarding sexual relations and prohibited marriage.[159] The Qumranites regarded those who did not follow their *mishpaṭim* as engaging in fornication.

Finally, a passage in the *Zadokite Fragments* (CDC 7:6-9, MS. A. Cf. 19:2-5, MS. B.) commands members that if they should dwell in camps and establish families:

ויתהלכו על פי התורה וכמשפט היסורים [160] כסרך התורה כאשר אמר . . .

> That they should live according to the Torah and the regulation (*mishpaṭ*) of the teachings according to the rule of the Torah as He said . . . (The quotation of Num. 30:17 follows.)

The group is to live according to the Torah and its sectarian interpretation. According to our passage, these regulations are regarded as stemming from the biblical text. This is the import of the words *ka-ʾasher ʾamar*, and of the subsequent quotation of Num. 30:17.

---

[154] On the use of a series of infinitives or "chain of *lameds*," see Licht, *MH*, 35-7.

[155] Reading *zenut* for *zonot* with Rabin and Schechter. Alternately, we can retain *zonot* and translate "women who had before been married incestuously" (Rabin, cf. CDC 4:20). Ginzberg (*MGWJ* 56 (1912), 43) notes that the reading *zwnwt* is confirmed by CDC 8:5. He suggests that the author was influenced by Hos. 4:14. The explanation of this form may lie elsewhere, however. The occurrence of a form *sodom* corresponding to the Greek form has been noted by Kutscher, 83f. DSD shows forms *kbwd*, *kwbd*, and *kwbwd* (Licht, MH, 45f.). It may be that at Qumran a principle of vowel assimilation operated so that mobile *shewa*ʾ was pronounced like a following vowel.

[156] We cannot read this as a passive part. *meṣuwweh* because it is parallel to *mishpaṭ*.

[157] Cf. Num. 30:15 (Ginzberg).

[158] Heb. *le-hibbadel*, a *nifʿal* serving (after the prep. *min*) as the reflexive of the *hifʿil*. See BDB, s.v. *bdl*, and Ges. rules 51e and f.

[159] Cf. CDC 5:6-11.

[160] Reading with MS. A and assuming that *hyswdym* in MS. B (according to Rabin's reading) should be read *hyswrym*. For the translation of this term see below, 49-54.

What has been said about the use of *mishpaṭ* in the *Zadokite Fragments* can be demonstrated as well for the *Manual of Discipline*. The devotion of one-third of each night to Bible study (DSD 6:6-8) has as its purpose *li-derosh mishpaṭ*, to derive the correct interpretation of the law.[161] An interpretation can now be proposed for DSD 9:14f.:

ובבחירי העת להחזיק על פי רצונו כאשר צוה ואיש כרוחו כן לעשות משפטו

> And to strengthen the chosen ones of the time according to His will as He commanded, and each one, according to his spirit,[162] thus to do His regulation (*mishpaṭ*).

In the first half of the clause, the *maskil* is admonished to strengthen the member of the sect in his observance of the *nigleh*, that which God commanded, and in the second part, he is told to strengthen the sectarian in his allegiance to the *mishpaṭ*, the regulations derived through the sectarian interpretation of the divine Law (*nistar*).[163]

CDC 7:1-2, already quoted,[164] contains a parallelism between the terms *mishpaṭ* and *miṣwah*. It is noteworthy that both areas of law mentioned here (prohibited unions and reproof) were the subject of peculiar sectarian legislation.[165] It would seem that the term *miṣwah* can be used interchangeably with *mishpaṭ* to connote the sectarian *halakhah*. In the Bible, *miṣwah* was used to denote all obligations whether "religious" or "secular." More specifically, this word referred to obligations ordained by God. Already in Jer. 35:14 the term was used to describe the regulations of a sect (the Rekabites).[166] The interchangeability of *mishpaṭ* and *miṣwah* in the sectarian

---

161 *Drš* and *midrash* are discussed below, 54-60.

162 *Ruaḥ* ("spirit") is a technical term in the scrolls. Line 16 provides, according to Licht, a definition of the "spirit." It is the man's rank in the sect measured by the perfection of his character or behavior and his ability to absorb ideas (*MH*, 196).

163 It is, however, possible to take the second clause here as parallel to what follows in the scroll: "And to bring near each man according to the purity of his hands, and according to his knowledge (*sekhel*) to draw him near." It is in accordance with this explanation that Wernberg-Møller translates our phrase, "He shall give everybody the treatment which is due him according to his spiritual quality."

164 P. 46.

165 See CDC 5:5-11 and 9:1-8.

166 I. Heinemann, "*Miṣwah*," *Enc. Bib.* 5, 229. Scholars have already realized the importance of the period of the return for an understanding of the sects of the Second Commonwealth. It may be that connections can be established between the Rekabites and the later sects. I refer here to the kinds of connections which have been established between the sect and the Karaites, not to any direct historical links. For the LXX translations, see Blank, 260-263. Cf. J. van der Ploeg, "Studies in Hebrew Law," 258.

literature was already evident to Schechter who translated both terms by "Law." [167] Elsewhere he translated *miṣwah* "commandment." [168] Rabin claimed that the *miṣwah* was the sect's oral Law.[169] It will be shown, however, that while *miṣwah* may describe the sectarian legal traditions, the comparison with oral Law is an oversimplification. The sectarian legislation shows no evidence of oral transmission or of a claim of authority based on oral tradition. These ideas are probably later. [170] Wernberg-Møller translated "regulations," and (referring to Jer. 35:14) suggested that the term might indicate a set of regulations.[171] Delcor has noted that the eight uses of the verb *ṣwh* in the *Manual of Discipline* all refer to God. It can thus be assumed that *miṣwah* is a divine commandment.[172] It must be remembered that laws derived by the sect through exegesis are regarded as divine, for the act of biblical exegesis is seen by the sect as divinely guided.

The term *miṣwah* also occurs in Rabbinic usage. Its most frequent meaning is a "commandment," one of the positive or negative obligations specified in the Torah. Yet in certain usages, *e.g.* M. Beṣah 5:2, it has been understood to describe a Rabbinic enactment. This is the view of G. Allon.[173] Bacher, however, does not recognize this definition, and Albeck disputes it.[174] If *miṣwah* actually does refer on occasion to Rabbinic enactments, it might be a development from the sectarian usage where it referred to the commandments of the Torah as interpreted by the sect. The same usage of the term *miṣwah* is found in DSD 8:17f.:

וכול איש מאנשי היחד [175] ברית היחד אשר יסיר [176] מכול המצוה דבר ביד רמה ...

---

[167] To CDC 7:1f.

[168] CDC 10:3.

[169] Commentary to CDC 10:3.

[170] See Introduction, n. 79.

[171] Translation and commentary to DSD 8:17.

[172] Delcor, "*Contribution*," 543.

[173] "*Shebut, Reshut, Miṣwah*," *Tarbiẓ* 7 (1935/6), 134-142, republished in *Meḥqarim Be-Toledot Yisrael* II, 111-119.

[174] Commentary and " *HWT*," to M. Beṣah 5:2, *Meḥqarim Bi-Baraita' We-Tosefta'*, 166f. Cf. Lieberman, *TK* V, 998f.

[175] Omit with MS. d, or it is possible that we are dealing here with a variant reading which has been incorporated into the text (van der Ploeg, quoted by Wernberg-Møller).

[176] Reading against Licht with Wernberg-Møller and Yalon. It is well-known that it is usually impossible to distinguish *waw* from *yod* in the Qumran documents. The sentence would then conform approximately to the wording of Josh. 11:15. See Yalon, *MMY*, 82, and (on *waw* and *yod*) 52-4, 72. Cf. above, 30f. n. 61.

> And any man from the men of the covenant of the community who shall intentionally leave undone [177] anything from the commandment (*miṣwah*)...

The next paragraph in DSD deals with the violator of *torat mosheh*. It may be deduced from this that the term *miṣwah* refers particularly to the law derived through the medium of exegesis by the sect.[178]

4. *Yissurim*

The root *ysr* is used quite frequently in the *Zadokite Fragments* and is also found in the *Manual of Discipline*. The noun *yissurim* signifies the teachings of the sect.

Schechter translated this term as "instructions." [179] Segal observed its connection with the noun *musar*.[180] In fact, *yissurim* may have regularly served as a substitute for *musar*, for some reason rejected by the sect. Rabin [181] accepted the translation of Schechter and noted that the singular of this term occurs in Ben Sira 40:29. Actually, he was citing a marginal reading from Segal's edition,[182] but the scroll found at Masada has confirmed this text.[183] In Ben Sira, however, the term is closer to its Mishnaic meaning, "sufferings inflicted as divine punishment," [184] in turn derived from the biblical usage.[185] Also interesting in the context of this study is the *ketib* of Jer. 17:13, according to which the *yissurim* of God would be written on the land.[186] This can be taken as a biblical use of *yissurim* foreshadowing the application of this word by the sect. The reference to writing will fit well with the written nature of the sect's legal material. Is. 28:26 may contain a parallelism of *ysr* and *yrh*. A number of commentators have seen *ysr* here in the sense of "to teach, instruct." [187] This is the same way in which the term is used in Qumran literature. Further, the mention of *mishpaṭ* in this verse would lend

---

[177] Translating with BDB, *s.v. swr*.

[178] Licht, *MH*, 183, Wernberg-Møller, *ad loc.*, and Rabin to CDC 10:3.

[179] Translation, to CDC 7:5.

[180] Commentary to CDC 7:5, and 7:8.

[181] Translation and Commentary to CDC 7:5.

[182] *Sefer Ben-Sira' Ha-Shalem* (1971/2), 275.

[183] Y. Yadin, *The Ben Sira Scroll from Masada* (1965), 16 (English).

[184] Rabin.

[185] See the note of Brownlee, *ad loc.*, who emends to *yissur we-da'at*.

[186] Cited by Rabin. This passage has presented considerable difficulty to the commentators. See, *e.g.*, Ehrlich, *ad loc.*

[187] Cf. Ibn Ezra, Kimchi, new JPS apparently following the Targum, Targum Onkelos to Deut. 8:5. But see also Rashi and Luzzatto.

support to the view that *mishpaṭ* and *yissurim* are synonymous at Qumran. Licht has interpreted the *yissure kabod* of 1Q 34, 3 II 7 as the laws of the Torah.[188] It should only be added that the *yissurim* are the laws of the Torah as *interpreted by the sect*. Wernberg-Møller [189] has suggested that this term in the singular is behind the peculiar Greek text of Ps. Sol. 3:4.[190] He also cites Yalon's attempt to compare *ysr* and *ḥzq* which appear in parallelism in Hos. 7:15 and Job 4:3 as well as in DSD 3:1. Yalon had assumed that both *ḥzq* and *ysr* meant "to bind" in these passages. Wernberg-Møller shows from the biblical and Qumran material that this explanation is not possible.

In CDC 7:5-6 [191] we read:

כל המתהלכים באלה בתמים קדש על פי כל יסורי[192] ברית אל באמנות להם לחיותם אלף דור

> As to all who live by these [193] in holy perfection, according to all of the teachings (*yissure*) [194] of God's covenant, they are dependable [195] for them to keep them alive a thousand generations.

Here the sectaries are described as living in accordance with the teachings (*yissurim*) of God's covenant, the Torah. These teachings, when followed, will guarantee the sectarian eternal life.

CDC 20:31f. has already been cited.[196] There the verb *ysr* is used in connection with the original regulations (*ha-mishpaṭim ha-rishonim*) in which the men of the sect were instructed. CDC 4:7-10, a similar

---

188 Commentary to DSD 3:1.

189 On the same passage.

190 Cf. the note in *Ha-Sefarim Ha-Ḥiṣonim*, ed. A. Kahana (1922/3) I, 441.

191 MS. A. Cf. MS. B, 19:1f.

192 The MS. clearly reads *yswrw* at this point, yet it is probable that this is a case of a confusion on the part of some scribe of *waw* and *yod*, which are identical in Qumran texts. See 30f. n. 61, 48 n. 176. The millenial gap in our knowledge of the history of the Zadokite text makes it impossible to know when such errors occurred. Alternately, it is possible to retain *yissuro* (a collective) and to posit a sentence break immediately thereafter. *Berit ʾel* would now become the subject of the next clause, on which see below.

193 The antecedent is the laws of the sect. Cf. CDC 8:2 (Rabin).

194 See Rabin to this passage as well as A. Ehrlich, *Mikra ki-Pheschuto* (1899-1901) III, 172-3, 215, and H. Yalon, *MMY*, 78f.

195 Hebrew *neʾemanot* is problematical as it would appear that we require a masculine to agree with *yissure berit ʾel*. Emendation is fruitless, even with reference to Ps. 89:29, because of the parallel in CDC 14:1 as well as the agreement of both MSS. of our text. Rather, the subject of *neʾemanot* may be identical with the antecedent of *ʾeleh* (see note 193), the *miṣwot*. This would explain the feminine pl. form. If we accepted the alternate reading proposed in note 192, we would have to emend to *neʾemenet* (sing).

196 Above, 43.

passage, has also been discussed.[197] It is to be noted that in this passage, the object of the verb *ysr b-* is *perush ha-torah*, the details of sectarian *halakhah* derived through exegesis. This would seem to confirm the interpretation of *mishpaṭim* in CDC 20:31f. as regulations (of a sectarian nature) rather than punishments.

DSD 9:10f. also confirms this interpretation:

ונשפטו במשפטים הרשונים[198] אשר החלו אנשי היחד לתיסר[199] בם עד בוא נביא ומשיחי אהרון וישראל

> And they will [200] be judged according to the original regulations (*ha-mishpaṭim ha-rishonim*) in which the men of the community began to be instructed (*lityasser*), until the coming of a prophet [201] and the anointed ones of Aaron and Israel.[202]

The members of the sect are to be judged according to the sectarian laws until the coming of the Messianic era. It is now possible to suggest an interpretation for the phrase *ha-mishpaṭim ha-rishonim*. The adjective "original" is used here to distinguish the sect's law, based only on the Bible and its interpretation, from that of the Pharisees, which, according to Josephus, had no basis in Scripture.[203] These regulations must have been considered new by the sect. In contradistinction they termed their *halakhah* "*ha-mishpaṭim ha-rishonim*" and in so doing emphasized its antiquity and identity with the Torah.

Rishon, "original," was also used by the tannaim to designate ancient practices and traditions. The term *ba-rishonah* preceded mention of older practices which had been replaced by more recent rulings. Z. Frankel points out that some of these were (1) teachings of the

---

197 Above, 38f.

198 Normally spelled *hr'šwnym*. Cf. Licht, *MH*, 47.

199 The *h* of the *hitpaʿel* is often omitted at Qumran. See Licht, *MH*, 46, *Megillat Ha-Hodayot*, 9. Cf. Ges. rule 54d.

200 Or "Lest they be," connecting this with the previous clause in DSD. See also Yalon, *MMY*, 78.

201 Cf. 1 Macc. 4:46, 14:41.

202 On the two-Messiah concept see Wernberg-Møller, *ad loc.*, A. Higgins, "Priest and Messiah," *VT* 3 (1953), 321-36, W. S. La Sor, "The Messiah of Aaron and Israel," *VT* 6 (1956), 425-9, R. Laurin, "The Problem of the Two Messiahs in the Qumran Scrolls," *RQ* 4 (1963), 39-52, J. Liver, *Toledot Bet Dawid* (1959), 117-147, "The Doctrine of the Two Messiahs in Sectarian Literature in the Time of the Second Commonwealth," *HTR* 52 (1959), 149-85, "*Ha-Mashiaḥ Mi-Bet Dawid Bi-Megillot Midbar Yehudah*," in *ʿIyyunim Bi-Megillot Midbar Yehudah* (1964), ed. J. Liver, G. Margoliouth, "The Two Zadokite Messiahs," *JTS* 12 (1910-11), 446-50, L. Silberman, "The Two Messiahs of the Manual of Discipline," *VT* 5 (1955), 77-82.

203 Ant. 13, 10:6.

Sages which were later changed, while other cases involved (2) popular practices of which the tannaim did not approve. Some of the first type are called *mishnah rishonah*.[204] There is an essential difference between the Qumran and tannaitic uses of *rishon*. The sect adheres to *ha-mishpaṭim ha-rishonim* and castigates those who have veered from them. The tannaim reject the original teaching (*mishnah rishonah*) and accept the innovations of the Sages. It may be tempting to assume that the *halakhah* of the sect is therefore identical to that referred to by the tannaim as "original." While such identity may be shown for some *halakhot*,[205] the evidence will not support such a general conclusion.

In DSD 3:1 the terms *yissure daʿat* and *mishpeṭe ṣedeq* appear in parallelism, emphasizing again the identity of the *yissurim* and *mishpaṭim*. Both of these are rejected by the enemies of the sect, further proof of their sectarian character.

A similar parallelism is found in DSD 3:5-6:

טמא טמא יהיה כול יומי מואסו במשפטי אל לבלתי התיסר ביחד עצתו

> Impure, impure [206] shall he be, all of the days [207] of his rejection of the regulations (*mishpeṭe*) of God, so that he not be instructed (*ysr*) in the community of His counsel.[208]

The sectarian usage of these terms is indisputable. Again in CDC 7:6-9, quoted above,[209] the sect, upon assumption of family life, is admonished to live according to the Torah and the *mishpaṭ ha-yissurim ke-serekh ha-torah*, "the regulation of the teachings [210] according to the rule of the Torah." This makes it clear that the *mishpaṭim* and *yissurim* are the sectarian laws derived through explanations of the Bible. These go hand in hand with Scripture as sources of sectarian law.

All of this clarifies the reading in CDC 10:4-7. There we must

---

[204] See Z. Frankel, *Darkhe Ha-Mishnah*, 146-150, 221, and Epstein, *Tannaim*, 21-23. E. E. Urbach, "*Ha-Derashah Ki-Yesod Ha-Halakhah U-Beʿayat Ha-Soferim*," *Tarbiẓ* 27 (1957/8), 168 suggests that some of these practices may be pre-Maccabean.

[205] Cf the discussion of *muqṣeh*, below, 117-119.

[206] This repetition occurs only in Lev. 13:45 as the formal declaration of the impurity of the *ṣaruʿa* made by the priest.

[207] On this Aramaicizing plural form, see Licht, *MH*, 44, Kutscher, 20, Yalon, *MMY*, 57, 72.

[208] The familiar construct of two synonyms. This is, no doubt, equivalent to the *ʿaṣat ha-yaḥad* (Wernberg-Møller).

[209] Above, 46.

[210] Another construct of two synonyms.

read *yissure ha-berit*,[211] "the teachings of the covenant." Here "covenant" is a synonym for the sect [212] and these teachings (*yissurim*) are mentioned alongside the *Sefer He-Hagu*, a term for the Torah. This, then, is another case in which the Torah and its sectarian interpretation are mentioned side by side.

The term *mesorot* which occurs quite frequently in the *War Scroll* will allow us to make a suggestion as to how *yissurim*, a term used primarily for "chastisement" or "punishment" in the Bible, can take on the primary meaning of "teaching" or "instruction" in the Qumran literature. According to Yadin,[213] the *mesorot* were subdivisions of the *serekh*, defined as "militia formations of the congregation." Yadin remarks that *srk* and *msr* have cognate meanings. He also mentions the tendency of terms for "tying" or "binding" to turn up as names for military units.[214] It would appear that some confusion of roots occurred, so that *mesorot* was viewed as connected with the root *ysr* rather than *ʾsr* from which it is derived in the lexicons.[215] Because of this, *yissurim* took on a meaning of "orders" or "instructions," derived from the term *mesorot* in the same way that *serekh*, a military formation, became and "order" or "rule" in the legal literature at the Dead Sea.[216]

There is evidence of this same confusion in biblical literature. Ezek. 20:37 contains the phrase *be-masoret ha-berit*. Even though spelled without an *ʾalef*, many commentators have taken this to be a nominal form of *ʾsr*.[217] In view of the cases in which initial *ʾalef* verbs lose their first root letter in various forms,[218] this would seem a most acceptable interpretation. While the reading behind the Greek (*ba-mispar*) is, no doubt, a corruption, the text in the Syriac seems

---

211 Against Rabin and Schecter and with Brownlee. Cf. CDC 14:6-8 in which parallel *mishpeṭe ha-torah* replaces *yissure ha-berit*.

212 See Licht, *MH*, 51f., DSD 8:17f. (and commentaries, *ad loc.*) and our 48 n. 175.

213 *War Scroll*, 40f.

214 P. 41.

215 Cf. Yalon's discussion of the root *ysr* and its equivalence to *ʾsr* in *MMY*, 78f.

216 P. 148, n. 11. Cf. DSW 3:3, 12.

217 Kimchi, Ehrlich, *ad loc.* Kimchi, *Sefer Ha-Shorashim*, *s.v.* *ʾsr* attributes this view to Judah Ibn Ḥayyuj. The connection of the root *ʾsr* with *berit* is not surprising in light of the connections of "tying" with covenants and oaths. The Masoretic note (*ḥaser ʾalef*) appearing in the printed Bibles seems to be a late addition.

218 Cf. the noun *moser* from *ʾsr*, Ges. rule 68i, k. This seems to have been a more common phenomenon in Mishnaic Hebrew (Segal, *Diqduq*, 138f.), perhaps as a result of Aramaic influence.

to take *masoret* as a derivative of the root *ysr*.[219] Is. 8:11 may represent a similar confusion. There *wa-yisreni* may mean "he bound me" so that I would not go.[220] It should also be noted that Aramaic *ysr* means "to bind."

5. *Drš*, *Midrash*

I. Heinemann has studied the development of the term *midrash*.[221] This noun occurs twice in the Bible (2 Chron. 13:22, 24:27). Both times the *midrash* appears as a source of additional historical information. The LXX has translated βιβλίον, γραφή and the Vulgate, *liber*. *Midrash* appears to be a synonym for *sefer*. Many scholars have followed Wellhausen[222] in taking *midrash* to be a denominative from *drš* and assuming it to have its later meaning. They have, therefore, seen these *midrashim* as exegetical or aggadic accounts of the period of the monarchy. Heinemann observes, though, that the verb *drš* is not used to describe exegetical activity in the Bible. Only in Deut. 13:15 does the verb mean "to investigate," but it applies to witnesses—not texts. Phrases such as occur in Is. 34:16 and Ezra 7:10 refer to assiduous investigation for the purpose of fulfilling God's Law. It may be, suggests Heinemann, that the noun *midrash*, as it occurs in Chronicles, must be taken in the sense of the root in Ps. 111:2. A *midrash* would then be a description (or account) of important deeds.

The phrase *bet midrash* first occurs in Ben Sira 51:23. Basing himself on the Greek text, Heinemann takes this reference as metaphorical. In the Dead Sea Scrolls, Heinemann will admit that the root has already acquired the exegetical meaning. He sees *midrash* in the 4Q Florilegium as the heading for a series of *pesharim*. This, as will be seen below, cannot be accepted.[223] Heinemann did not discern the technical difference between the two kinds of exegesis. Nevertheless, he correctly observes that the Qumran uses of the root

---

[219] See G. A. Cooke, *Ezekiel*, 221, 225.

[220] Note that this is the only occurrence of *ysr* in the *qal* in the Bible. This interpretation of Is. 8:11 would be consistent with Yalon's view mentioned above (and n. 215). Jonah Ibn Janaḥ, *Sefer Ha-Shorashim*, *s.v. ysr*, advances an explanation for this passage which seems to show that it belongs under *ʾsr*. This confusion was quite persistent.

[221] I. Heinemann, "*Midrash*," *Enc. Bib.* 4, 695f. Cf. his previous studies cited in the bibliography, p. 701, E. E. Urbach, "*Ha-Derashah*," 171f., and Epstein, *Tannaim*, 501.

[222] *Prolegomena to the History of Ancient Israel* (1965), 227.

[223] Below, 59f.

correspond to the tannaitic. He sees this new exegetical connotation as a development from the various meanings of *drš* in the Bible.

Segal [224] has raised objections to Heinemann's analysis. Basing himself on Ben Sira [225] as well as sources contemporary with this book, he concludes that the process of "midrashic" exegesis must go back even further than Ben Sira. Segal justly takes issue with Heinemann's assumption that the Greek translator of Ben Sira took the phrase *bet midrash* metaphorically. Rather, the translator understood *midrash* as a process of study (Heb. "*limud we-talmud*"). The "house" was then the place in which Ben Sira instructed his students. Segal makes no attempt, however, to claim that Ben Sira was a teacher of the oral Law. Instead, he seems to have been continuing the tradition of the ancient wisdom schools known from biblical literature as well as throughout the ancient Near East. At any rate, by this time *bet midrash* must have been a well-known technical term describing a school for adults (as opposed to the *bet sefer*).

Segal, while agreeing with Heinemann that Wellhausen's explanation for biblical *midrash* is untenable, suggests that the Chronicler referred to the two works as *midrash* to distinguish them from the *sefarim*,[226] those works taught in the *bet sefer*. The term *midrash* would refer to those works the study of which was reserved for the *bet midrash*. Those who aspired to join the ranks of the *soferim* would attend this institution of higher learning.

While Segal's strictures seem justified in regard to the period of Ben Sira, and while some biblical usages might support an early date for the beginnings of the midrashic process, it is doubtful if Segal's explanation of the term *midrash* can be accepted. Segal had rejected Wellhausen's view because it assumed that the term had developed to the full extent of its Rabbinic use by the time of the Chronicler. It seems, though, that Segal's theory would require even fuller development of the term than Wellhausen's. Only after the process was called *midrash* could one refer to the school in which it was practiced as a *bet midrash*. Only then could books studied in this school acquire the name *midrash*. Heinemann's understanding of *midrash* is further in accord with the ancient versions and its context in Chronicles. It would seem, then, that while accepting generally the account given by Heinemann, it is necessary to push

---

[224] "*Drš, Midrash, Bet Midrash,*" *Tarbiẓ* 17 (1945/6), 194-6.
[225] Cf. his *Sefer Ben Sira' Ha-Shalem*, 362, and the note in Charles, *ad loc.*
[226] See above, 33 n. 75.

the date of the exegetical use of *drš* and *midrash* at least back to the time of Ben Sira. This would make it easy to understand why the Qumran texts, probably composed shortly after Ben Sira, exhibit such a wide use of this root in its exegetical and technical sense.

It is now time to turn to the uses of this root in the sectarian literature. Rabin has translated *doresh ha-torah* as "Searcher of the Law," [227] apparently because he did not realize that already at Qumran this term had taken on a technical, exegetical significance. He likewise translated *midrash ha-torah* as "investigation of the Law," meaning "investigation according to the Law," [228] a translation which also disregards the technical sense of this term.

Delcor [229] points to the centrality of the study of the Law in Qumran literature. But the question must be answered whether *midrash* is simply study or if it denotes a particular literary genre. He assumes that the Chronicler's citations of *midrash* show that there was already such a genre in his time. This view cannot be supported in light of the studies of Heinemann and Segal.

Delcor next surveys the verbal uses of the root in the *Manual of Discipline*. *Drš* can signify interrogating someone. The verb is also used with *mishpaṭ* in the sense of "studying" or "searching" the Law, or in a religious sense, "to seek God." Finally, the root can mean "to study" or "teach" the Torah. He sees these usages as identical with those of the Bible except that the meaning "to seek an oracle" is not attested at Qumran.

Delcor continues by stating that *midrash ha-torah* must, above all, signify the study of the Torah. While this is dependent on his view of the biblical material which is not supported by the sources, his conclusion is nevertheless correct in light of the occurrence of the term *midrash* in Ben Sira. Delcor rightly observes that for the sect, the best way to seek God is to study His Law. Failure to study the *nistarot* as well as errors in their interpretation have led Israel to transgress. Most important, Delcor draws the distinction between the *midrash ha-torah*, the product of exegesis, and an oral Law, such as is described in M. ʾAbot 1:1.[230]

The *midrash ha-torah*, in the view of Delcor,[231] must have occurred in a *bet midrash*, a "house of study." He suggests that the main building

[227] To CDC 6:7.
[228] Trans. and commentary to CDC 20:6.
[229] "*Contribution*," 66-69.
[230] P. 537.
[231] P. 72-75.

at Qumran may have been designated for this purpose. Noting the occurrence of the term in Ben Sira, Delcor proposes taking *midrash* as an elipsis for *bet midrash* in some passages, but admits that these passages are subject to another interpretation. They may be using the word *midrash* in its usual meaning of "study." He also acknowledges that *bet midrash* never occurs at Qumran. He points out that the expression *bet ha-torah* (CDC 20:10, 13) must be understood figuratively, as a description of the sect, yet he suggests that the image may be based on the fact that, in essence, the Qumran community was a school of exegesis.

In tannaitic technical terminology, the verb *drš* and its nominal formation, *midrash*, are used in the sense of "to derive the law through Scriptural exegesis." [232] It is precisely this usage which is encountered at Qumran.[233] DSD 8:11f. cited above,[234] mentions the *ʾish ha-doresh*, the man who publicly expounds the law and its sectarian interpretation.

In DSD 5:7-12 the purpose of inquiring (*drš*) into God's laws is to learn the *nistarot*, the "hidden interpretations." This must have been the main function of the *doresh ha-torah*, the expounder of the Law.[235] From DSD 5:6f. it is clear that members of the sect served alternately as *doresh ha-torah*.[236]

In CDC 6:1-11 there is an "aggadic" exegesis of Num. 21:18. There we find (ll. 7f.):

והמחוקק הוא דורש התורה אשר אמר ישעיה מוציא כלי למעשיהו

> And the "staff" ("lawmaker") is the expounder of the Law, about whom Isaiah said (Is. 54:16): "He brings forth a tool [237] for His work."

---

[232] See Bacher, *ʿErkhe Midrash*, 19-21, 173-175, Strack, 6, I. Heinemann, *Darkhe Ha-ʾAggadah* (1970), 115, "*Midrash*," *Enc. Bib.* 4, 695-701, "*Hitpatḥut Ha-Munaḥim Ha-Miqṣoʿiyim Le-Ferush Ha-Miqraʾ*," *Leshonenu* 14 (1945/6), 185f. and M. D. Herr, "Midrash," *EJ* 11 (1971), 1507f.

[233] But contrast the view of Baumgarten, "Unwritten Law," 26f. and notes.

[234] Above, 28.

[235] On the *doresh ha-torah*, see N. Wieder, "The Law-Interpreter of the Sect of the Dead Sea Scrolls: The Second Moses," *JJS* 4 (1953), 158-75, "The Idea of a Second Coming of Moses," *JQR* N.S. 46 (1955-6), 356-64 (with a postscript by S. Zeitlin, 364ff.), P. Winter, "Notes on Wieder's Observations on the *Doresh Ha-Torah* in the Book of the New Covenanters of Damascus," *JQR* N.S. 45 (1954-5), 39-47.

[236] Wernberg-Møller, *ad loc.*

[237] Ginzberg, *MGWJ* 56 (1912), 38, compares the phrase *keli le-dibberot* used of Moses in the *Mekhiltaʾ De-Rabbi Ishmael*, beginning. This reading, however, is based on emendation (cf. the note of Ginzberg and the apparatus in ed. Horovitz-Rabin).

It is possible that the connection of the verse in Isaiah with the text being expounded here (Num. 21:18) is based on the similarity of the roots *yṣ'* and *mṣ'*. This kind of similarity is often the basis of *midrashim* found in Rabbinic literature.[238] The association would then be with the *nimṣa'*, the sectarian derivation of the law through exegesis.[239] The *meḥoqeq*, lawmaker, is identified with the expounder, whose main function, the derivation of the sectarian regulations, is described (according to the interpretation of the *Zadokite Fragments*) in Is. 54:16.

The result of the efforts of the *doresh ha-torah* is the *midrash* or *midrash ha-torah*, another term for sectarian law. In connection with the man who has been deprived of his status in the sect because of deviations from its *halakhah*, CDC 20:6-7 states:

ובהופע מעשיו כפי מדרש התורה אשר יתהלכו בו אנשי תמים הקדש אל יאות איש עמו ...

> And until [240] his deeds appear according to the interpretation of the Law (*midrash ha-torah*) by which the men of the holy perfection [241] shall live, let no man agree [242] with him...

The man's punishment will extend until he conforms to the regulations of the Torah as understood by the sect, the *midrash*.

DSD 8:25f. lays down the qualifications for a suspended member seeking readmittance to full-fledged membership in the sect:

אם תתם דרכו במושב במדרש ובעצה...

> If his way shall become perfect in [243] the session, the exegesis (*midrash*) and the counsel...[244]

If these qualifications are met, the violator can be readmitted. Here, too, *midrash* refers to the peculiar halakhic exegesis of the sect.

It is also the *midrash ha-torah* by which the sect is to be judged. At the head of a list of punishments for offenses against sectarian

---

[238] Cf. CDC 7:14-16 and our comments above, 31f.

[239] Cf. the use of *nimṣa'* with the verb *drš* in CDC 8:11.

[240] The syntax necessitates the assumption that the prep. *b* can mean "until." Rabin's suggestion that the author forgot how he started the sentence seems less likely.

[241] *Sc.* the sect.

[242] The same usage occurs in 2 K. 12:9.

[243] Licht's interpretation seems to require "according to." Cf. Wernberg-Møller, ***ad loc.***

[244] For this clause MS. d reads *we-shab ba-midrash u-ba-ʿeṣah.*

halakhah this formula appears (DSD 6:24):

ואלה המשפטים אשר ישפטו בם במדרש יחד על פי הדברים

> And these are the regulations by which they shall judge in the interpretation (*midrash*)[245] of the community, according to the(se) cases.

What has been said here about *midrash* should enable us to comment on DSD 8:15-16 discussed above.[246] The *midrash* in that passage is the sectarian interpretation of the Torah which God had commanded through the agency of Moses, *i.e.* (as the passage continues) the exegesis of the *nigleh*. *Midrash*, then, is the sectarian interpretation of the *nigleh*, and, hence, equivalent to *nistar*.

The last legal passage to be discussed dealing with the term *midrash* is a variant reading to DSD 5:1. The reading in the St. Mark's manuscript is:

וזה הסרך לאנשי היחד המתנדבים...

> And this is the rule (*serekh*) concerning the men of the community who volunteer...

Milik has cited [247] this variant:

מדרש למשכיל על אנשי התורה המתנדבים...

> An interpretation (*midrash*) for the *maskil* concerning the men of the Torah who volunteer...

This is most probably a case of the well-known phenomenon of synonymous variants.[248] *Midrash* here would seem to be a synonym of *serekh*, which will be discussed later.[249]

A final word should be said about the technical or specific meaning of the term *midrash*. The 4Q Florilegium [250] contains a short exegesis

---

[245] See the comments of Wernberg-Møller, *ad loc.* The words *bam be-midrash yaḥad* are omitted in MS. g.

[246] P. 26.

[247] "*Le travail d'édition des fragments manuscrits de Qumrân,*" *RB* 63 (1956), 61, cf. Licht, *MH*, 123.

[248] At first glance *le-ʾanshe ha-yaḥad* and *la-maskil ʿal ʾanshe ha-torah* may not appear synonymous. The texts must be understood as follows: The St. Mark's MS. must be taken as giving the rule concerning the volunteers. The variant addresses this rule (here called *midrash*) to the attention of the *maskil*, the sectarian teacher. The men of the Torah are the same as those of the sect (*yaḥad*).

[249] See 60-68.

[250] J. M. Allegro in *DJD* 5, 53-57, "Further Messianic References in Qumran Literature," *JBL* 75 (1956), 176f., and "Fragments of a Qumran Scroll of Eschatological Midrašim," *JBL* 77 (1958), 350-354. Cf. Y. Yadin, "A Midrash on 2 Sam. vii and Ps. i-ii (4Q Florilegium)," *IEJ* 9 (1959), 97. (I first made the suggestion to follow in my Brandeis University honors thesis, "Scriptural Allusions in the Hodayot Scroll," May, 1970, p. 9, and I here repeat those conclusions making some modifications in wording).

of Ps. 1:1 and 2:1f. The *'aṣat resha'im* of 1:1 is understood as "those who turn from the path (of righteousness)." This interpretation is supported in the usual midrashic manner by Is. 8:11 which is understood as referring to the "end of days" and by a quotation from Ezekiel, probably from 37:23,[251] identifying the sect with the *bene ṣadoq*. Ps. 2:1f. is also understood as a reference to the elect of Israel, *i.e.* the sect, in the "end of days."

On the basis of this passage an interesting suggestion can be made. The explanation of Ps. 1:1 is called a *midrash* while that of Ps. 2:1f. is called a *pesher*.[252] The essential difference between these interpretations is that the first brings testimony from another biblical passage to confirm its suggestion, while the second gives no such supporting evidence. It would appear, then, that the distinction between *midrash* and *pesher* lies in the use of evidence from the Scriptures. A *midrash* requires such references, while a *pesher* does not.[253]

All of the passages discussed thus far would seem to indicate that *midrash* can refer only to halakhic exegesis. This is not correct. This florilegium indicates that *midrash* can be used for halakhic or "aggadic" exegesis, although its halakhic application is more common in the scrolls.[254]

6. *Serekh* [255]

Ever since Solomon Schechter's discovery of the *Zadokite Fragments*, the peculiar use of the word *serekh* has puzzled scholars. In commenting on its first occurrence (CDC 7:6a, 19:15), Schechter pointed to its affinity with Rabbinic *serekh* and *sirkha'*, and translated "usage." [256] Charles pointed to the correspondence of *serekh* to Greek τάξις in the Testaments of the Twelve Patriarchs, and to the use of

[251] So according to Yadin. Allegro is more inclined to accept Ezek. 44:10.

[252] On this term see Yalon, *MMY*, 65 (first published as "*Pesher Habaqquq*," *Qiryat Sefer* 27 (1950/1), 172), I. Heinemann, "*Hitpatḥut Ha-Munaḥim*," 20-28, Delcor, "*Contribution*," 69ff., I. Rabinowitz, "*Pēsher/Pittārōn*. Its Biblical Meaning and its Significance in the Qumran Literature," *RQ* 8 (1973), 219-232. For the medieval use of the roots *ptr* and *pšr* cf. P. R. Weis, "The Date of the Habakkuk Scroll," *JQR* N.S. 41 (1950/1), 126-131. Weis accepts a medieval dating of the scrolls.

[253] A check of the material in *DJD* reveals no exceptions. This was not noticed by M. R. Lehmann, "Midrashic Parallels to Selected Qumran Texts," *RQ* 3 (1961-2), 545-551.

[254] The halakhic *midrash* is most probably earlier. See above, 19 and n. 77.

[255] This material was read under the title "Aspects of the Halakhic Terminology of Qumran: *Serekh*," American Oriental Society, Mar. 21, 1973.

[256] *Documents* I, XXXIX, cf. XI.

sarkhin in Dan. 6:3-5, etc. as well as the parallel *ḥoq* in MS B. Accordingly, he translated "order." [257] These views were echoed by M. H. Segal who also cited Rabbinic *serekh bittah* (B. Niddah 67b).[258]

Ginzberg [259] suggested that it is difficult to derive *serekh* in the *Zadokite Fragments* from Talmudic *serekh*, German "*Folge*." Even so, he pointed out that R. Ḥananel, in his commentary to B. Yoma' 30a, explains *serekh* as *minhag*, "custom," and that this is the sense in which *serekh* appears in the fragments. He also cited the Greek parallel in the Testaments according to which *serekh* would have to be translated "*Ordnung, Regel*." Ginzberg suggested that *serekh* in the fragments was probably derived from a root different from that of Talmudic *serekh*.

With the publication of the Qumran texts, there was renewed interest in the *Zadokite Fragments*. Rabin,[260] like Schechter, failed to realize the existence of two independent roots *srk*. He added material citing Ethiopic *sirak*, "line, way," and Soqotri [261] *sīrīk*, "*entrave*," [262] as well as biblical *serokh*, "string." He followed Charles's translation of "order," also repeating his citation of the reference from the Testaments.

The editors of the *Manual of Discipline* faced the same problem. W. H. Brownlee translated "order," explaining *serekh* as "practice, orderly procedure, ritual," but added little to the discussion.[263] He cited the reference in the *War Scroll* which will be taken up below. Wernberg-Møller summarized the evidence cited thus far and added, apparently independently of Yadin, that the full range of meanings of Greek τάξις could be applied to Hebrew *serekh*.[264] Licht [265] pointed out that the basic meaning of the root *srk* is "order, series (*shurah*)," and that only in DSD 1:16 did *serekh* actually serve as a name of the sect. Its general meanings were (a) "a series of decrees or statements arranged in a small collection" [266] and (b) "a series of people arranged according to a particular rule," as in its use for a military

257 *APOT* II, 815, followed by Delcor, "*Contribution*," 544.
258 "*Sefer Berit Dameseq*," *Ha-Shiloaḥ* 26 (1912), 491.
259 *MGWJ* 56 (1912), 45.
260 *The Zadokite Documents*, 27.
261 A survival of OSA spoken on the island of Socotra in the Indian Ocean (C. Rabin, "Semitic Languages," *EJ* 14 (1971), 1153).
262 French for "shackle, fetter, hobble."
263 *Manual*, 7.
264 *MD*, 44.
265 *MH*, 66.
266 *E.g.* DSD 5:1, 6:8, *Serekh Ha-ʿEdah* 1:1, DSW 9:10.

unit.[267] After citing the parallel with τάξις, Licht goes on to say that Josephus uses the term τάγμα [268] for the Essene brotherhood (Wars 2:122, 166).

B. Levine [269] has recently surveyed the uses of the root *srk*. He has concluded that it is necessary to distinguish between (1) the root *srk* which occurs in verbal forms in biblical and Rabbinic usage and in nominal *serekh* or *sirkha'*, and whose basic meanings are "to adhere to, follow, tie, wind one's way," etc., and (2) the root primarily represented by nominal forms *serekh* or *sirkha'* meaning "custom, practice, rule." Levine states that "it can be shown that the [Dead Sea] term *serek*, and related forms, convey the basic sense of governance and administration and not the notion of 'following, adhering' or the like. The same is probably true for some Talmudic occurrences of *serek/sirka'*." Levine follows Rosenthal in deriving the Aramaic *sarakh* (Dan. 6:3-5) from Avestan *sara*, "head," [270] and suggests that the correct translation is "prescription, procedure, statute/code." He explains the verbal uses in the *War Scroll*, to be discussed below, as denominative from the form in Daniel. Accordingly, he translates *serekh* in the Persepolis texts as "administration."

An additional word must be said about the Avestan derivation of *sarakh*. *Sara* meaning "head" is attested in Avestan as well as in

---

[267] *E.g.* DSD 2:20, 5:23, DSW 5:4 and, militarily, DSW 7:1.

[268] "The noun *taxis* is cognate to the verb *tasso*, and to the noun *tagma*. The verb *tasso* has several related meanings: 1. 'to arrange, put in order, array, marshal,' etc. 2. 'to appoint, to assign a task, to order one to do a thing,' 3. 'to place in a certain order, to lay down rule; to impose laws.' The term *tagma* means: 'that which has been ordered or arranged,' especially; 'an ordinance, command.'... Greek *tagma* also means: 'a regular body of soldiers, a division; an order or rank.' " (B. Levine, "Aramaic Texts from Persepolis," *JAOS* 92 (1972), 74. Cf. Liddell-Scott, *Greek-English Lexicon*, *s.v.*). Licht also points to the use of διαταγμάι and διαταξείς for collections of regulations in the early church document *Constitutiones Apostolicae*. Cf. also S. Mowinckel, "The Hebrew Equivalent of Taxo in Ass. Mos. IX," *Supplements to VT* 1 (1953), 88-94, and Delcor, "Contribution", *RB* 62 (1955), 60-66.

[269] "Persepolis," 72-75. To his references add S. Lieberman, *TK* IV, 745 (commenting on T. Kippurim 1:16, *ṣorekh bittah*, a phonetic corruption) and L. Ginzberg, *Perushim We-Ḥiddushim Ba-Yerushalmi* II, 321-325. Cf. also R. A. Bowman, *Aramaic Ritual Texts from Persepolis* (1970), 22-24.

[270] F. Rosenthal, *A Grammar of Biblical Aramaic* (1963), 58, rule 189. Cf. also A. Kohut, *'Arukh Ha-Shalem*, *s.v.* and addenda (Vol. 9), *s.v.*, as well as L. Ginzberg, *Ginze Schechter* I, 252, and S. Feigin, "Etymological Notes," *AJSLL* 43 (1926), 54. This same derivation is accepted by A. A. Bevin, S. R. Driver (BDB, *s.v.*), H. Bauer, P. Leander, *Kurzgefasste Biblisch-Aramäische Grammatik* (1965), 77. Cf. J. Levy, *Wörterbuch über die Talmudim und Midraschim* (1876-89) III, 593, *s.v. sarkha'*.

Pahlavi.[271] The ending *ka* in Old and Middle Persian indicates the doer of an action. *Sari tir*, literally "head of an arrow," is used in classical Persian for "a learned, distinguished man, one who administrates justice." [272]

Most recently, M. Weinfeld has discussed *serekh*.[273] After pointing out that Akkadian *riksu*, *rikistu*, *rikiltu* indicates the tie of obligation to the covenant, he remarks that the actual origin of *serekh* in the Dead Sea Scrolls is the meaning "tie," like Heb. *śrk* (*serokh ha-naʿal*). According to Weinfeld, the actual meaning of *serekh* is "binding" and "tightening," sometimes "dragging" or "drawing." He therefore cites *serekh bittah* (B. Niddah 67b), and *serekh terumah* (B. Ḥullin 106b). He also compares the Arabic root *šrk*. Weinfeld concludes that *serekh* must be explained as *berit* ("covenant"). He claims that the military use of *serekh* strengthens his case in that words for "tying" are often used in this context. As an example, he cites Akkadian *riksa*, *rākasu* which literally means "to tie a knot," but can be used for (1) to make a covenant, (2) to make an arrangement for a sacrifice in the cult or set a table (*paššura rākasu*), (3) to draw up a battle or military formation. This Akkadian root is semantically parallel to Hebrew *ʿrk*.[274] The root *ʾsr* is also similar. In Num. 30:4 it refers to a covenant. In Ps. 118:27 it is used cultically and it appears in a military usage in 2 K. 20:14. The same range of meanings, Weinfeld observes, is present in Greek τάξις. The main problem with Weinfeld's analysis, though, is that he ignores the appearance of this root in the Bible as a *nomen agentis*, as well as the derivations proposed for this noun. Finally, *srk* can also be used to represent a leader, to which Weinfeld's Akkadian material offers no parallel.

Yadin has discussed *serekh* in its military context.[275] He writes:

> DSW uses it as meaning disciplinary rule, custom, order... as do the other scrolls but extends its uses further:... it appears as a verb to indicate the action to be accomplished in a certain sequence or according to rule and those responsible for carrying it out... the word *serekh* occurs in this scroll to indicate the actual body or unit as arrayed into a formation or acting according to a prescribed order...

[271] C. Bartholomae, *Altiranisches Wörterbuch* (1904), 1565, *s.v. sarah*, H. S. Nyberg, *A Manual of Pahlavi* (1964), 202, D. N. MacKenzie, *A Concise Pahlavi Dictionary* (1971), 74.

[272] F. Steinglass, *Persian-English Dictionary* (1892), 665. To the ending *ka*, Levy compares *ganzakh* (1 Chron. 28:11).

[273] "'*Ha-Berit We-Ha-Ḥesed*—,' *Ha-Munaḥim We-Gilgule Hitpatḥutam Be-Yisrael U-Ba-ʿOlam Ha-ʿAtiq*," *Leshonenu* 36 (1972), 85-105. See especially 104f.

[274] Cf. 2 Sam. 23:5 (*ʿrk* + *berit*).

[275] *War Scroll*, 148-50, 151f. See also Yalon, *MMY*, 39, n. 34.

The fundamental problem in understanding the use of *serekh* as a legal term is that of realizing its military origins. Yadin seems to be purposely non-committal on the question of which usage is original, the military or the legal. It would be more logical to assume that the original use of this term is in the military context. It is a common phenomenon in language for terms of military command or rank to assume legal function. This was the case with *shofeṭ* and *shoṭer*, two terms originally used as military officers' titles, and Latin *iudex* and *praetor*, terms which seem to have travelled the same path.[276] Yadin lists these examples of the military usage of *serekh* in the *War Scroll*:

1. 'Upon the trumpets of the formations they shall write "Serekh of God" ' (3:3)
2. 'The horsemen of the Serekh' (6:13)
3. 'The men of the Serekh' (7:1)
4. 'And his brother priests and the Levites and all the elders of the Serekh' (13:1)[277]

Yadin then mentions the well-known parallel between *serekh* in the Aramaic fragment of the Testament of Levi and Greek τάξις and suggests that an examination of the various meanings of this Greek term will throw light on the usages of *serekh*. According to Yadin, the Greek term also can represent "not only a tactical, numerically defined sub-unit of the Hellenistic phalanx but also a formation of indeterminate size . . ." and a congregation or group of people making up a religious or political body.

In line with this last definition is the use of *serekh* as a name for the sect.[278] The military terms "men of the *serekh*" or "elders of the *serekh*" would then refer to the members of the sect.

The Targumim also make use of *sarkha'* and its plural forms as military terms in translating *shoṭerim*.[279] In the *War Scroll* there are officers called *sorekhe ha-maḥanot*, or "camp prefects." Their duties were keeping law and order and supervising the execution of orders.

---

[276] See C. Burney, *The Book of Judges and Notes on the Hebrew Text of the Book of Kings* (1970), xxxiii, 1 (Judges), G. A. Cooke, *A Textbook of North-Semitic Inscriptions* (1903), 115f., H. Donner, W. Röllig, *Kanaanäische und Aramäische Inschriften* (1968) II, 53, R. Yaron, "Semitic Elements in Early Rome," Read at Am. Academy for Jew. Research, 1971.

[277] Cf. Luke 1:8, Heb. 5:6, 10, 6:20, 7:11, 17, 21 (A. R. C. Leaney, *The Rule of Qumran and its Meaning* (1966), 124).

[278] DSD 1:16, *serekh ha-yaḥad*.

[279] Yadin, 151f. Cf. Targumim to Deut. 1:15, 20:5, Pr. 6:7, etc.

They may also have been responsible for assigning the different units their places in the camps.

Two passages in the *War Scroll* allow us a glimpse of the verbal usage of the root *srk*. DSW 2:1-2 contains this regulation:

ואת ראשי הכוהנים יסרוכו[280] אחר כוהן הראש ומשנהו ראשים שנים עשר להיות משרתים בתמיד לפני אל

> And they shall appoint [281] the chiefs of the priests after the Chief Priest and his deputy, twelve chiefs to be attendants for [282] the daily offering before God.

From DSW 2:6 it appears that these appointments were made in the Sabbatical year:

את כול אלה יסרוכו במועד שנת השמטה

> All these they shall appoint at the time of the Sabbatical year.[283]

From these passages, the *serekh*, a battle array or legal instruction, is that which results from the activity of the *sorekh*, the one who issues the order or makes the arrangement. The verb *srk* denotes that act of issuing an order, putting something into order, or arraying.

Two passages in the *War Scroll* link *serekh* with *perush*. DSW 4:6 provides that when the sect goes forth to battle certain attributes of God be written on their banners followed by *kol serekh perush shemotam*, "the whole list of their names in full." [284] Lines 7 and 8 contain similar prescriptions to be enacted when the army closes in for battle and returns from battle. Here, however, the phrase *kol perush shemotam* is found. The word *serekh* can be omitted because *perush* means exactly the same thing as *serekh perush*.[285]

Line 11 of the same page contains another clause with both *perush*

---

[280] For this unusual verb form, see Licht, *MH*, 46, Kutscher, 31, Yalon, *MMY*, 23-26, 72.

[281] With Levine, "Persepolis," 74, Yadin: "dispose."

[282] The phrase comes from 2 Chron. 29:11. We translate *mesharetim* with new JPS to Num. 11:28.

[283] It is also possible that the sect interpreted the phrase *be-mo'ed shenat ha-shemiṭṭah* (Deut. 31:10) to refer to the beginning of the first year of the new cycle, as did the amoraim. This would mean that the sect's appointments occurred in the fall of the first year of the cycle. Cf. Targum Jon., B. Rosh Ha-Shanah 12b, Rashi, and B. Epstein, *Torah Temimah*, to Deut. 31:10.

[284] The translation is Yadin's.

[285] Another example in Qumran literature of the use of synonyms, one in construct with the other.

and *serekh*:

ופרוש שמותם יכתובו [286] עם כול סרכם

> And they should write the list (*perush*) of their names with their complete order (*serekh*).[287]

It is of particular interest that in these passages the *serekh* is a written roster as is the *perush* a written list of names. A similar list is mentioned several times in the *Zadokite Fragments* [288] as well as in DSD 5:23:

וכתבם בסרך איש לפני רעהו לפי שכלו ומעשיו להשמע הכול איש לרעהו הקטן לגדול

> And he [289] shall write them in an order (*serekh*) each before his neighbor, according to his knowledge and deeds, so that all should be heard [290] each by his neighbor, from the least to the greatest.

A more complete picture of this roster is given in CDC 14:3-6:

וסרך מושב כל המחנות יפקדו כלם בשמותיהם הכ[הני]ם לראשונה והלוים שנים ובני ישראל שלשתם והגר רביע ויכתבו בש[מות]יהם איש אחר אחיהו הכהנים לראשונה והלוים שנים ובני ישראל שלושתם והגר רביע וכן ישבו וכן ישאלו לכל

> And the list (*serekh*) of the session of all the camps: They shall all be mustered [291] by their names, the pr[ies]ts first,[292] and the Levites

---

[286] See 65 n. 280.

[287] Cf. lines 12f. and *War Scroll*, 42, n. 1. The identity of *serekh* with *perush* is further attested by a comparison of CDC 12:19 and 14:17 in which the same formulation appears as a solemn conclusion to a body of laws, with the substitution in the second passage of *perush* for *serekh*. Along the same lines, the phrases *serekh ha-torah* (CDC 7:6a, MS. A, cf. 19:5, MS. B) and *perush ha-torah* (CDC 4:7, 6:14) are apparently equivalent in meaning.

[288] CDC 2:13, 4:4f. (from which it appears that a copyist left out an actual list of sectarians which may have once been part of the text). Cf. Neofiti Targ. Gen. 6:4, Targ. Jon. Num. 2:3, M. Rosh Ha-Shanah 2:9, T. Rosh Ha-Shanah 1:18 (2:3) (in MS. Erfurt, London and *ed. princ.* MS. Vienna reads *sipper*. See Lieberman, *TK* V, 1035) for the use of *prš shemot*.

[289] On the possibility that we are dealing here with a plural form written defectively, see Wernberg-Møller, *ad loc.*

[290] Wernberg-Møller is correct in identifying the verb form as *nifʿal* but has totally missed the point. His translation, "obey," obscures the fact that we are dealing with a practice similar to that of the tannaim who, in cases of capital crimes, required the students, lest they be influenced, to cast votes before their teachers. (M. Sanhedrin 4:2. On the text of this *mishnah*, see Albeck's "*HWT*," 445 who corrects according to the readings in the Babylonian and Palestinian Talmuds). The next passage to be cited containing the phrase *we-khen yishaʾalu* confirms our interpretation here.

[291] So Rabin.

[292] The strange forms of the ordinal numbers (first through fourth) have given rise to numerous emendations. It is interesting that in our passage the sequence is repeated with only minor orthographic variations. This would seem to indicate at least that the scribe of our MS. copied his text accurately.

> second, and the children of Israel third, and the proselyte fourth. And they shall be written down by their na[mes], each after his brother,[293] the priests first, and the Levites second, and the children of Israel third, and the proselyte fourth. And thus [294] shall they sit and shall they be asked about everything.

Here again military language is used to describe the arrangement (*serekh*) of the members in order. Members are mustered in the proper sequence so that a written list can be prepared. The function of this list was to provide for roll call votes in the *moshab ha-rabbim*, the sectarian legislative and judicial assembly, and to guarantee each member the right to speak in turn. New members were entered on the roster immediately after admission (DSD 6:21-23), as were members who had been temporarily suspended upon readmittance (DSD 8:19, 9:2). When DSD 7:2 refers to the priestly members of the sect as *ha-kohanim ha-ketubim ba-sefer*, "the priests who are recorded in the document," the reference is to this roster. The use of *sefer* is added evidence for the written nature of this list.[295]

The usual usage of *serekh* in the Dead Sea Scrolls is in the introduction to a set of regulations. It may now be stated with assurance that in this context a *serekh* is a list of *halakhot*. The development of the term would then have been as follows: Originally *sarkha'* was a loan-word into Aramaic (and probably Hebrew) during the Persian period when it denoted an official of the Achaemenid bureaucracy, probably associated in some way with the military.

The link between the bureaucracy and the military is best illustrated by the satrap. Not only did he control the civil affairs of his province, but he was also the leader of its levies. When his men went out to battle, he accompanied them as commander.[296] Since the armies were traditionally broken into sub-units,[297] one may assume that some of the officials under the satrap also had military functions. From the Jewish colony at Elephantine comes additional confirmation. There the governor of the nome, or *fratarak*, was the immediate superior of the *rab ḥaila'*, the "chief of the force." Final appeal was always to the satrap.[298]

---

[293] On this form cf. Licht, *MH*, 44f. Yalon, *MMY*, 55f., and M. H. Goshen-Gottstein, "Linguistic Structure, etc.," 116f.

[294] Or "in this order."

[295] Cf. the phrase *sefer serekh* in DSW 15:5 (partly restored by Yadin), and the variant to DSD 1:1 cited by Licht.

[296] A. T. Olmstead, *A History of the Persian Empire* (1959), 59, 239.

[297] Olmstead, 239.

[298] Olmstead. 244f.

A denominative verb meaning "to administrate, issue an order or array" came into use, followed by a noun meaning "battle array, order, instruction." This military use of *serekh* led to its employment for a list of names in a military context. Since the sect saw itself as a militia preparing for the eschatological war, it appropriated the term for a roster of its members. At the same time, *serekh* became a general term for a series of orders or instructions and was used for a list, body, or code of *halakhot* (usually on one subject) and even as a general term for sectarian law.

7. *Moshab Ha-Rabbim*

E. F. Sutcliffe [299] has devoted a study to the *moshab ha-rabbim*. He notes that this body was the general council of the community and functioned democratically. All decisions concerning law, property, and judgment were made by this group. The members are called *rabbim*, a term including all those who have passed two years of the novitiate and taken the oath of initiation.

Rabin [300] has observed that *moshab* ("session") occurs five times in the *Zadokite Fragments* and that four of these occurrences precede groups of laws. DSD 7:11 makes it clear that the session lasted a limited time and was a recurrent event. DSD 6:8-13 establishes that certain matters of policy were discussed at these meetings and that *rabbim* can serve as a synonym for *moshab ha-rabbim*.

DSD 6:8-10 reads:

וזה הסרך למושב הרבים איש בתכונו הכהנים ישבו לרשונה והזקנים בשנית ושאר כול
העם ישבו איש בתכונו וכן ישאלו למשפט ולכול עצה ודבר אשר יהיה לרבים להשיב
איש את מדעו לעצת היחד

> And this is the rule for the session of the assembly: Each man in his proper place.[301] The priests shall sit first, and the elders second, and the rest of the entire people shall sit each in his place. And thus shall they be asked for regulation(s) (*mishpaṭ*), for any counsel or case [302] which the assembly would have, to answer each to his acquaintance,[303] for the council of the community.

Mishpaṭ, the sectarian law, was determined at public legislative sessions during which disputes were also settled.

---

[299] "The General Council of the Qumran Community," *Biblica* 40 (1959), 971-983. On *rabbim*, see Delcor, "*Contribution*," 548f.

[300] See *QS*, 103.

[301] So Licht, *ad loc.*

[302] For the forensic use of *dabar*, see BDB, *s.v.*

[303] See Licht's references, *ad loc.*

Rabin[304] suggests that the laws of CDC were discussed at these sessions and issued in scrolls at the end of the deliberations. Further, the session administered the sect's finances, accepted new members and served as a court of law. He likens the *moshab ha-rabbim* to the Rabbinic *yeshibah* (a tannaitic term for *bet midrash* and *bet din*) because both were educational and judicial institutions. Rabin also notes that seating in both the *yeshibah* and *moshab* followed a fixed order according to which opinions were expressed when the assembly functioned as a court. Rabin compares the lists of laws (following the word *moshab*) in CDC to the list of eighteen decisions reached by voting mentioned in M. Shabbat 1:4. Here Rabin failed to notice that the Mishnah only mentions the eighteen decrees. There is no listing. Indeed, commentators have debated the identity of these decrees from the amoraim to our own day.[305] This *mishnah* is not a parallel for a list of decisions voted at one session (*moshab*).

Rabin[306] sees allusion to the voting process at Qumran in DSD 7:10-12:

וכן לאיש הנפטר במושב הרבים אשר לוא בעצה וחנם עד שלוש פעמים על מושב אחד
ונענש עשרת ימים ואם יזקפו ונפטר ונענש שלושים יום

> And likewise, as to the man who is absent from[307] the session of the assembly, without permission,[308] and without (good) cause[309] three times[310] in one session, he is fined[311] ten days. And if they stand up[312] and he absent, he is fined thirty days.

---

[304] *QS*, 103f.

[305] Cf. Albeck, "*HWT*," *ad loc.*, T. Shabbat 1:16 and Lieberman, *TK* III, 13-16.

[306] *QS*, 105f. Cf. E. Ferguson, "Qumran and Codex 'D,' " *RQ* 8 (1972), 75-80.

[307] Licht, *ad loc.* takes *nifṭar* to mean "slouches," but is hard pressed for any justification of this translation. Wernberg-Møller translates, "who goes away." The root *pṭr* is used intransitively in the *qal* to mean "escape" in 1 Sam. 19:10 where it is followed by *mipne*. So DSD is not following biblical usage here. Tannaitic Hebrew regularly makes use of the *nifʿal* of this verb (not attested in the Bible) for "to take leave, to depart" (Jastrow). This is clearly the usage of DSD. Our form would be a present participle. From this it would follow that the *b* of *be-moshab* must be another example of the interchange of the prepositions *bet* and *mem* in Qumran Hebrew. See 27f. n. 44.

[308] This means not in accordance with the decision of the assembly.

[309] Yalon and Milik read *hnm*. The fact that the scribe originally wrote an *ʿayin* which he later corrected would make a reading of *ḥnm* certain (Licht). See 32f. n. 73.

[310] This is a rare use of *ʿad* for "during." Cf. BDB, 724b, and Jastrow, *s.v.*

[311] This refers to the reduction of his food ration by one-fourth for the duration of his punishment. See DSD 6:25. Rabin translates "punished," as he does not realize the technical sense of *ʿns*. The use for "fine" is biblical (*e.g.* Deut. 22:19).

[312] See *QS*, 105f. Rabin sees the as a *nifʿal*, "to stand up from a sitting position." For other views, see E. F. Sutcliffe, "The General Council of the Qumran Community," *Biblica* 40 (1959), 974-6.

Rabin's suggestion that the verb *zqf* (l. 11) is to be seen as the semantic equivalent of tannaitic *'md* and that both can mean "to vote" must be accepted. Voting was presumably accomplished by rising from one's seat and remaining standing while the votes were being counted. It has been pointed out that the list of members kept by the sect had as its purpose making sure that all *bona fide* Qumran sectarians would get a chance to express their views and vote at the meetings of the *moshab ha-rabbim*.[313] In short, it can be said that the sectarian assembly functioned like a New England town meeting rather than a constituant assembly.

Among the roles of the priesthood in the biblical period was that of judging.[314] Deut. 17:8-13 enjoins that in difficult cases requiring fuller investigation the litigants go up to the chosen city to be judged by "the Levitical priests and the judge." Deut. 21:5, perhaps reflecting an ideal command, requires that all law suits be decided by priests. M. Haran has noted that the priestly literature does not make reference to the judicial function of the priesthood.

The priest was also a teacher of the Torah. This is alluded to in Deut. 33:10. His knowledge of the law must have been derived from legal discussions held before him. The priest also rendered decisions in matters of impurity and diseases. Such a decision was called a *torah*. Further, the priesthood had a large part in the preservation of books.

DSD 9:7 indicates that the Aaronides had the greatest part in the determination of the *halakhah* at Qumran:

רק בני אהרון ימשלו במשפט ובהון ועל פיהם יצא והגורל לכול תוכן אנשי היחד

> Only the sons of Aaron shall have control over law and property [315] and according to them shall the decision [316] go forth for every norm [317] of the men of the community.

The same idea is found in DSD 5:2-3, except that a role is assigned to non-Aaronides in the decision-making process, and the Sons of Zadok appear as the dominant priests. The language of this passage is almost identical with that cited above.[318] Nevertheless, Rabin

[313] Above, 67.

[314] For a survey, see M. Haran, "Priests and Priesthood," *EJ* 13 (1971), 1079f.

[315] The rest of the quotation is omitted in MS. d.

[316] Assuming the *w* of *whgwrl* to be otiose (Licht and Wernberg-Møller).

[317] So Wernberg-Møller.

[318] For a similar formulation cf. DSD 5:8f. Wernberg-Møller, *MD*, 134, suggests that the older custom may have given the priests absolute authority whereas by the time of our text, the laymen had begun to share in the decision-making process.

has ignored the parallel of DSD 9:7, as well as the historical precedents, and emended the text of DSD 5:2 in such a way as to conclude that the Zadokite priests are subordinate to the "majority of the men of the community" and are an "executive body." [319] To the extent that the Zadokite's authority rested on the consensus of the "majority," Rabin is correct. Yet the texts are describing the day-to-day administration of the sect, clearly under the control of this priestly group.

DSD 5:15f. prohibits members of the sect from answering questions of *halakhah* according to the views of outsiders:

ואשר לוא ישיב איש מאנשי היחד על פיהם לכול תורה ומשפט

> And that no man from the men of the community should answer according to them about any law or regulation.

Members of the sect must live only according to the law as discovered by sectarian exegesis. They may not make use of laws dependent on outside sources of *halakhah*. Most important, the law must be decided under the supervision of the Zadokite priests.

The importance of the *kohen* in the law-making process is such that DSD 6:3-4 provides that:

ובכול מקום אשר יהיה שם עשרה אנשים מעצת היחד [320] אל ימש מאתם איש כהן ואיש כתכונו ישבו לפניו וכן ישאל לעצתם לכול דבר

> In every place in which there are ten men from the counsel of the community, there should not be absent [321] from them a priest, and each man according to his proper place shall sit before him, and thus shall they be asked for their counsel on any matter.

The Qumranites are commanded to have a priest among them so that they can establish a *moshab ha-rabbim* to derive the correct law.

A natural extension of the role of the priest in the interpretation of the law was his authority in its application in court.[322] CDC 14:6-8 dealing with the priestly *paqid* or supervisor of the assembly has been cited.[323] CDC 10:4-7 describes the "judges of the congregation:"

וזה סרך לשפטי העדה עד עשרה אנשים ברורים מן העדה לפי העת ארבעה למטה לוי ומישראל ששה מבוננים בספר ההגו וביסורי הברית מבני חמשה ועשרים שנה עד בני ששים שנה

[319] *QS*, 105, omitting the *we-* of *we-ʿal pi*.
[320] The MS. has *hḥyd*, an obvious metathesis.
[321] A jussive of the verb *mwš* (Rabin to CDC 13:2).
[322] Cf. G. F. Moore, *Judaism* (1927-30) I, 261, *Sifre* Deut. 153.
[323] Above, 44.

> And this is the rule for the judges of the congregation, up to ten men,[324] chosen [325] from the congregation according to the time,[326] four of the tribe of Levi, and from Israel, six learned [327] in the *Sefer He-Hagu* [328] and in the teachings [329] of the covenant, from twenty-five years old to sixty years old.

These Levites may be Zadokite priests, or, it is possible that while priests were required for the law-making process, Levites were sufficient for judging everyday cases. Indeed, CDC 13:3 even provides for the possibility that in the absence of a competent priest, a Levite may stand in.

The *Manual of Benedictions* 3:22-5 contains a *berakhah* to be uttered by the *maskil* [330] in honor of the Zadokite priests:

אשר בחר בם אל לחזק בריתו [לעולם ולב]חון כול משפטיו בתוך עמו ולהורותם כאשר צוה ויקימו מאמ]ת בריתו] ובצדק פקדו כול חוקיו ויתהלכו כא[שר] בחר

> Whom God chose [331] to strengthen His covenant [eternally and to ex]amine [332] all of his laws in the midst of His people and to instruct them as He commanded, and who established [His covenant of tr]uth, and in righteousness [333] commanded all of His laws and lived a[s] He had chosen.

From this passage the role of the priest as an instructor of the law, and of its correct (sectarian) interpretation is apparent. The sect believed that the Zadokites had been chosen from among God's people to fill this role. This passage also indicates beyond a doubt that the term *bene ṣadoq* is not a general term for the sect, as if so, to whom would they teach their secret interpretations? Obviously, *bene ṣadoq* refers to a segment of the sect entrusted with the duty of

---

[324] On courts of ten, see Rabin, *ad loc.*, M. Megillah 4:3, and M. Sanhedrin 1:3.

[325] See BDB, *s.v. brr*, M. Sanhedrin 3:1 (Rabin) and P. Qiddushin 4:5 (66a) (Schechter), but to the last passage commentaries translate, "pure," in the sense of having proper lineage.

[326] Like the *doresh ha-torah* discussed above, these offices apparently rotated.

[327] See 44 n. 142.

[328] The Torah. See 44 n. 144.

[329] Reading *yissure* for MS. *yesode*. Cf. 46 n. 160.

[330] On *maskil*, see 25 n. 24.

[331] Cf. the quotation from Ben Sira, below, 74.

[332] This text was first published in *DJD* I, 124. This word is there translated "*d'authentifier*," "to make legal and binding." It can also mean to "examine" or "scrutinize" (cf. BDB, *s.v.*). The examination of the law would be equivalent to its study. The priests are commanded here to publicly teach the law.

[333] Note the paranomasia of *ṣedeq* and *ṣadoq*. Cf. P. Wernberg-Møller, "*Ṣedeq, Ṣadiq* and *Ṣedaqah* in the Zadokite Fragments, the Manual of Discipline and the Habakkuk Commentary," *VT* 3 (1953), 310-15.

teaching and interpreting the law to the others. That is why the *bene ṣadoq* are mentioned in connection with *rob ʾanshe beritam*, the majority of the members of their covenant, those whom they instruct in the proper observance of the Law.

Here again, the sect was following biblical precedent. It is not important whether the sectarian use of *bene ṣadoq* is to be taken literally (genealogically) or figuratively. What is important is that at Qumran the priestly leaders were identified as descendants of Zadok. Ezek. 44:6-16 limited the priestly role to the Sons of Zadok. The prophet accused Israel of having brought foreigners and foreign worship into the Temple and the Levites of allowing this to happen and participating in it. The priests of the house of Zadok had not engaged in this worship and, therefore, they alone would continue to serve God.

The importance of the house of Zadok was clear even earlier in biblical history. An examination of the biblical passages relating to Zadok and Abiathar can only lead to the conclusion that the Bible was overwhelmingly prejudiced in favor of Zadok. In eleven passages (2 Sam. 8:17, 15:24ff., 17:5, 19:12, 20:25, 1 K. 4:4, 1 Chron. 15:11, 18:16, 24:3, 6, and 31), all those in which Zadok and Abiathar or their sons are mentioned together, Zadok or his son always comes first. In 2 Sam. 15:24ff., the account of David's fleeing from Absalom, Zadok clearly plays the leading role. In 2 Sam. 18:19, when either the son of Zadok or Abiathar is to be a messenger, Ahimaaz, son of Zadok, fills the post. In 1 K. 1:8 Zadok supports Solomon, the winning side (1 K. 1:32, 34, 38, and 39).[334]

Certainly, the account of Zadok's anointing Solomon in 1 K. 1:39, before the expulsion of Abiathar (1 K. 2:26-27), would seem to indicate that, with the victory of Solomon over the forces of Adonijah, Abiathar had *de facto* lost power. Solomon's act (1 K. 2:26-27) simply made this expulsion *de jure*.

In 1 Chron. 29:22 there is a tradition that Zadok was anointed at the same ceremony as Solomon. According to P, priests were to be

[334] The only contrary verse is 1 K. 2:35 in which, after his coronation, Solomon replaced Abiathar with Zadok. This presumes that Zadok and Abiathar were not on equal footing before. This is contrary to all the sources. One of two conclusions can be drawn from this text. One can assume it to be an anomaly and simply accept the tradition as valid that Zadok ministered with Abiathar. Or it can be a remnant of the accurate history. This would mean that pro-Zadokite editors had doctored the historical books of the Bible, and that Zadok actually began to minister in the time of Solomon.

anointed. In Ex. 40:12-15 anointing is the symbol of eternal priesthood. In some passages anointing is reserved for the high priest; elsewhere it appears that all priests were anointed.[335] Most scholars interpret the anointing of Zadok as an anachronism. This is based on the post-exilic dating of P.[336] Accepting the view of Kaufmann [337] as to the antiquity of P, one can interpret the anointing of Zadok as a sign of his eternal priesthood. Since such a promise had been made to Eli (1 Sam. 2:30), it was necessary for Solomon to have had Zadok anointed to show his ascendency over the House of Eli.

Abravanel [338] explains that Ezekiel's vision of the Zadokites as the only legitimate priests is due to the anointment of Zadok. What will happen to the (anointed) House of David in the eschatological future will also happen to the (anointed) House of Zadok.

This interpretation is very interesting in light of the Hallel of Ben Sira.[339] Liver [340] considers this passage earlier than Ben Sira itself. If Ben Sira is dated to about 180 B.C.E.,[341] the Hallel is within a few hundred years of Chronicles. Here we find:

הודו למצמיח קרן לבית דוד כי לעולם חסדו
הודו לבוחר בבני צדוק לכהן כי לעולם חסדו

Give thanks to the one who causes a horn
to sprout forth for the House of David,
For His love [342] is eternal:

Give thanks to the one who chooses the
Sons of Zadok to serve (as priests),
For His love is eternal:

We may be certain that the canonical books, with the exception of Daniel, were familiar to Ben Sira.[343] This passage may be an exegesis of 1 Chron. 29:22, the anointment of Zadok.

Throughout the First Temple period the Zadokites were in

---

[335] R. de Vaux, 105.

[336] *Idem.*

[337] Cf. *Toledot* I, 140f.

[338] *Perush ʿal Nebiʾim ʾAḥaronim*, to Ezek. 43:19.

[339] S. Schechter, C. Taylor, *The Wisdom of Ben Sira* (1899), p. (22), chapter 51:12c 1-15 and Segal, *Sefer Ben Siraʾ Ha-Shalem*, 355 (and note on 357). This text is not found in the versions.

[340] "*Bene Ṣadoq She-Be-Kat Midbar Yehudah*," *Ereṣ Yisraʾel* 8 (1967), 78.

[341] B. Metzger, *The Oxford Annotated Apocrypha* (1965), 128.

[342] See N. Glueck, *Ḥesed in the Bible* (1967) for the covenant connotations of this term.

[343] Schechter and Taylor, 35.

power. Only at a few points do interruptions occur, usually at times when non-Israelite worship was introduced.[344] It is logical that in his vision of the rebuilt Temple and reconstituted cult Ezekiel would have retained the House of Zadok as high priests. This is even more logical accepting Zadok's Levitical and Aaronide descent.[345]

In First Temple times, although the Zadokites controlled the high priesthood, others ministered in the Temple. This is certainly true as P delegates the priestly duties to all Aaronides, and Ezekiel's prophecy is based on that assumption.

The priesthood of the Second Temple was not limited to Zadokites. Nevertheless,[346] the high priests from the founding of the Second Temple until the Maccabean revolt were of the Zadokite line. Since the Hasmoneans were not of this descent, there must have been those who rejected the Hasmonean claim to the high priesthood. Some groups may have gone so far as to believe that any priest having authority ought to be a Zadokite. This may be why the Qumran dwellers looked only to the *bene ṣadoq* for leadership both in the "period of wickedness" and the soon-to-arrive eschaton.

Based on CDC 3:21ff., Licht has concluded that "Sons of Zadok" referred to the entire sect at Qumran. Yet this is only a *pesher* exegesis of Ezek. 44:15 and should not be taken literally. The leaders of the sect were drawn from the Zadokite priests. It is even possible that the Qumran sect originated when discontented Zadokites left Jerusalem in protest against the Maccabean takeover of the cult. The Zadokites must have regarded the Hasmoneans as usurpers.

Summary: *The Derivation of Halakhah at Qumran*

The Dead Sea sect regarded the laws of the Bible as falling into two main categories, the *nigleh* and *nistar*. The *niglot* ("revealed") are those laws the interpretation of which is obvious to anyone. The *nistarot* ("hidden") are those precepts for which only the sect has the correct interpretation. The mainstream of Israel is responsible for violation of both types of laws. The correct interpretation known only to the sect is derived by biblical exegesis (believed by the sect to be divinely

---

344 See H. J. Katzenstein, "Some Remarks on the Lists of the Chief Priests in the Temple of Solomon," *JBL* 81 (1962), 377-384.

345 It is most probable that Ezekiel's limitation of the priesthood to Zadokites is part of his general tendency toward greater stringency in matters of Levitical law.

346 For the following, see J. Licht, "*Ṣadoq, Bene Ṣadoq Bi-Yeme Bayit Sheni*," *Enc. Bib.* 6, 677f.

inspired) which was carried on continuously. It was also believed that successive revelations of inspired interpretation would allow the law to change with the times. Both categories of commandments would be affected in this way. Although the sect attacked its opponents for transgression of the *nistarot*, the interpretation of these commandments was not revealed to those outside the sect. At times *nigleh* can appear as a synonym for the Torah. There is no similarity between these terms and the written and oral Laws of Rabbinic thought.

All necessary guidance in matters of *halakhah* came from biblical exegesis. While there are a large number of terms for study or legal interpretation of Scripture found at Qumran, the two most important are undoubtedly *perush* and *midrash*. *Perush* refers to an exegesis of the text which does not involve the citation of corroborative material from elsewhere in Scripture. The *midrash* is an exegetical form in which a passage is interpreted in light of a second passage. *Midrash* involves the harmonization of two biblical sources. Both forms of exegesis were performed on a written text and took place in regular sessions presided over by the *'ish ha-doresh*.

The laws were then arranged in written lists called *serakhim*. Written, not oral transmission was the norm at Qumran. Each *serekh* dealt with a specific subject. Many of these laws were probably derived at the sessions of the *moshab ha-rabbim*, the sect's legislative and judicial assembly. Possibly, after each session, the newly derived laws were officially promulgated. Decisions of the assembly were reached by voting, although greater authority was given to the priests of Zadokite lineage. They played a leading role in the work of the assembly as well as in the courts. Priests also functioned as instructors of the law. It is clear, though, that there were also lay instructors (*maskilim*).

Thus far, a number of technical terms from the sect's vocabulary have been discussed. It has been demonstrated in each case that these terms indicate a *halakhah* derived only from direct exegesis of the biblical text.[347] If interpretation of the Torah were its only source of *halakhah*, the sect could not have had a dual-Torah concept or an oral Law.

---

[347] Baumgarten, "Unwritten Law," 23-9, sees Qumran law as dependent on revelation as a continuing process. In view of the preceding study, his conclusion cannot be accepted. In chap. 3, we will show that exegesis (not revelation) was the basis of Qumran Sabbath legislation.

CHAPTER TWO

INTRODUCTION TO THE QUMRAN SABBATH CODE

1. *The Sabbath in Qumran Literature*

The Sabbath code of the *Zadokite Fragments* (10:14-11:18) is not the only text which deals with the Sabbath in Qumran literature. Yet this code is the only halakhic material relating to the seventh day available thus far. Below, reasons will be evinced for regarding this unit as complete. What must be done now, however, is to glean from the rest of the fragments, as well as from the other material, whatever will contribute to a general picture of the Sabbath in the Dead Sea community.

CDC 3:12-16 states that God fulfilled His eternal covenant with Israel by revealing to those who had held fast to the commandments the secrets (*nistarot*) in which all Israel had erred. Included in these secrets are "His holy Sabbaths." The sect felt that Israel had gone astray in its Sabbath observance, not possessing the correct interpretation (*nistar*) of the Sabbath law. The sect had calendar differences with the Jerusalem establishment as to the correct days for the observance of the festivals. It need not be assumed that because this passage mentions both Sabbath and festivals, there were also differences as to the timing of Sabbath observance. However, some have claimed that the sect may have disagreed with the established views as to when the Sabbath began and ended.[1]

In a "chain of *lameds*,"[2] CDC 6:15 mentions the obligation of the sectarian "to observe the Sabbath according to its specification (*ke-ferushah*)." It has been shown that *perush* can mean a list,[3] and *ke-ferushah* is followed by a list of prescriptions (CDC 10:14-11:18). Unlike many of the other series of *halakhot* on a given subject, that pertaining to the Sabbath is not headed by *serekh*. The use of *perush*, already shown to have a sectarian connotation,[4] also emphasizes that this is the particular Sabbath law of the sect, as opposed to the (in their view) mistaken practices of the general Jewish community.

---

[1] See the discussion of CDC 10:14-17 below, 84-87.
[2] For this construction see Licht, *MH*, 35f.
[3] Above, 65f.
[4] See above, 38-40.

CDC 12:3-6 ordains that if a man went astray and violated the Sabbath, he was not to be put to death. Rather, he was deprived of his position in the congregation (*qahal*) for seven years, during which time he was observed. If he had mended his ways, he was readmitted. This is a definite break with the view of Jubilees which commands death for any Sabbath violation.[5] Apparently, the sect rejected this penalty for accidental transgression. Rabin[6] attempts to show that the sect "abolished" the death penalty even for those who purposely transgressed. Since the death penalty is biblical in origin, the term "abolish" here is inappropriate. One must bear in mind that even if the death penalty remained "on the books," it need not ever have been carried out.[7]

Yadin[8] explains that the *Zadokite Fragments* gives guidance to the sect only about how to observe the Sabbath in the current "period of wickedness." While CDC does not allow offerings in the Temple because the clergy is illegitimate and the procedure faulty, the sect still looks forward to the restored Jerusalem cult. The description of this cult may be the actual purpose of the Temple Scroll.[9] The restored cult includes the institution of *ʾanshe maʿamad*,[10] "who stand by on their festivals, on their new moons and on the Sabbaths, and on all days of the year..." (DSW 2:4). As opposed to the Rabbinic tradition in which most of these Israelites would assemble in their home towns while the priests were in Jerusalem,[11] the sect may require that all the Israelites be present at the sacrifices (DSW 2:4f.).

The Angelic Liturgy, or 4Q *Serekh Shirot ʿOlat Ha-Shabbat*,[12] enumerates blessings which certain angels are to recite on each Sabbath of the year. These praises were intended to replace the sacrifices

---

[5] Rabin, *QS*, 86. The Falashas also follow Jubilees here (Wurmbrand, 239).

[6] To CDC 12:3. Cf. S. T. Kimbrough, "The Concept of Sabbath at Qumran," *RQ* 5 (1964-6), 498-500, Baumgarten, "Unwritten Law," 12 n. 1.

[7] Cf. B. Sanhedrin 30a where there is a view that punishment of a *ben sorer u-moreh*, "rebellious son," had never taken place and that the laws had as their intention only the reward one received for studying them. See below, 88.

[8] *War Scroll*, 198-207.

[9] See Y. Yadin, "The Temple Scroll," *New Directions in Biblical Archaeology*, ed. D. N. Freedman, J. Greenfield, 162-5.

[10] See J. Licht, D. Sperber, "Mishmarot and Maʾamadot," *EJ* 12 (1971), 89-93.

[11] M. Taʿanit 4:2 (and Albeck, "*HWT*," *ad loc.*), T. Taʿanit 3 (4):3 (and Lieberman, *TK* V, 1103).

[12] See J. Strugnell, "The Angelic Liturgy at Qumran— 4Q *Serek Šîrôt ʿÔlat Haššabbāt*," *Suppl. to VT* 7 (1960), 318-345 and H. Ringgren, *The Faith of Qumran* (1963), 227-229. Fragments of this text were found at Masada (Y. Yadin, *Masada, First Season of Excavations, 1963-64* (1965), 118-20.

in which the sectarians could not take part. Much of this material is in the style of the *Hekhalot* literature.[13] J. M. Baumgarten[14] has observed, based on this text, that each Sabbath at Qumran had its own specific character and liturgy. Num. 28:10, *ʿolat shabbat be-shabbato*, was understood as "the sacrifice for each particular Sabbath on that Sabbath."[15] He relates to this the practice of counting Sabbaths as well as the use of priestly courses for calendric purposes.

The War Scroll specifies that fighting cease during the first Sabbatical year.[16] In the descriptions of the eschatological war, the account deducts subsequent Sabbatical years from the years of combat.[17] DSW 2:8f. gives a reason for the cessation of hostilities, calling the year a *shabbat manoaḥ* ("Sabbath of rest").[18] Yadin[19] suggests that the prohibition of fighting during Sabbatical years was derived from the words *shabbat shabbaton* (Lev. 25:4). This explanation assumes that the cessation of warfare during the Sabbatical year was indirectly derived from its prohibition on the Sabbath. Any one of the uses of *shabbat* in connection with the Sabbatical year[20] could have resulted in an analogy (*heqesh*)[21] whereby it was reasoned that some Sabbath prohibitions applied to the year of release. Accordingly, Yadin alludes to material relating to the refusal to fight even defensively on the Sabbath in the early second Commonwealth. There are accounts of

---

[13] Cf. G. Scholem, *Jewish Gnosticism, Merkabah Mysticism, and Talmudic Tradition* (1965), 3f. It is apparent that the whole problem is in need of reevaluation. Of interest is the comparison of DSD 4:7f. (cf. *middot*, Ps. 133:2) and Scholem, 57-64, 132. Cf. J. Greenfield, "Prolegomenon," to H. Odeberg, *3 Enoch or the Hebrew Book of Enoch* (reprinted, New York, 1973), xi-xlvi and my forthcoming contribution to the Festschrift for Alexander Altmann.

[14] "The Counting of the Sabbath in Ancient Sources," *VT* 16 (1966), 277-86.

[15] Cf. *Sifre* Num. 144.

[16] There is no mention of this in the paraphrases of Lev. 25 and Deut. 15 in *DJD* I, 94f. (The Words of Moses).

[17] Yadin, *War Scroll*, 20f.

[18] In DSW 19:9 *manoaḥ* describes the cessation of fighting at night. In DSH 11:8 *shabbat manoaḥ* is applied to the Day of Atonement (*yom ṣom*). Cf. the phrase *shabbat menuḥah* in M. Tamid 7:4 (some texts and the Grace after Meals in Ashkenazic prayerbooks read: *shabbat u-menuḥah*), and *shabbat manoaḥ* in some Ashkenazic MSS. of the additional service for Rosh Ha-Shanah (D. Goldschmidt, *Maḥazor La-Yamin Ha-Noraʾim* (1970) I, 149).

[19] P. 20, n. 1.

[20] Cf. Jub. 50:3ff., 12f.

[21] The Rabbinic *heqesh* was always based on some common element relating the two Scriptural texts to be compared ("*Heqesh*," *Enc. Tal.* 10, 557-575, Lieberman, *Hellenism*, 60f. The logic of CDC 5:8-11 is similar.). Cf. R. North, "Maccabean Sabbath Years," *Biblica* 34 (1953), 501-515.

military failure in Sabbatical years,[22] due, no doubt, to shortage of supplies. Yadin must be correct in noting that the abandoning of the siege of Dagon by John Hyrcanus[23] shows that fighting was prohibited by analogy with the Sabbath and that food supply was not the only consideration. For this reason John Hyrcanus pulled back. In cases of defensive warfare, the Jews labored under serious disability due to shortage of supplies, making it easier for sieges against them to succeed.[24]

2. *A Form-critical Note on the Sabbath Code*

It would appear that the body of Sabbath law in the *Zadokite Fragments* constitutes a unity because the first and last precepts only are accompanied by Scriptural citations or proof-texts. These biblical quotations form an *inclusio*, or what the medieval commentators called *ḥatimah me'en petiḥah*.[25]

Another aspect to be considered is the internal form, that of the individual *halakhot*. In the field of biblical law, the distinction between casuistic and apodictic law has long been known.[26] The casuistic laws are those which state the law applying to given conditions, always in the form "If... then...." The apodictic are those laws stated as imperatives. You are to do this; you are not to do that. The negative of the imperative would normally be *'al* followed by the jussive, but the apodictic law usually uses the stronger *lo'* followed by the indicative.

Bright has noted that when *'al* and the jussive are used for a negative command, it is "a specific command for a specific occasion, with future occasions not in view."[27] These he calls *'al* prohibitives. The *lo'* prohibitive occurs with second person masculine, singular or

---

[22] I Macc. 6:49, 53 and the forthcoming study of N. M. Sarna, "The Sabbatical and Jubilee Years as a Factor in Biblical History."

[23] Wars 1, 2:4, Ant. 13, 8:1. Note that the food shortage in a Sabbatical year would be acute only in the spring, summer, and fall of the following year.

[24] Cf. below, 124-8.

[25] Note also the order of subjects. It is similar in its logic to that of Ezra's eighteen decrees (Neh. 10:31-40). The last Sabbath regulation (CDC 11:17f.) deals with the application of Sabbath law to the cult. Immediately following are laws relating to the cult and sanctity of the holy city (CDC 11:18-12:1).

[26] For a thorough discussion see A. Alt, "The Origins of Israelite Law," *Essays on Old Testament History and Religion* (1968), 103-171. Cf. D. Patrick, "Casuistic Law Governing Primary Rights and Duties," *JBL* 92 (1973), 180-184 and J. van der Ploeg, "Studies in Hebrew Law," *CBQ* 12 (1950), 416-427.

[27] J. Bright, "The Apodictic Prohibition: Some Observations," *JBL* 92 (1973), 186.

plural, or third person plural verbs. "No discernible difference can be detected between the three forms." [28] "Whereas the *ʾal* prohibitive expresses a specific command for a specific occasion, the *loʾ* prohibitive expresses a categorical prohibition of binding validity both for the present and the future"[29] and is stronger. Bright admits that there are rare exceptions to these definitions. The *ʾal* form is used consistently in the wisdom literature. In the legal sections of the Pentateuch Bright finds 373 *loʾ* prohibitives to 13 with *ʾal*. The *loʾ* form was particularly suitable for the divine command.[30] After an investigation of questionable cases,[31] Bright concludes that the two forms (*ʾal* and *loʾ*) are not interchangeable.

The characteristic basis of laws in Mishnaic Hebrew is the participle. A negative law is usually stated with *ʾen* followed by a participle.[32] Positive and negative participles are found together in clauses such as *ba-meh madliqin u-ba-mah ʾen madliqin*, "With what may we light (the Sabbath lamp) and with what may we not?" (M. Shabbat 2:1). Often prohibitions are stated in the form of *loʾ* followed by the third person singular imperfect (jussive). This is the case in M. Shabbat 1:3: *loʾ yeṣe ha-ḥayyaṭ be-maḥaṭo samukh le-ḥashekhah*, "A tailor may not go out with his needle close to dusk." This form is not far from that of some biblical apodictic laws. But Mishnaic jurisprudence does not use the biblical forms.[33] Only abstract formulation is common to both groups of laws.

The laws of the sect have a different form. The Sabbath laws are stated in the form of *ʾal* followed by the jussive.[34] In most cases, the jussive is followed by *ʾish*, "anyone." Sometimes the conjunction *waw* appears before the negating particle. Subsidiary conditions may be described by *ʾim* just as occasionally in biblical law one meets a conflation of the forms.[35] The entire collection of Sabbath material in the fragments is concerned with cataloging the prohibited activ-

---

28 Bright, 187.

29 *Ibid.*

30 Bright, 187f.

31 Bright, 189-98. He finds "textual fluidity" in the bulk of the cases which seem exceptional, but does recognize a small number of exceptions.

32 See Neusner, *Rabbinic Traditions* III, 73, "Types and Forms in Ancient Jewish Literature," *History of Religions* 11 (1972), 363f. Cf. Alt, 142-146 for possible biblical background.

33 Neusner, *ibid.*

34 See Neusner, *Rabbinic Traditions* III, 76, "Types and Forms," 366f. Delcor, "*Contribution*," 540, n. 6.

35 *ʾIm* is characteristic of the casuistic law.

ities, hence its negative form is not surprising. It does, however, stand in contrast to the form of the tannaitic thirty-nine categories. After a general statement that these activities are the categories of prohibited labor, thirty-nine positive participles follow. Only the heading indicates that they are forbidden on the Sabbath (M. Shabbat 7:2).

The question remains as to why the sect used *ʾal* and the jussive for the negation of its "apodictic" laws. This phraseology is common to what are usually called the priestly writings of the Pentateuch. This is not to say that use of this negative is limited to these writings; rather, use of this particle as a means of introducing a law formulated in the negative seems to occur primarily in Leviticus.[36] Since the leaders of the sect were apparently drawn from the Zadokite priesthood, and the priestly writings occupied the primary place in the curriculum of the priestly schools, one can assume that the language of these writings was a factor in the statement of law by the leaders of the sect. It is interesting that Ex. 16:29 (usually assigned to J[37]), an important Sabbath prescription about which there was much debate, also appears in the form of *ʾal* followed by the jussive. Apparently, then, the distinction made between the *ʾal* and *loʾ* prohibitives noted by Bright was no longer operating when the laws of the *Zadokite Fragments* were put into this form.

A final point relates to the heading. The first law is preceded by a heading: *ʿal ha-shabbat, le-shomrah ke-mishpaṭah*, "Concerning the Sabbath, to observe it according to its regulation(s) (CDC 10:14)." Such headings are found throughout the *Zadokite Fragments*, often beginning with the term *serekh*. While biblical law seems to run from subject to subject without well-defined limits or headings, the sectarian law sets off some topics by providing them with titles.[38] It is well known that the Mishnah is organized according to subject, even though remnants of earlier mnemonic divisions and Scriptural (midrashic) order are present. It is usually assumed that arranging the Mishnah in subject order was the work of R. Akiba.[39] The existence

---

[36] Lev. 10:6, 9, 11:43, 16:2, 18:24, 19:4, 29, 31 (twice), 25:14, 36. This has been called the "second apodictic formula." Cf. van der Ploeg, 426. For a similar impersonal usage in Persian see M. Weinfeld, "The Origin of the Apodictic Law," *VT* 23 (1973), 63-75. See the discussion in Bright, 194-197.

[37] S. R. Driver, *An Introduction to the Literature of the Old Testament* (1956), 30.

[38] Cf. CDC 9:8 (L. Ginzberg, "*Eine unbekannte jüdische Sekte*," *MGWJ* 56 (1912), 424).

[39] For a summary of views and problems see Ch. Albeck, *Maboʾ La-Mishnah*, 63-98.

of such subject collections in the Qumran library may indicate that when R. Akiba provided the tradition with this organization, he was drawing on ancient techniques. It is even possible that the beginnings of such organization may be seen in biblical materials.[40]

---

[40] Subject organization seems especially the case in the priestly writings. For the order of the books of the Bible see N. M. Sarna, "The Order of the Books," *Studies in Jewish Bibliography, History and Literature in Honor of I. Edward Kiev*, ed. C. Berlin (1971), 407-413.

CHAPTER THREE

THE QUMRAN SABBATH CODE: TEXT AND COMMENTARY

1. *CDC 10:14-17: The Tosefet Melakhah*

אל יעש איש ביום השישי מלאכה מן העת אשר יהיה גלגל השמש רחוק מן השער מלואו כי הוא אשר אמר שמור את יום השבת לקדשו

> No one shall do work on Friday from the time when the sphere of the sun is distant from the gate [1] (by) its (the sun's) diameter, for this is (the import of) that which He said,[2] "Observe (*shamor*) the Sabbath day to sanctify it (Deut. 5:12)."

This passage refers to what the Rabbis termed the *tosefet melakhah*,[3] the addition of the last part of Friday (immediately before sunset) to the Sabbath. This law prohibits all labor, thus making the *tosefet* similar in observance to the Sabbath itself. According to Rabin, P. Shebiʿit 1:1 (33a) indicates that this addition was considered optional. In fact, the Palestinian Talmud only informs us that the *tosefet* was considered by some to be Rabbinical in origin, while others attributed it to the Torah.[4]

This passage in CDC has been the subject of considerable argument. S. Talmon [5] has suggested that as part of its solar calendar the Qumran sect began the Sabbath observance in the morning, and that the Sab-

---

[1] Ginzberg *MGWJ* 56 (1912), 424, relates this gate (*shaʿar*) to the heavenly portals of Enoch 72:2ff. (Fragments of Enoch were found in Cave 4 (Cross, *Ancient Library*, 44) and have not yet been published.) The "gate" would be the horizon. Cf. *Enumah Elish* 5:9, *ANET*, 67 and Ps. 78:23. The same idea is found in the evening and Sabbath morning liturgies (Baer, *Siddur ʿAbodat Yisrael*, 164, 210). Alternately, the gate can be that of the city. This would mean starting the Sabbath quite a bit earlier. See also P. Berakhot 4:1 (7c) and L. Ginzberg, *Perushim We-Ḥiddushim Ba-Yerushalmi* III, 67f. Y. Gilat, "*Le-Qadmutam shel ʾIssure Shabbat ʾAḥadim*," *Bar-ʾIlan, Sefer Ha-Shanah Le-Madaʿe Ha-Yahadut We Ha-Ruaḥ*, 1963, 116-9 has taken the *shaʿar* as the city gate. Cf. his *Mishnato shel Rabbi ʾEliʿezer ben Hyrcanos* (1968), 102-106 for a discussion of the Rabbinic *tosefet melakhah*.

[2] For this formula see Ex. 16:23. Note the interchange of *ʾmr* for *dbr*.

[3] B. Yomaʾ 81a, b, *Sifraʾ* ʾEmor 14:7-9.

[4] See M. Margalit, *Marʾeh Ha-Panim* to P. Shebiʿit 1:1 (ed. Zhitomir), B. Rosh Ha-Shanah 9a and *Tosafot*, *s.v. we-rabbi*.

[5] "The Calendar Reckoning of the Sect from the Judaean Desert," in *Aspects of the Dead Sea Scrolls* (1958), 187-196, "*Maḥazor Ha-Berakhot shel Kat Midbar Yehudah*," *Tarbiz* 28 (1959), 6f. J. Z. Lauterbach, *Rabbinic Essays*, 445-51, note on 452, takes the view that the original Israelite calendar reckoned the day from morning to morning. Cf. Rashbam to Gen. 1:4.

bath lasted until the following morning. He has supported these conclusions by citing DSD 10:10,14 which lists the daily prayers in the sequence of morning, afternoon, evening. Our passage has been cited as clear evidence against Talmon's assertion.[6] Talmon claims that the presence of this *halakhah* in CDC is the result of the editorial activity of a later copyist. It is difficult to understand why a copyist should here insert a normative Rabbinic law while ignoring many other blatantly schismatic elements in this text.[7]

The medieval sect of the Mishawites taught that the Sabbath should be observed from morning to morning.[8] This group also proposed to adhere strictly to a solar calendar. Talmon has suggested a literary link between these two sects. This ninth century calendar, however, was never put into practice, probably because of the principle of this sect that in all disputed matters, the Rabbinite practice should be followed. "All coins are counterfeit, so one might as well use the one at hand." [9]

The Karaites opposed beginning the Sabbath on Saturday morning, as well as Mishawism in general. The Falashas, like the Rabbis, begin the Sabbath on Friday evening.[10]

The *tosefet melakhah* is one of the few *halakhot* in the *Zadokite Fragments* which is expressly derived from a Scriptural quotation. This might be taken by some as an argument against its authenticity. On the contrary, the Sabbath code in our text is set within a literary framework, the first and last laws being supported by biblical references.

---

[6] Wieder, *JSK*, 54f., D. Leibel, "*Shabbatah shel Kat Midbar Yehudah*," *Tarbiz* 29 (1960), 296, J. M. Baumgarten, "The Beginning of the Day in the Calendar of Jubilees," *JBL* 77 (1958), 355-360 (He shows conclusively that by the time of our text the normal reckoning of the Jewish day was evening to evening.), S. Zeitlin, "The Beginning of the Day in the Calendar of Jubilees," *JBL* 78 (1959), 153-6 and Baumgarten, "Reply," *JBL* 78 (1959), 157, and A. A. Akavyah, "*Ha-ʾEmet ʿal Ha-Luaḥ shel Kat Midbar Yehudah*," *Sinai* 47 (1960), 39-41. See Talmon's defense, "*Le-ʿInyan Ha-Luaḥ shel Kat Midbar Yehudah*," *Tarbiz* 29 (1960), 394f.

[7] Several studies have attempted to clarify the relationship between the *Manual of Discipline* and the *Zadokite Fragments* (*e.g.* M. Margaliot, "*Mi-Berit Dameseq ʿad Serekh Ha-Yaḥad*," *Sinai* 30 (1951/2), 9-21). It has been observed that although the two texts are obviously part of the same literature, the sectarian organization outlined in the documents is different in some details. There is a remote possibility, if Talmon is correct, that this factor may account for the difference here. One group may have begun the Sabbath in the morning while the other began it on the evening before. This solution would appear unlikely, though, as such a change would be too important to have gone unnoticed.

[8] See Z. Ankori, *Karaites in Byzantium*, 372-416. Cf. Ibn Ezra to Ex. 16:25.

[9] J. Heller, L. Nemoy, "Karaites," *EJ* 10 (1971), 766.

[10] A. Z. Aescoly, *Sefer Ha-Falashim* (1943), 30.

The last regulation is CDC 11:17f. which is of sectarian origin, not a late addition.

This *midrash halakhah* is based on the word *shamor* in Deut. 5:12. Perhaps the sect was bothered by the question of why the word *zakhor*, "remember," was replaced by *shamor*, "guard or observe," when the decalogue was repeated. The word *shamor* indicated to them that it was necessary to add to the Sabbath in order to prevent its accidental violation. The tannaim applied this verse to the addition of time *after* the Sabbath,[11] at least sharing with the sect the application of this source to the *tosefet melakhah*.

Lev. 19:3, also containing the root *šmr*, was likewise interpreted by the Karaite Eliezer Bashyatchi to refer to the *tosefet melakhah*.[12] Yet the Rabbinite influence on this scholar must not be forgotten.[13] The Falashas are reported to have begun the Sabbath at three o'clock, Friday afternoon. Ginzberg cites a parallel from Ant. 16, 6:2 which relates that Augustus assured the Jews that they would not be forced to come to court to testify after three o'clock, Friday afternoon.[14] Although this statement confirms the Friday eve beginning of the Sabbath, it does not prove that there existed a custom of abstaining from labor from 3:00 P. M. on. Josephus specifically refers to Friday as the day of preparation for the Sabbath. Thus, the excuse from appearing in court on Friday after three o'clock was designed not to interfere with the Sabbath *preparation*.

A *baraita'* in B. Pesaḥim 50b states that no blesssing will be derived from work done on Friday afternoon after *minḥah* (three-thirty P. M.).[15] This, however, like Josephus, supports the custom of ceasing work on Friday at three o'clock. Yet the onset of the Sabbath, the period during which violations were punishable, was not until shortly before sunset.[16] According to T. Sukkah 4:11 it was the custom to sound the trumpet on Friday afternoon to signal the ending of work. Mai-

---

[11] *Mekhilta' De-Rabbi Shim'on ben Yoḥai* to Ex. 20:8 (ed. Epstein-Melamed, 148), *Mekhilta' De-Rabbi Ishmael*, Yitro 7, *Midrash Tannaim* I, to Deut. 5:12 (Ginzberg, 426). Cf. Neusner, *Rabbinic Traditions* I, 185-7.

[12] *Sefer Ha-Miṣwot Ha-Niqra' 'Aderet 'Eliyahu* (Eupatoria, 1835), chap. 9, 27b.

[13] "Bashyazi," *EJ* 4 (1971), 297f.

[14] For this and the following see Ginzberg, 427. These times are for the equinoxes. Other dates would require adjustment to match our reckoning since their solar hours would not equal our fixed-length hours.

[15] This is the *minḥah qeṭanah*. Cf. Rashi to B. Pesaḥim 50b, B. Berakhot 26b and Rashi, *ad loc.*

[16] Cf. Gilat, "*Le-Qadmutam*," 118 and *Mishnato*, 104f. He assumes that originally *melakhah* was prohibited from 3:30 P.M. Friday.

monides (M. T. Shabbat 5:20)[17] rightly understands this to occur at the time of *minḥah* (three-thirty). A later set of blasts (T. Sukkah 4:12) signaled the actual onset of the Sabbath and the concomitant abstention from *melakhah*. Josephus refers to this practice in Wars 4, 9:12. The inscription *le-bet ha-teqiʿah* followed by the letters *lh*, found on a parapet stone from the top of the southwest corner of the Herodian Temple, may indicate the place from which the trumpets were blown.[18]

2. *CDC 10:17-19: Discussion of Business*

וביום השבת אל ידבר איש דבר נבל ורק אל ישה ברעהו כל אל ישפוט על הון ובצע אל ידבר בדברי המלאכה והעבודה לעשות למשכים

> And on the Sabbath day,[19] no one shall speak a wicked or vain word.[20] Let him not lend [21] his neighbor anything. Let him not dispute [22] about wealth [23] or profit.[24] Let him not speak of things (relating to) the work and the labor to be done the next morning.[25]

[17] Cited by Lieberman. Cf. his comprehensive notes in *TK IV*, 894ff.

[18] This find was announced in Jan., 1971, having been discovered in the debris lying immediately above the Herodian pavement. The piece was of Jerusalem limestone, one meter high and two meters wide and weighed 8 tons. Carved into the stone was a niche in which a man could stand.

Josephus uses the term παστοφόριον for the niche. A survey of the uses of this term in Hellenistic Gk. (cf. LXX to Jer. 35:4,42:4 in the Gk. numbering) shows that it referred to a chamber at the top of the wall. This *bet ha-teqiʿah* could not have been used for the blowing of trumpets connected with the sacrifices as it would be senseless to blow them across the valley toward the city.

[19] The usual form of these *halakhot* is that they conclude with reference to the Sabbath. This law deviates and begins with such a reference. It may be that through a series of errors this phrase (*ba-yom ha-shabbat*) was moved from its original position after the law to a position at its beginning.

[20] On the translation of *nabal* see below. Note that biblical *nebalah* has been replaced (Licht, *MH*, 163). The phrase is dependent on Is. 32:6, to which the Targum translates *nabal* as *rishʿaʾ*, "evil," and Is. 9:16, where Targ. translates *sheqar*, "falsehood" (note the phrase *nablut we-khaḥash* in DSD 10:22). Cf. Job 2:10. Deut. 32:47 is the source of *dabar req*. New JPS there translates, "a trifling thing." Ginzberg (428) calls attention to *hebel wa-riq* (Is. 30:7) which he suggests was the original reading. The impossibility of Schechter's reading *we-raq* is also shown by Ginzberg.

[21] Note the use of biblical *nšh* (Deut. 15:2, 24:10) meaning "to lend" or "become a creditor" (BDB, *s.v.*). There is a tendency in the Qumran legal materials to use biblical alternatives to the standard post-biblical terminology (see Rabin, *QS*, 108f.)

[22] Reading here *yšpwṭ* and assuming that the *waw* was introduced by a scribe who was unaware of the *nifʿal* (reciprocal) usage of this root. It is easy to see how a sloppily written *ṭet* can appear like the letter *kaf*, *waw*, but we cannot say if this error was first introduced by the copyist of our MS. or if it was found in his text.

[23] This is primarily a wisdom term for wealth or financial resources. Here again, note the biblicizing tendency of Qumran terminology.

[24] It is hard to tell if *beṣaʿ* here is just or unjust gain. Regardless, the proscrip-

(Note 25 p.t.o.)

The first clause is one of general introduction, against discussing business affairs on the Sabbath.[26] It passes a value judgment on the three subcategories which follow. If these exchanges take place on the Sabbath, they become wicked or vain (perhaps even offensive) and fall into the same category as those for which DSD 7:9 prescribes a three month punishment.[27] There is no mention of punishment in CDC, but it is possible that there were set punishments recorded in writing for violators of the "ritual" law.[28] The sect may have punished only infractions against its organizational structure while leaving all other offenses in the hands of Heaven.[29]

As to the three specific offenses here forbidden, the first is lending anything to a neighbor. Rabin makes the remark that lending is permitted in M. Shabbat 23:1. In fact, this *mishnah* indicates that lending might be accomplished only by circumlocution, and that making a loan using the terminology of money-lending was not permitted. There is a principle of Rabbinic law that it is better to allow the continuation of practices in error than to admonish the people who will continue their former practices, but now with full knowledge of what they are doing. This principle is discussed immediately after M. Shabbat 23:1 in the Babylonian Talmud. That this *mishnah* represents a tannaitic

---

tion is due to the fact that the discussion of business would be involved.

[25] See M. Bikkurim 3:2 (Schechter and Rabin) and Albeck's "*HWT*," *ad loc.* for other uses of this expression. Cf. Lieberman, *Greek*, 135 n. 151.

[26] Ginzberg (428) sees the first clause as unrelated to the following. E. Slomovic, "Toward an Understanding of the Exegesis in the Dead Sea Scrolls," *RQ* 7 (1969), 9f., has shown that the grouping of these clauses may be the result of a *gezerah shawah* based on the word *dabar* in Deut. 32:47, 15:2 and 17:8.

[27] DSD 7:9 is a general regulation, not one for the Sabbath. Apparently, the sectarian was expected to avoid foolish-wicked-obscene remarks at all times. The phrase *nablut we-khaḥash* in DSD 10:22 and the Targum of *nabal* as *sheqar* mentioned above (n. 20) may require that we take the law of DSD 7:9 as a punishment for lying. Cf. Wars 2, 8:6, 7 (S. T. Kimbrough, "The Concept of Sabbath at Qumran," *RQ* 5 (1964-6), 488). If this interpretation is correct, it eliminates the inconsistency between the CDC Sabbath code and DSD. For a possible Falasha parallel, see Aescoly, 33. See also Gilat, "*Le-Qadmutam*," 112-16.

[28] DSD 6:24-7:25 contains only penalties for offenses against the sectarian organization.

[29] See above, 78. Ex. 31:14 prescribes excision (*karet*) as the punishment for one who does labor on the Sabbath. While it is possible that originally *karet* may have been some kind of exile or excision from the people, the Rabbis interpreted it as *mitah bi-yede shamayim*, "death at the hands of heaven." This meant that they took no action to punish such offenders. See S. Loewenstamm, "*Karet*," *Enc. Bib.* 4, 330-332. It may be that the sectarian documents do not prescribe punishments for these Sabbath infractions because they are all subsumed under the heading of *melakhah* and, hence, their punishment is up to God.

compromise and acceptance of reality is further attested in P. Shebiʿit 8:4 (38a).[30] In other words, the Rabbis felt that even the making of loans through circumlocution should have been forbidden, but that the acceptance of this practice was so firmly ingrained in the populace that it could not be eliminated by Rabbinic edict. This Qumran law is, then, in complete harmony with the Rabbinic ideal.

The second aspect, disputing about money on the Sabbath, has been likened to M. Beṣah 5:2 which prohibits judgment on the Sabbath. Schechter and Ginzberg, in suggesting this, failed to perceive the unity of this group of restrictions[31] which are all forbidden because they involve the discussion of business on the seventh day. The Qumran *halakhah* here forbids not the formal court session, but the private business argument on the Sabbath.

Finally, one is forbidden to make plans on the Sabbath regarding the work which he intends to do the following morning. A similar prohibition is found in Philo,[32] and according to the reading of L. Finkelstein,[33] also in Jubilees 50:8: "...Whoever says that he will do something on it, that he will set out on a journey[34] in regard to buying or selling... shall die." There is no way of knowing if the sect would have agreed with the verdict imposed upon the violator by Jubilees.[35]

It is clear that these regulations, like their tannaitic counterparts,[36] are derived from a *perush* exegesis of Is. 58:13. The first part of the verse prohibits the conduct of normal business on the Sabbath. The crux of this verse is the last two words, *we-dabber dabar*. Ehrlich[37] makes the obvious statement that the Sabbath could not have been a day of silence.[38] The Targum here translates *u-malala*ʾ *milin de-*ʾ*onas*. This

---

[30] Albeck, "*HWT*" to *Seder Moʿed*, 423. Cf. Gilat, *Mishnato*, 137.

[31] Ginzberg (428) points out that if the passage is understood to prohibit litigation on the Sabbath, it should read *yishafeṭ* (cf. the *nifʿal* of *špṭ* + *ʿal* in Jer. 2:35). See above, 87 n. 22. In support of his interpretation, Ginzberg cites a parallel from the *Teʾezaza Sanbat* which links the prohibitions of litigation and doing business.

[32] Belkin, 200f.

[33] "The Book of Jubilees and the Rabbinic Halaka," *HTR* 16 (1923), 48f.

[34] Reading with two MSS. cited by Charles which omit "thereon."

[35] See above, 78.

[36] M. Shabbat 23:1-3, T. Shabbat 7(8):5-7, B. Shabbat 150a, b.

[37] *Mikra ki-Pheschuto* III, 145.

[38] But cf. the late Rabbinic avoidance of superfluous conversation (B. Cohen, "Sabbath Prohibitions Known as Shebut," in *Law and Tradition in Judaism* (1959), 145f. who compares our passage in CDC (n. 51). Cohen's article originally appeared in *Proceedings of the Rabbinical Assembly* 9 (1949), 123-161.).

same phrase occurs in the Targum to Is. 58:9 as a translation of *dabber 'aben*, "to speak iniquity or wickedness."[39] Both the Rabbis and the sect took the phrase *we-dabber dabar* to mean that discussion of business (*ḥafaṣekha*) was forbidden. The sect and the Targum considered such prohibited discussion to be wicked (*nabal*). One must remember the relationship between wickedness and foolishness in the wisdom tradition. The wicked man acts as he does because of lack of understanding or foolishness. Hence, in the Bible the same term, *nabal*, can be used for a morally foolish or ignoble man.

This law, like many others in the *Zadokite Fragments* and the *Manual of Discipline*, assumes that there was private property at Qumran and that sectarians could enter into business dealings for profit. Otherwise, how could arguments erupt? Most probably the new member surrendered all of his property for *use* by the sect, but he retained ownership. Thus, he could be fined or could engage in business. Communal use, not communal ownership, seems to have been the rule at Qumran.[40]

3. *CDC 10:20f.: Walking in the Field*

אל יתהלך איש בשדה לעשות את עבודת חפצו השבת

> No one shall walk about in the field to do his desired [41] labor on the Sabbath.[42]

Whether the text is accepted as it stands or is emended to read *'aḥar ha-shabbat*,[43] this law may prohibit walking to the furthest extent of the Sabbath limit in order to leave on a journey immediately after nightfall. This same prohibition is echoed in M. Shabbat 23:3 and T. Shabbat 7(8):10-13.

Ginzberg, however, understands this regulation somewhat differently. He sees it as prohibiting walking about in the field in order to determine what work needs to be done after the Sabbath. He supports

---

[39] Cf. Kimchi to Is. 58:13.

[40] See Rabin, *QS* 22-36, and Licht, *MH*, 10-13. I hope to develop my view in a future study.

[41] Translating with the Targum to Is. 58:13 yields, "the work he requires" (Rabin).

[42] Schechter emends to *ba-yom ha-shabbat*. Ginzberg suggests *'aḥar ha-shabbat* on which see below.

[43] Ginzberg's discussion on pp. 428f.

this interpretation by citing a *baraita'* in B. 'Erubin 38b which prohibits this very action.[44]

According to this second interpretation, this law easily follows from the one immediately before. Ginzberg would then read *ḥefṣe ha-shabbat* and translate, "*die Arbeit für die Woche.*"

Whichever interpretation is accepted, this law was derived through a *perush* of Is. 58:13 as shown by the key words *la-'asot* and *ḥefṣo* which parallel the phrase *me-'asot derakhekha mi-meṣo' ḥefṣekha.*[45]

4. *CDC 10:21: A One Thousand Cubit Sabbath Limit*

אל יתהלך חוץ לעירו על אלף באמה

Let him not walk about outside of his city MORE THAN A THOUSAND CUBITS.[46]

This law is clearly the result of a *midrash halakhah*. Ex. 16:29 was understood by means of *perush* to apply not only to the desert period but to all time. However, the verse did not define the limits of *taḥtaw* or *meqomo*. The process of *midrash* was used to define these terms. The sect, like the tannaim later on, cited the description of the boundaries of the Levitical cities in Num. 35:2-5 and used this definition of the city limits. A man was permitted to go as far as these limits on the Sabbath but no further.

Although both the sect and the tannaim made use of this passage in Numbers, both had trouble interpreting the text. The Rabbis eventually decided that only the "two thousand cubits" referred to the *teḥum shabbat*, "Sabbath limit," while the other figure of "one thousand" referred to the Levitical pasture land (*migrash*).[47] The sect probably con-

44 Ginzberg reads *be-tokh* where the Vilna text has *le-sof*. Both readings have ample support in DS, *ad loc. Be-tokh* is also supported by the reading *ba-sadeh* in *Midrash Ha-Gadol*, Yitro 20:10 (but note Margaliot's critical apparatus), cited by Lieberman *TK* III, 286. This passage, however, in light of the late completion of the text, seems to be a conflation of the two clauses of the *baraita'* cited in B. 'Erubin 38b, 39a and is certainly dependent on that recension. Cf. also *Mekhilta' De-Rabbi Shim'on b. Yoḥai*, ed. Hoffmann, 108, the note in ed. Epstein-Melamed, 150, *Wa-Yiqra' Rabbah* 34:16 and the notes in ed. Margaliot, and Cohen, 145.

45 Cf. Targum, *ad loc.* '*Abodat* would be an explanatory gloss. Slomovic, 11-13 suggests that Is. 58:13 served as a mnemonic for the entire series of laws in CDC 10:19-11:6. He compares M.T. Shabbat 24:1 and 2.

46 After a large *'alef* through which the scribe has drawn a line to indicate erasure come the last three words in larger writing. They are in the same hand but apparently made with a larger pen (Rabin). On this Qumran *halakhah*, cf. Gilat, *Mishnato*, 142-5.

47 M. Sotah 5:3, but see the sources quoted in Albeck's "*HWT*" *ad loc.*, which indicate that the Levitical pasturage was 2000 cubits.

The square character of the *migrash* of Num. 35:2-5 is unquestionable (in accord

cluded that there were two Sabbath limits, the one described here of one thousand cubits beyond which a man could not walk on the seventh day, and the other of two thousand cubits, beyond which he could not walk if pasturing his animals (CDC 11:5f.).[48] In other words, the Sabbath limit was 1000 cubits which could be extended another thousand for the pasturing of animals.

Rabin is correct in observing that there is a difference between simply walking and going after an animal.[49] Whereas the Mishnah ruled that "The feet of the animal are like those of the owner" (M. Beṣah 5:3), the sect's *halakhah* could be formulated as the reverse: The feet of the owner are like those of the animal.[50] Since the animal is permitted to go 2000 cubits (the size of the *migrash* ("pasturage")), the man following him may go a similar distance although he alone would be subject to a 1000 cubit Sabbath limit. This view, according to Rabin,[51] would agree with that of R. Eliezer ben Yose Ha-Gelili in M. Sotah 5:3.

Rabin [52] assumes from this *halakhah* that the original limit was 1000 cubits and only later was it widened to 2000. J. Brand,[53] although dating the fragments to the fifth century B.C.E., adopts a similar view. However, as a principle of hermeneutics the sect maintained that in groups of numbers each had to have some significance. This rule also prevails in regard to the law of testimony of CDC 9:17-22

---

with the view of the sages in M. ʿErubin 4:8). Cf. G. B. Gray, *A Critical and Exegetical Commentary on Numbers* (1903), 467f., S. D. Luzzatto, *Perush Shadal ʿal Ḥamishah Ḥumshe Torah* (1965), 493-7, N. H. Tur-Sinai, *Peshuto shel Miqra*ʾ (1962-7) I, 196 (who reads *ʾalpayim* in v. 4 with LXX), and Naḥmanides, *ad loc.* See especially M. Greenberg, "Idealism and Practicality in Numbers 35:4-5 and Ezekiel 48," *Essays in Memory of E. A. Speiser*, ed. W. Hallo (1968), 59-66. There is no evidence that the "squaring off" of the Sabbath limit described in tannaitic sources (Greenberg, 61) was known in the Second Temple period. The evidence from Gezer, described below, seems to confirm this.

48 Note the parallels: Num. 35:4, . . . *ha-ʿir wa-ḥuṣah ʾelef ʾammah* . . ., CDC 10:21, . . . *ḥuṣ le-ʿiro* . . . *ʾelef be-ʾammah*, Num. 35:5, . . . *mi-ḥuṣ la-ʿir* . . . *ʾalpayim be-ʾammah* . . ., CDC 11:5, . . . *ḥuṣ me-ʿiro* . . . *ʾalpayim be-ʾammah*. The dependence is unquestionable.

49 Commentary, *ad loc.* So also Yadin, *War Scroll*, 74.

50 The formulation is that of J. Rosenthal, "*ʿAl Hishtalshelut Halakhah Be-Sefer Berit Dameseq*," *Sefer Ha-Yobel Mugash Li-Khbod Ha-Rab Shimʿon Federbush* (1960), 302.

51 *Ad loc.*, and *QS*, 90f.

52 *QS*, 91.

53 "*Megillat Berit Dameseq U-Zemanah*," *Tarbiz* 28 (1958/9), 26. Cf. Rosenthal, 302.

as derived from Deut. 17:6.[54] For this reason, the sect concluded that there were two limits.

DSW 7:6f. provides for the placing of latrines at least 2000 cubits from the camp.[55] This distance is a definite addition to the law of Deut. 23:13 which simply requires that these facilities be placed outside of the camp. The scroll is here linguistically dependent on Josh. 3:4, a passage associated in Rabbinic literature with the Sabbath limit.[56] The Joshua passage deals with the distance which must separate the sanctuary from the tents of Israel and, according to Yadin, was most probably used by the sect to indicate the required "minimum distance between the holy camps and the place of the 'hand' " (latrine).[57] Yadin also raises the possibility that this requirement is in some way connected with the Sabbath limit, and that the latrine had to be placed at such a distance as to allow use on the Sabbath. Since CDC has two limits, 1000 cubits for walking about and 2000 for pasturing animals, one would then have to assume either that the sectarians also permitted going 2000 cubits to the latrines or that, like the Essenes of Josephus,[58] they refrained from using these facilities.

Yadin has since pointed out that in the (still unpublished) *Temple Scroll* there are requirements dealing with the sanctity of (eschatological?) Jerusalem.[59] These regulations similarly place the latrine 2000 cubits from the Temple precincts [60] and would involve as great an inconvenience during the week as the *War Scroll* seems to require on the Sabbath. Why not assume that both these texts are ideal in nature and need not represent the actual practice of the sectarians at Qumran or anywhere else they may have lived?

---

[54] Cf. B. Levine, "Damascus Document IX, 17-22. A New Translation and Comments," *RQ* 8 (1973), 195f., J. Neusner, "'By the Testimony of Two Witnesses' in the Damascus Document IX, 17-22 and in Pharisaic-Rabbinic Law," *RQ* 8 (1973), 197-218, H. van Vliet, *No Single Testimony, A Study of the Adoption of the Law of Deut. 19:15 par. into the New Testament* (1958), Y. Yadin, "Pesher Nahum (4QpNahum) Reconsidered," *IEJ* 21 (1971), 6-8, J. M. Baumgarten, "Does *tlh* in the Temple Scroll Refer to Crucifiction?" *JBL* 91 (1972), 472f. and my "The Qumran Law of Testimony," to appear in *RQ*, no. 32.

[55] See Yadin, *War Scroll*, 73-5.

[56] *Tanḥuma* Be-Midbar 9 (49bf.), *Be-Midbar Rabbah* 2:9 (cited by Yadin, 74 (n. 1)). Cf. *Tan. B.* Be-Midbar 4bf. and Kimchi to Josh. 3:4. The lateness of the sources of these otherwise unattested traditions must be recognized.

[57] P. 74.

[58] Wars 2, 8:9. Cf. Rosenthal, 299f.

[59] See Yadin, "The Temple Scroll," 163. On the "New Jerusalem," cf. *DJD* I, 134f., III, 84-9, 184-193.

[60] *Ibid.*, 165.

There is no reason to assume either that going to the latrine 2000 cubits from the camp on the Sabbath was necessarily permitted, or that the sect shared the asceticism of the Essenes. The sect could have accepted the notion of *ʿerub teḥumin* by which the city limits can be extended, so that by placing something at a distance of 1000 cubits from the original limit, a person would then be permitted to walk a second 1000 cubits. This would enable the sect to conform to its strict rules of camp purity as well as to its Sabbath code. Alternately, the tannaim defined the city limits by the presence of houses.[61] It is possible that for purposes of Sabbath law the sectarians considered the latrines to be within the city limits. The camp would then be the central portion of the city with such places as latrines (and possibly barns) on the outskirts.

Some scholars read *ʾalpayim* for *ʾelef* in our regulation[62] and assume that in an earlier copy *ʾalpayim* had been abbreviated. This abbreviation was misunderstood at some point and became *ʾelef*.[63] If so, this law and CDC 11:5f. would be in complete accord with one another and with the Rabbinic law. But even B. ʿErubin 51a (amoraic), in evaluating a *baraitaʾ*[64] connecting Ex. 16:29 with Num. 35:2-5, asks why the Sabbath limit might not have been one thousand cubits. This question would seem to strengthen the possibility that the sect considered both numbers authoritative.

The writing of the words *ʿal ʾelef be-ʾammah* in larger letters need not be taken as an indication that the copyist was unsure of his text. Rather, he regarded the reading as strange and wanted to make sure that no modification would take place. This technique was an ancient practice among Hebrew scribes.[65]

J. Rosenthal has investigated this Qumran *halakhah* at length,[66] beginning with the post-biblical data. He says that Jubilees 50:12 has been seen by many as a literal interpretation of Ex. 16:29.[67] Why then

---

[61] M. ʿErubin 5:1. T. ʿErubin 4(6):1-8.

[62] Schechter, *ad loc.*

[63] So Ginzberg, 429f.

[64] Cf. Targum Jonathan to Ex. 16:29, P. ʿErubin 4:1 (21d), *Sifre Zutaʾ*, ed. Horovitz, p. 287 and parallels mentioned there. Rabbinic sources all take *taḥtaw* as referring to the four cubit limit in carrying on the public domain and *meqomo* as referring to the Sabbath limit.

[65] *E.g.* the large *ʿayin* and *dalet* in Deut. 6:4. For a complete list and discussion of biblical examples, see "*ʾOtiot*," *Enc. Tal.* 1, 190-192.

[66] The complete study occupies pp. 292-303. Cf. J. Z. Lauterbach, *Rabbinic Essays*, 444.

[67] Albeck, *Jubiläen*, 9.

would Jubilees go on to mention specific prohibitions such as riding, as this would be assumed by a general prohibition of leaving the house? Tchernowitz, therefore, assumes that this passage prohibits only the undertaking of a long journey on the Sabbath.[68]

The Falasha *halakhah* is usually similar to that of Jubilees. The *Te'ezaza Sanbat*, the Falasha Sabbath code, mentions this subject twice. Once this text says that whoever does not remain in his dwelling place on the Sabbath shall die. A second passage (like Jubilees 50:12) decrees that whoever goes on a journey on the Sabbath shall die. Even today the priests of the Falashas sleep in the synagogue, not leaving its portals on the Sabbath. The Falashas go to the synagogue on the seventh day but do not leave their villages.[69] They have no law of *teḥum shabbat* ("Sabbath limit").[70]

Although the ancient versions (LXX, Vulgate, Peshitta) all translate Ex. 16:29 literally, this is no indication that any prohibition on leaving the house existed. On the contrary, according to Rosenthal, Josephus's writings show that this verse was understood only to prohibit long journeys.[71] In his time it was customary to attend the synagogue on Sabbath mornings and afternoons.[72] Rosenthal concludes that already in ancient times the *maqom* ("place") of Ex. 16:29 was given the wider interpretation of dwelling place, village, or city.

The Rabbinic *halakhah* of the Sabbath limit (*teḥum shabbat*) may also be shown to reach back into the Second Temple period.[73] M. Yoma 6:4-5 reports that on the Day of Atonement the honored citizens of Jerusalem accompanied the one who sent forth the scapegoat as far as the first booth (*sukkah*) which was one *mil* (equal to 2000 cubits) from Jerusalem. Others who had made the booths their dwelling places for the Sabbath would accompany this man from booth to

---

68 IV, 367. So also Ginzberg, *Eine unbekannte jüdische Sekte*, 196, 202 and Epstein, *Tannaim*, 279.

69 According to Aescoly (30), Falashas leave their houses only to attend the synagogue and go to the bathroom. Contrast Wars 2, 8:9 regarding the Essenes.

70 Rabin, *QS*, 90 (n. 1) writes, "Dr. J. Tubiana of Paris kindly informs me that the Falashas now walk as far as the nearest watercourse, but do not cross it." This report, if accurate, contrasts with the material cited by Rosenthal, 294 nn. 9, 10.

71 Ant. 13, 8:4 and 14, 10:12. Cf. the philological notes of Rosenthal, 295 n. 15.

72 Cf. Schürer II, ii, 75-83, Belkin, *Alexandrian Halakhah*, 21-25.

73 For biblical attribution, see Cohen, 147 n. 56. Cf. Gilat, "*Le-Qadmutam*," 107-112 and *Mishnato*, 118f.

booth.[74] A *baraita'* in B. 'Erubin 30a would support a *terminus ante quem* of the time of the houses of Hillel and Shammai. M. Rosh Ha-Shanah 2:5 also pushes the Sabbath limit back to the time of Rabban Gamliel I (flourished 20-50 A.D.). S. Zeitlin [75] has deduced from this *mishnah* that the original widening of the term *maqom* allowed a person to go 2000 cubits in any direction. Only later was he permitted to go anywhere in the city (even if further than 2000 cubits). Finally, immediately preceding or following the destruction, it was decided that a man might travel 2000 cubits beyond his city limits. Rosenthal [76] rejects this view and prefers a two stage development. First, the word *maqom* was widened to include the entire city and then, by analogy with the Levitical cities, *maqom* was extended to 2000 cubits beyond the city boundaries. From these several sources it is established that the Sabbath limit was in existence during the Second Commonwealth.

The excavations at Gezer unearthed a set of boundary stones which stood 2000 cubits from the nearest point on the city wall. These were inscribed *teḥum geẓer*, "the boundary (or limit) of Gezer," and probably date from Herodian times.[77] During the same period the Mount of Olives is mentioned as a Sabbath day's journey from Jerusalem (Acts 1:12). The Mount of Olives is approximately 2000 cubits from St. Stephen's gate.[78]

Even so, there were groups in the Second Temple period that did not accept this broadening exegesis of Ex. 16:29. The Samaritans still leave their houses on the Sabbath only to pray in the synagogue. Thus they agree that Ex. 16:29 applied not only to the gatherers of the manna but to all Israel throughout the generations. Even though the Mishnah generally accepts the reliability of the Samaritans as regards the observance of the Sabbath,[79] it disqualifies them as witnesses to the Sabbath limit because they did not accept the legality of

---

[74] Cf. T. Kippurim 3(4):13, and Lieberman, *TK* IV, 794.

[75] S. Zeitlin, *The Zadokite Fragments*, *JQR* Monograph Series 1 (1952), 12, cf. his "The Takkanot of Erubin, a Study in the Development of the Halaka," *JQR* N.S. 41 (1950/1), 351-7.

[76] P. 297f.

[77] S. Macalister, *The Excavation of Geẓer* (1912) I, p. 38, nos. 1-3, 6 (Rabin). Cf. Schürer I, i, 261f. (note).

[78] Rabin, *ad loc.* and T. S. Kepler, "Sabbath Day's Journey," *IDB* 4, 141. Cf. Targum to Ruth 1:16 and Schürer II, ii, 102f.

[79] M. Nedarim 3:10.

these limits.[80] There are, however, no early Samaritan sources for the interpretation of Ex. 16:29, and their medieval texts are no doubt influenced by Karaite and Arabic material. Rosenthal suggests that the Samaritans derived the permissibility of attending the synagogue on the Sabbath either from Lev. 23:3 where the Sabbath is called *miqra' qodesh* ("a holy convocation"), or from Ex. 33:7 from which it would appear that even on the Sabbath one could visit the *'ohel mo'ed* ("tent of meeting"). This same conclusion was drawn by Benjamin al-Nahawandi (ninth century) who may have been influenced by the Samaritans.[81] The military colony of Elephantine (Yeb, present-day Aswan) was quite strict in regard to Sabbath laws. The soldiers were careful to tie their animals in barns on Friday so that they could not escape on the Sabbath. From this Rosenthal concludes that they must have taken Ex. 16:29 in its narrowest sense and remained in their houses on the Sabbath.[82]

Nothing is known about the Sadducean interpretation of Ex.16:29. From Josephus [83] it is clear that the Essenes were quite strict in their Sabbath code. Nevertheless, only from Hippolytus (third century C.E.) [84] is there a report of Essenes who would not even leave their beds on the Sabbath. They must have taken Ex. 16:29 literally.

In dealing with the Karaites, the problem is more involved. Anan is said to have taken *meqomo* and *taḥtaw* metaphorically, *maqom* being a wide (enlarged) place and *taḥtaw* indicating permission to travel up to 2000 cubits to the house of study or the synagogue. The latter seems not to apply in a city in which there are (a majority of ?) gentiles.[85] Most later Karaite authorities agree with Anan and do not admit the permissibility of the *'erub teḥumin*. The Karaites, then, did not take Ex. 16:29 literally. Nahawandi interpreted *taḥtaw* to mean that one could not go further than 2000 cubits from his city and that such travel was only permitted *le-ṣorekh ha-bore'* ("for the need of the Creator"), *i. e.* to fulfil a commandment.[86] Qirqisani quotes Nahawandi

---

[80] M. 'Erubin 3:2, B. 'Erubin 31b, B. Niddah 57a. Cf. M. 'Erubin 6:1, Albeck's "*HWT*," *ad loc.* and B. Revel, *Karaite Halakhah*, 39f.

[81] Rosenthal, 298f.

[82] P. 299.

[83] Wars 2, 8:9.

[84] J. Donaldson, A. Roberts, eds., *Ante-Nicene Fathers* (1907) V, 136.

[85] A. Harkavy, *Mi-Sifre Ha-Miṣwot Ha-Rishonim Li-Bene Miqra'* (1903), 163, and the sources cited by Rosenthal, 300 nn. 42, 43. Cf. Revel, 40f.

[86] The same is recorded in *Mishnat R. 'Eliezer*, most probably an 8th century work (ed. Enelow (1933), 368). Cf. also the view of Sahl b. Maṣliaḥ (Rosenthal, 301).

and takes issue with his point of view. Qirqisani permits travelling within the city (thus not taking Ex. 16:29 literally) but refuses to accept the notion of *teḥum shabbat*.[87] From Haddasi [88] it appears that there were some Karaites who remained in their houses on the Sabbath. R. Petaḥiah of Regensburg (twelfth century), the famous traveller, met such people in southern Russia. According to his report, they remained in one place all day.[89] To summarize the views of the Karaites, all interpreted Ex. 16:29 loosely to include the entire city. Some agreed to the *teḥum shabbat* but limited its use to religious purposes.[90]

5. *CDC 10:22f.: Preparation of Food Before The Sabbath*

אל יאכל איש ביום השבת כי אם המוכן ומן האובד בשדה

> No one shall eat (anything) on the Sabbath day except that which has been prepared (*mukhan*) (in advance) or from that which is decaying [91] in the field.

The term *mukhan* for prepared food is used in similar context by the tannaim.[92] The *halakhah* of Jubilees also contains this same prescription (2:29, 50:8).

It is probable, though, that the Rabbinic and Qumran injunctions are differently derived. The starting point of the tannaim was the prohibition of "baking" or cooking on the Sabbath.[93] If an item was prepared on the Sabbath in violation of the law,[94] it was forbidden to make use of it. Hence, all cooking and baking had to be done before the Sabbath.

The sect did not allow one to eat *anything* which was not prepared in advance, possibly including even vegetables not peeled before the Sabbath. This law was based on their interpretation of Ex. 16:5 and 23.

---

87 So also Yefet ben Ali (Rosenthal, 301).

88 *ʾEshkol Ha-Kofer* 144, p. 54c.

89 A. Kahana, *Sifrut Ha-Historiyah Ha-Yisraelit* (1922/3) I, 219, J. Mann, *Texts and Studies in Jewish History and Literature* (1931, 5) II, 39 n. 7.

90 All the Karaite views are detailed and documented by Rosenthal, 300-302.

91 Cf. Joel 1:11f. (which shows that the harvest is drying up), P. Shebiʿit 9:1 (38d top) and the commentary *Pene Mosheh, ad loc.* See also M. Giṭṭin 3:8 and P. Giṭṭin 3:8 (45a) which equates *ʾbd* and *qlql*. If we translated "lost," there would be no reason why these foods should be permitted, but cf. CDC 9:10-12 where *ʾobed* clearly means "lost."

92 M. Beṣah 3:4, B. Beṣah 6b, (But note that these passages refer to that prepared for festivals, not Sabbath), M. Shabbat 24:4, B. Pesaḥim 56b, B. Ḥullin 14a. Cf. Gilat, *Mishnato*, 123-8.

93 M. Shabbat 7:2. Cf. B. Shabbat 74b and commentaries.

94 M. Shabbat 3:4, B. Shabbat 38a. Cf. "*Hakhanah*," *Enc. Tal.* 9, 103-125.

The exegesis of these verses in Exodus resulted for the sect in a positively stated commandment to prepare all food in advance of the Sabbath. This derivation of the sect's *halakhah* is supported by the use of the term *mukhan* based on *we-hekhinu* in Ex. 16:5. It is an example of *perush* exegesis.[95] It may be that the sect and Jubilees here represent a more ancient and rigorous *halakhah* than that of the tannaim.[96] The Falashas are also required to prepare all food for the Sabbath on Friday.[97] It would seem from Josephus [98] that the Essenes only prohibited cooking and baking of food on the Sabbath, but not other kinds of preparation. Otherwise, why would Josephus cite fear of making a fire on the Sabbath as the reason for preparing food before the holy day?

In regard to the Karaites, Ginzberg [99] sees the references in Anan's *Sefer Ha-Miṣwot* as ambiguous, yet points out that the later Karaites attributed to Anan the requirement that preparation (*hakhanah*) be completed before the Sabbath. It would seem, however, that Ginzberg's claim of ambiguity is overstated, especially in light of the later tradition which he cites. Benjamin al-Nahawandi did permit the eating of that not prepared before the Sabbath.[100]

As to the second part of this law, Ginzberg [101] says that it is impossible that the author of the fragments would allow the plucking of fruit to save it from rain or other damage. He goes on to suggest reading *ha-ʾagur ba-ʾoṣaroh*,[102] "that which is stored up in his storehouse." Although this reading would connect well with what follows,

---

[95] Cf. Targum Jon. to Ex. 16:5, 23.

[96] But see the *baraitaʾ* quoted by R. Mana (or R. Huna—both amoraim) in B. Shabbat 114b, Cohen, 140f. and nn. 36-38, and Gilat, *Mishnato*, 122f.

[97] Aescoly, 31, 33, Wurmbrand, 238.

[98] Wars 2, 8:9 (Kimbrough, 489).

[99] P. 430 (and n. 1), citing Anan, 70, 73. See also 147 (Hadassi, *ʾEshkol Ha-Kofer*, 72c is the original source), 152.

[100] Harkavy, *Mi-Sifre Ha-Miṣwot*, 136, 152 (cited from Hadassi's *Sefer Ha-Miṣwot*, in S. Pinsker, *Liqqute Qadmoniot* (1860) II, 95. On the authorship of these fragments, see p. 93.) It should be noted that Pinsker used transcriptions prepared by A. Firkovich in publishing this text, yet Harkavy points out that even P. F. Frankl accepted the attribution of the text to Hadassi. Frankl's criticisms of Pinsker's collection were published in "*ʾAḥare Reshef Le-Baqqer Be-Sifrut Ha-Qaraʾim*," *Ha-Shaḥar* 7 (1875/6), 646-50, 701-13, 8 (1876/7), 29-31, 119-27, 177-84. If this attribution is correct, we would have a preliminary work, in biblical order, done in preparation for the *ʾEshkol Ha-Kofer*, much the same way as Maimonides' *Sefer Ha-Miṣwot* served as a preliminary to the *Mishneh Torah*.

[101] P. 430f.

[102] Ginzberg refers to a similar spelling, *bmh* in line 12, but this may be for *be-mey*, "in water of." His reading is better supported by reference to Ges. rule 91e.

its weakness is that it is dependent on speculative emendation. Finally, Ginzberg fails to realize that *ha-'obed ba-sadeh* need not refer to that which is still on the tree, but rather to that which has fallen from the tree and is lying "on the field." Ginzberg also suggests that (retaining *ba-sadeh*) this law can be understood as prohibiting the use of that which has been brought by a non-Jew on the Sabbath from outside the Sabbath limit. This interpretation is also dependent on tenuous emendation and contradicts CDC 11:14f. which prohibits spending the Sabbath in the vicinity of gentiles.

The second part of this law permits the eating of fruits which have presumably fallen from the tree and are lying in the field decaying. This same matter was the subject of a disagreement between the tannaim and the "men of Jericho."[103] The men of Jericho ate fruits found under a tree on the Sabbath, while the Rabbis, afraid that the fruit may have fallen off on the Sabbath, did not sanction this practice.[104] Apparently, the men of Jericho were not willing to abstain from eating these fruits on the mere possibility (*safeq*) that they had fallen off on the Sabbath.[105] The sect took a midway position. It allowed the eating of the fruit if it had started to decay. If decay had already set in, the fruit could be presumed to have fallen before the Sabbath.[106] It is probable that the sect did not have a concept such as *safeq de-'orayta' le-ḥumra'*, "in case of doubt relating to a biblical injunction, one should be strict." [107] There was for them no reason why such fruits, obviously coming under the category of *mukhan* (prepared before the Sabbath)[108] could not be eaten. They did, however, take care

---

[103] M. Pesaḥim 4:8 (See Albeck, "*HWT*," 448), T. Pesaḥim 3(2):19, 21 (See Lieberman, *TK* IV, 540f. and note especially the omission of *ba-shabbat* in many texts.). Cf. the view of Finkelstein, *Pharisees* I, 69.

[104] According to P. Pesaḥim 4:9 (31b) (see commentaries *ad loc.* and *Tosafot* to B. Pesaḥim 56b, *s.v. maḥaloqet*). A. Büchler, *Ha-Kohanim We-'Abodatam* (1966), 122 shows that these traditions must deal with the time of the Temple.

[105] Finkelstein (*Pharisees* I, 69) suggests that the rural "men of Jericho" could not accept the extension of the prohibition of reaping to include the plucking of fruits since the distinction was clear to them as farmers. Their practice is reflected in the actions of the disciples of Jesus (Matt. 12:1, Mk. 2:23, Luke 6:1). Büchler (124f.), based on the variant readings omitting *ba-shabbat* from the Mishnah, takes this as referring, like the clause above in the Mishnah, to the eating of the fruit of sanctified trees (*heqdesh*). If he were correct, this *mishnah* and the attendant traditions would be irrelevant to our passage in CDC, but Ginzberg, 430, accepts their relevance.

[106] Thus answering the question of *Tosafot*, *ibid.* (*u-qeṣat temah* etc.).

[107] B. Beṣah 3b, etc.

[108] See B. Pesaḥim 56b. Note that this entire *sugya'* is built around the Tosefta rather than the Mishnah.

to see that fruits which had actually fallen on the seventh day would not be consumed. As would be expected, the Karaites agreed with the Rabbis in this stringency.[109]

6. *CDC 10:23: Eating and Drinking within the Camp*

ואל יאכל ואל ישתה כי אם היה במחנה

Let him not drink or eat except if he (or: that which [110]) is in the camp.

If the first translation proposed above is correct, the sect used *midrash halakhah* to widen the meaning of *meqomo* [111] in interpreting the law of Ex. 16:29. The sect shared the view of the tannaim that *taḥtaw* referred to the distance that a man could carry in a public domain. The tannaim created a four cubit (six foot) square in which a man may carry in *reshut ha-rabbim* ("public domain").[112] The sect, however, felt no reason (as even the Rabbis could cite no Scriptural prooftext) to extend the meaning of this word, and so concluded that the distance one would be allowed to carry was nil. In other words, nothing in the public domain might be moved even the slightest distance on the Sabbath. Hence, no eating or drinking outside the camp was permitted. But this interpretation might lead to the conclusion that the sect allowed food to be moved or water to be drawn [113] within the camp. Since this would contradict CDC 11:7-9,[114] the second explanation may be preferable.

It is also possible to supply (in thought) *'asher* [115] after *ki 'im* and to relate this law to CDC 10:22f. In favor of this second interpretation is the apparently logical sequence in which the laws are arranged in the code. This second interpretation would mean that the sect did not permit the eating of food that had not been brought into the camp before the Sabbath. This would limit the decaying fruits of CDC 10:22f. to those already within the city limits before the Sabbath.

---

109 Samuel al-Magribi, *Al-Muršid*, Discourse IV, 9:4, translated in Nemoy, 210.

110 Schechter, *ad loc.* For the ramifications of this translation see below.

111 See the discussion of CDC 10:21, above, 91-98.

112 Targum Jonathan to Ex. 16:29, T. ʿErubin 3(4):11, B. ʿErubin 48a (tannaitic), P. ʿErubin 4:1 (21d), and other sources cited in *TK* III, 347f.

113 So Rabin, *ad loc.* See the discussion of the next law.

114 See below, 113-115.

115 See Ges. rules 155f-l, Gen. 15:4.

7. *CDC 11:1f.: Drinking and Washing on a Journey*

בדרך וירד לרחוץ ישתה על עומדו ואל ישאב אל כל כל[י]

> On the road, if he goes down to wash [116] let him drink where he stands, but let him not draw (water) into any vessel.[117]

This law takes for granted the permissibility of washing. No doubt, washing here refers to the ritual cleansing of the hands (and feet?) [118] performed upon rising and before eating. These ablutions would have been especially important to the sectarians, judging from their emphasis on laws of ritual purity.[119]

There is a more compelling reason for translating "wash." The regulation here is speaking of someone who is kneeling next to a water source and who can drink without having to draw water into any vessel.[120] Such a person must be washing and not bathing, otherwise the words *ʿal ʿomdo*, "where he stands," would be inappropriate. So although the sect may have allowed bathing on the Sabbath, our text is clearly dealing with washing.

But was bathing the entire body permitted on the Sabbath? M. Beṣah 2:2 contains an argument between the houses of Hillel and Shammai regarding Rabbinically ordained ritual immersion (*de-rabbanan*)[121] on the Sabbath. The Hillelites allowed the immersion, probably by analogy with the man who had had a seminal emission (*baʿal qeri*)[122] who was permitted to immerse on the Sabbath. The discussion in the Babylonian Talmud indicates that even bathing for pleasure (to cool off) was permitted according to this view.[123] The Shammaites did not permit ritual immersion because it changed the

---

[116] Translating with Schechter against Rabin (whose translation "bathe" is based on Ex. 2:5). The possibility that we are dealing with a ritual bath is extremely unlikely as it would be unusual for anyone to drink from it. (See Cross, *Ancient Library*, 68.) Here we must be dealing with some kind of natural running water suitable for drinking as well as bathing.

[117] Reading with Schechter and Rabin. It is also possible that this is an otherwise unattested singular *kel* on which the pl. *kelim* may have been built (Ges. rule 96, p. 286).

[118] See N. Wieder, *Hashpaʿot ʾIslamiot ʿal Ha-Pulḥan Ha-Yehudi* (1957), 10-22.

[119] They may also have laved before prayer. Cf. Ringgren, 84f., 124f., CDC 10:10-13.

[120] Ginzberg, 433f.

[121] The discussion was about purification before festivals on which see B. Rosh Ha-Shanah 16b. Cf. also Albeck's "*HWT*" to *Seder Moʿed*, 481.

[122] P. Beṣah 2:2 (61b), but note the possibility raised in the commentary *Ṣiyyun Yerushalayim* by J. S. Nathanson, *ad loc.*, that *le-qeruyo* means "to cool himself" making the interpretation of the Palestinian Talmud the same as that of the Babylonian.

[123] B. Beṣah 18a, b.

status of a person previously unfit for a specific purpose and rendered him fit for that purpose.[124] There is no reason to assume, then, that the Shammaites did not allow bathing for pleasure. Therefore, it is also possible that the sect would have allowed bathing as well as ritual immersion.[125] The Falasha *Teʾezaza Sanbat*, however, forbade bathing on the Sabbath.[126] The Samaritans permit ritual immersion.[127]

The necessity of drinking in his place, directly from the water source, follows logically from the prohibition of drawing water into any vessel. Mishnaic law permitted the drawing of water from a well within the private domain. An *ʿerub* would also permit drawing of water from a flowing watercourse. Under no circumstances could water be taken from a source in the public domain.[128] M. ʿErubin 10:6 [129] allows one to drink in the public or private domain provided that the head and torso are in the same domain as the water. In the public domain, where water-drawing was prohibited, the action permitted would be that of bending over and drinking directly with the mouth. This Mishnaic tradition accords completely with the Qumran *halakhah*. Perhaps the sect permitted the drawing of water within the confines of the camp.

Jubilees 2:29 and 50:8 prohibit drawing water directly from its source but allow the taking of water from a reservoir or cistern. This, of course, would only apply within the private domain. In the field all water-drawing is forbidden by Jubilees. The Karaite Hadassi[130] appears to agree with Jubilees. There is, however, a difference between their views. Jubilees sees the prohibition as based on the fact that the water was not prepared for use before the Sabbath (*hakhanah*). After mentioning this reason, Hadassi goes on to say that water-drawing (from a natural source) is in itself a forbidden labor (*melakhah*).[131] The Falashas also forbid water-drawing in the Sabbath.[132]

---

[124] This may have fallen under the category of *ha-makkeh ba-paṭish* (M. Shabbat 7:2) in the Shammaite view. To the Hillelites this category only applied to *kelim*, but the Shammaites understood it more generally.

[125] So Ginzberg, 432.

[126] *Ibid.*

[127] S. Lowy, "Some Aspects of Normative and Sectarian Interpretation of the Scriptures," *Annual of Leeds University Oriental Society* 6 (1969), 113.

[128] M. ʿErubin 8:6-8 (Rabin), cf. M. Shabbat 11:4.

[129] See the note in Ginzberg, 434 where the reference to Maimonides is found in chapter 15 (not 14).

[130] *ʾEshkol Ha-Kofer* 147, p. 56a, Charles to Jub. 50:8, and Ginzberg, 433.

[131] Ginzberg, *ibid.*

[132] Aescoly, 33, Wurmbrand, 238. Ginzberg (433) notes that only running water is forbidden.

Ginzberg [133] here proposes an emendation from *ba-derekh* to *ha-ba' min ha-derekh*. He refers to a parallel in P. Yoma' 8:1 (40d) and understands this law of CDC to permit one who has returned from travelling on Friday afternoon to cleanse himself on the Sabbath of the dust of the journey. Two objections can be raised. First, the emendation is unsupported.[134] Second, the parallel cited does not refer to the Sabbath but to the Ninth of Ab. This interpretation also assumes a different punctuation than the one proposed above. Ginzberg breaks the sentence into two separate laws, placing a period after *lirḥoṣ*.

8. *CDC 11:2: Performance of Sabbath Work by a Non-Jew*

אל ישלח את בן הנכר לעשות את חפצו ביום השבת

Let him not send a foreigner to do his desire on the Sabbath.

Rabin, basing himself on Is. 56:3 and 6,[135] assumes that this passage refers to converts. The law would then prohibit a Jew's sending a convert to do work for him on the Sabbath. Anticipating the obvious question of why anyone would ask a convert to violate the Sabbath, Rabin makes reference to Schürer's discussion of proselytes in Hellenistic Judaism.[136] During this period many people practiced certain Jewish observances, particularly relating to the Sabbath and forbidden meats, without actually fulfilling the legal requirements of conversion—circumcision, immersion, and the offering of a sacrifice. According to Rabin, the text here prohibits the sending of a semi-proselyte who would otherwise observe the Sabbath to perform forbidden labors.

This analysis immediately raises the question of the history of the institution of conversion in Israel. In the time of Ezra there was

---

[133] P. 431f.

[134] Ginzberg quotes the P.T. as reading *ha-ba'*. The reading of the printed editions, supported by the syntactic context, is *be-ba'*. No text agreeing with that of Ginzberg can be located except that of the *Tur* in which the modification is clearly the result of his omitting the name of the tradition's author. Cf. B. Ratner, *'Ahawat Ṣion Wi-Yrushalayim*, Yoma', 86.

[135] These are the only two passages in which the phrase *ben ha-nekhar* (as opposed to *ben nekhar*) occurs. This phrase is associated with *nilwim*, apparently a term for "converts." Nevertheless, in Isaiah the *ben ha-nekhar* is still not an Israelite. It would appear, then, that there is no real difference between *ben nekhar* and *ben ha-nekhar*. Cf. M. Weinfeld, "*Nekhar, Nokhri, Nokhriyah*," *Enc. Bib.* 5, 866f., Kaufmann, *Toledot* IV, 135-7. J. M. Baumgarten, "The Exclusion of '*Netinim*' and Proselytes in 4Q Florilegium," *RQ* 8 (1972), 87-96 has suggested that *ben ha-nekhar* was a term for the *netinim* at Qumran.

[136] *History* II, ii, 311-327. On the *halakhot* of conversion, see "*Gerut*," *Enc. Tal.* 6, 426-449.

apparently no system for the acceptance of proselytes, as can be seen from the story of Ezra's expulsion of the foreign wives (Ezra 9 and 10). Kaufmann [137] is probably correct in assuming that there could not have been an institution for religious conversion at this time. He takes the view that originally conversion was accomplished by attachment to the land and collective fate of the people of Israel. The early Second Commonwealth, however, was a period of transition. The old process, followed by Ruth for example, had gone out of use,[138] yet the later methods of conversion, based on a conception of Judaism as a religion rather than Israel as a national entity, had not yet been developed. It is only in this light that one can understand why the technique of conversion was not used to avoid the separation of families and the hardships it must have brought about.

It may be that the foundations of religious conversion had already been laid by the time of the *Zadokite Fragments*. Even in the time prior to Ezra, when conversion was an ethnic rather than religious phenomenon, people were absorbed or assimilated into Israel in varying degrees.

The factor which really motivates Rabin's analysis of this passage is his desire to avoid a contradiction between this regulation and that of CDC 11:14f. which prohibits spending the Sabbath in an area close to non-Jews (*goyim*).[139] The apparent contradiction is based on the assumption that our law is meant to prohibit giving the non-Jew instructions *on the Sabbath*. Hence, the law must deal with converts or semi-proselytes. As support for this explanation, Rabin calls attention to an identical law found in tannaitic literature.[140]

All of this is incorrect. Although the sectarian may not spend the

---

[137] *Toledot* IV, 296-301. Tchernowitz III, 108 suggests that men could convert by circumcision but that no method was available for women.

[138] The return to Judea did not result in a revival of this process. Apparently the effects of the exile were too strong.

[139] On this term see "*Goy*," *Enc. Tal.* 5, 286-289 where it is shown that the biblical terms for a non-Israelite, *nokhri* and *ben nekhar*, were replaced in Rabbinic parlance by *goy*. Apparently, the sect, standing somewhere between the language of the Bible and that of the Mishnah, is still using the older terminology although the new term has already been coined.

[140] Considered a biblical ordinance in *Mekhilta' De-Rabbi Ishmael*, Pisḥa', 9. See commentaries in ed. Friedmann, 9b, Horovitz-Rabin, 30f. and Berlin, 37. Later authorities, however, considered it Rabbinical. Cf. B. Shabbat 150a (Kimbrough, 491) which is amoraic, "*'Amirah Le-Nokhri Shebut*," *Enc. Tal.* 2, 42-45, and M. Shabbat 16:6. It may be that in tannaitic times it was a *melakhah*. Cf. B. Cohen, 148f.

Sabbath among non-Jews, it would still be possible for him to give instructions to a non-Jew on a weekday to be carried out on the Sabbath. However, the sect had ruled that this, too, is a violation of the Sabbath law. The Qumranites, then, adopted a law which is in accord with the view of the Shammaites and stricter than that of the Hillelites who permitted non-Jews to perform labors if asked to do so before the onset of the Sabbath.[141] There is no contradiction here with CDC 11:14f. The sectarian may not spend the Sabbath among non-Jews, and he may also not send them to violate the Sabbath on his behalf.

In this discussion, the non-Jew is sent to perform tasks forbidden to the Jew on the Sabbath. Since the non-Jew is now acting as an agent for the Jew, it is as if the Jew himself were violating the law.[142] Philo understands the commandment of Ex. 20:10 and Deut. 5:14 to mean that the master may not benefit from any work done by the servant on the Sabbath, even if permitted.[143] It is probable that the sect also would have extended this law (CDC 10:21) to include even tasks which do not involve forbidden labor (*melakhah*). The sect, like the *Mekhilta'*,[144] must have derived its law using the *perush* method from either Ex. 12:16 (assuming the law was the same for Sabbaths and festivals) or from the commandment of Ex. 20:10 and Deut. 5:14.

9. *CDC 11:3f.: The Cleanliness of Sabbath Garments*

אל יקח איש עליו בגדים צואים או מובאים בגז כי אם כיבסו במים או שופים בלבונה

> No one shall put on [145] filthy garments or (those) put [146] in storage [147] unless they have been washed [148] with water or are rubbed [149] with frankincense.[150]

---

[141] M. Shabbat 1:7-9 and Albeck's commentary, *ad loc.*, T. Shabbat 1:21, 22, Lieberman, *TK* III, 19-22.

[142] For other explanations see the encyclopedia article cited in n. 140.

[143] Belkin, 203.

[144] See n. 140.

[145] *Lqh ʿal* means "to put on" in 2 Sam. 13:19 (Rabin) and Jud. 19:28.

[146] *Hofʿal* of *bw'* + *b* = "to be introduced, put." Cf. Ex. 27:7, Lev. 11:32.

[147] So Rabin basing himself on "Talmudic *gazzā* (from Persian)." The *zayin* is quite clear in the MS.

[148] Reading *kubsu* with Segal, *ad loc.* Such an error must have arisen in ancient times when the *waw* and *yod* were still identical. We can imagine that shortly after the two diverged, scribes copying texts from scrolls several hundred years old with which they were unfamiliar must have confused the two letters quite often.

[149] Ginzberg (436, n. 1) reads *shufam*: "Unless he had rubbed them."

[150] A. Büchler, "Schechter's 'Jewish Sectaries,'" *JQR* N.S. 3 (1912/3), 452 would translate "on a brick." See Jastrow, *s.v. lebenta'* and B. Shabbat 50b.

Reading *ba-goy*, Schechter [151] has proposed comparison with the ancient law,[152] now surviving in Falasha *halakhah*, to the effect that anything touched by a non-Jew was ritually impure. Ginzberg [153] objects on linguistic grounds, saying that the text should read *min goy*. Recent discoveries of the use of the preposition *b* to mean "from" as well as evidence that this usage was alive even in the post-biblical period would obviate this criticism.[154] His second objection is more substantial: This is a Sabbath code, so what would such a law of ritual purity be doing in this context? [155] He answers by referring to 2 Macc. 12:38 which mentions purification as part of preparation for the Sabbath.[156] This still leaves some difficulty. He asks how frank-

---

[151] P. XXV.

[152] *Sifra'*, Parashat Zabim 1 (to Lev. 15:2), reading *ka-zabim* with Elijah of Vilna, and Codex Assemani LXVI (p. 311), *ad loc.*, T. Zabim 2:1, B. Niddah 34a, where the reading *ka-zabim* is further confirmed by the context. Elijah of Vilna to T. Zabim 2:1 remarks that the impurity was a Rabbinical ordinance (so B. Niddah 34a). See also John 18:28, Acts 10:28 (all cited by Ginzberg, 434 n. 3).

[153] Pp. 434-436.

[154] See above, 27f. n. 44.

[155] Possibly the familiar phrase *ba-yom ha-shabbat* has been omitted at the very beginning of this regulation by haplography (the regulation of CDC 10:17 begins with *ba-yom ha-shabbat* also). Some of the laws encountered later in this code are manifestly applicable only to the Sabbath and yet bear no specific label to that effect.

[156] 2 Macc. 8:25-28 tells us that when pursuing the routed army of Nicanor, the Jews stopped in order to prepare for the Sabbath. In addition, they did not divide the spoils until after the Sabbath since this was probably forbidden as a type of commercial activity. Similarly, in 2 Macc. 12:38, Judah took his men into a town as the Sabbath was approaching, "and they purified themselves in accordance with their custom, and celebrated the Sabbath there." R. Marcus, *Law in the Apocrypha* (1927), 80, explains the purification as being necessary after the shedding of blood (cf. Num. 31:19). It is possible that such a purification was required, or the passage may refer to the cleansing of the body in honor of the on-coming Sabbath. (So Albeck, *Das Buch der Jubiläen und die Halacha* (1930), 7f. Cf. G. Allon, *Meḥqarim* I, 306f. for a possible Christian reference to this custom.) Ginzberg (435 n. 3) refers to the tannaitic *halakhah* which required non-priests to be pure only for the three pilgrimage festivals. See *Sifra'* Shemini 4:9 to Lev. 11:8, B. Rosh Ha-Shanah 16b. *'Oṣar Ha-Geonim, ad loc.*, cites traditions indicating that later, purity for the Sabbath was associated with what originally was just a requirement of cleanliness. Hadassi, *'Eshkol Ha-Kofer*, 56b refers to *reḥiṣah* before the Sabbath from which one can understand simply a requirement of cleanliness. It should be noted that the only reason for the requirement of purity on festivals is that the pilgrim would enter the Temple precincts. So even in ancient times, there would have been no reason for the entire population to be ritually pure on the Sabbath. It is possible that in Maccabean and sectarian circles, dominated as they were by priests, ritual purity was required for every Sabbath.

incense can be used for purification, when the Bible only ordains the use of water.[157]

Ginzberg therefore suggests reading *seubim be-gel*,[158] "soiled with excrement." The law would then deal not with ritual purity but with the cleanliness of garments on the Sabbath. The garments would then be washed and the frankincense used to remove the odor, all before the holy day. The reading adopted above, that of Rabin, accords well with Ginzberg's interpretation, yet involves no emendation of the text.

The regulation demands that if garments have become dirty, they must be washed; if they have been stored, they must be deodorized before they can be worn on the Sabbath. The tannaim also require the wearing of clean clothes on the Sabbath, as well as on festivals and on the Day of Atonement.[159] There seems to be no mention in Rabbinic literature of any prohibition against wearing clothes in need of this "dry cleaning." It is, however, a natural extension of the respect given the Sabbath.

E. Neufeld [160] has drawn attention to the practice of using spices as deodorants in ancient Israel. Ps.45:9 mentions their use for clothes. Song 3:6 may refer to this practice. These aromatic substances were used by all elements of the population and were cultivated extensively. The odors were emitted during cumbustion of the plants.[161] It is

[157] Ginzberg (436 n. 2) cites the only exception, Num. 31:23. Although the Rabbinic tradition (cf. Targum Jon. and *Torah Temimah*, *ad loc.*) has taken this use of fire as for the purpose of *hagʿalah* ("kashering"), modern scholars have seen it in context as a form of ritual purification (see Luzzato, *ad loc.*, and M. Noth, *Numbers*, 231). Ginzberg (n. 3) also cites a report of Herodotus (I, 198) to the effect that spices were used by the Babylonians to purify themselves after sexual intercourse.

[158] Ginzberg does not vocalize, but *gel* is the putative sing. absolute form of the construct *gelal-* (BDB, 165a). It is also possible to vocalize *gal* and assume an Aramaism. Cf. Targum Ezek. 4:12, 15 and read *galle* (Jastrow, *s.v. gallaʾ*).

[159] *Mekhiltaʾ De-Rabbi Shimʿon b. Yoḥai* Yitro 20:8, ed. Epstein-Melamed, 149, Hoffmann, 107. For festivals see *idem*, Boʾ 12:16 ed. Epstein-Melamed, 18, Hoffmann, 16, *Mekhiltaʾ De-Rabbi Ishmael* Pisḥaʾ 9, ed. Friedmann, 9a, Horovitz-Rabin, 30, *Sifre* Num. 147, ed. Friedmann, 54b, Horovitz, 194, *Sifraʾ* ʾEmor (8) 12:4 and for the Day of Atonement, B. Shabbat 119a. Jubilees 31:1, taken by Rabin to indicate that clean clothes were also required on the new moon, may simply refer to the particular event it describes. B. Babaʾ Qammaʾ 82a explains the purpose of Ezra's institution (*taqqanah*, described there) of washing clothes on Thursday as being "in honor of the Sabbath."

[160] "Hygiene conditions in Ancient Israel (Iron Age)," *BA* 34 (1971), 57-9, originally appeared in *Journal of the History of Medicine and Applied Sciences* 25 (1970).

[161] Note the words *ke-timerot ʿashan, mequṭeret* in Song 3:6.

possible that this practice is referred to in tannaitic sources.[162] Neither disinfectant nor antibiotic, these substances served to mask the previous odor with a stronger or more pleasant smell.[163]

The use of frankincense for perfuming purposes is well known,[164] and it is possible that the priestly connections of the sect rendered its members especially familiar with its use.[165] It still would be interesting to know why clothes were stored. Did the sectarians have seasonal clothes suited to given climates? This must be left for experts in the history of costume.

The remaining question is how the sect derived the requirement of clean clothes from the Torah. The *Mekhilta' De-Rabbi Shim'on b. Yoḥai* derived this regulation from Ex. 20:8 (*le-qaddesho*). On the other hand, B. Shabbat 119a derives a similar prescription for the Day of Atonement from Is. 58:13.[166] A different exegesis of this same Isaiah passage found on the same page of the Talmud, associated it with the Sabbath, although deriving from it a different law. It is probable that the sect derived its regulation from one of the two passages: Ex. 20:8 or Is. 58:13. In either case, the exegesis is strictly that of *perush*.

10. *CDC 11:4f.: Entering a Partnership*

אל יתערב איש מרצונו בשבת

No one shall enter partnership[167] by his own volition[168] on the Sabbath.

---

[162] A *baraita'* in B. Shabbat 18a and P. Shabbat 1:5 (3d), according to Rashi and *Qorban Ha-'Edah*. The reading of the same *baraita'* in T. Shabbat 1:23 omits *taḥat ha-kelim* ("clothes"). Cf. B. Shabbat 18b. Instead, the Tosefta seems to refer to the practice of burning incense (*mugmar*) to deodorize a room. Since other occurrences of the word *mugmar* (*e.g.* M. Berakhot 6:6) all refer to the deodorizing of a room, it seems doubtful if the version of the Talmudim can be accepted. Further, since even the Tosefta version mentions *kelim* in reference to *gafrit* ("sulphur"), it is easy to understand how the corruption might have occurred. Cf. *'Arukh Ha-Shalem*, *s.v. mgmr*. *Mugmar* is also mentioned in 11Q Job Targum Col. 36:6 (to Job 41:12). See J. van der Ploeg, A. S. van der Woude, *Le Targum de Job*, 82f., 127 and S. Kaufman, "Job Targum," 322.

[163] Neufeld, 58.

[164] Song 3:6, 4:6, 4:14.

[165] See CDC 11:19.

[166] On this passage see Berlin's commentary to *Mekhilta' De-Rabbi Ishmael*, 36.

[167] On the technical use of this verb in the scrolls, see Licht, *MH*, 150 (note) and the texts cited there. It is clear that this verb cannot mean "to make an *'erub*" as that meaning commonly requires a *pi'el* in Heb. and a *pa'el* in Aram. For the *hitpa'el* in our passage, cf. BDB, *s.v. 'rb*. Note that normally the *hitpa'el* of *'rb* in the Qumran literature requires that the preposition *b* follow. Our passage is an exception. See further S. Hoenig, "An Interdict against Socializing on the Sabbath," *JQR* N.S. 62 (1971), 78f. Hoenig's attempt (81-3) to relate Karaite

(Note 168 p.t.o.)

This law has given rise to several emendations. Nevertheless, it is possible, and may be preferable, to adhere to the text as it stands. The law would then prohibit declaring on the Sabbath any private property to be available for communal use.[169] This prohibition would be the result of *perush* exegesis of Is. 58:13. This regulation is similar to CDC 10:17-19 which prohibits the discussion of business affairs on the Sabbath and which was similarly derived. If the interpretation above is correct, there would be no Rabbinic parallel, as the content of this law is purely sectarian, applying only in a community which shared the use of its property.

Several scholars[170] have sought to emend *yitʿareb* to *yitraʿeb* or *yitʿaneh* and to translate, "Let no man starve himself voluntarily on the Sabbath."[171] They have taken this to refer to the prohibition of fasting on the Sabbath known from Jub. 50:12, Judith 8:6, the Falasha *halakhah*,[172] M. Nedarim 9:6, and a *baraitaʾ* in the Babylonian Talmud.[173] Josephus (Life 54) and the Palestinian Talmud[174] insist that one eat before noon. Presumably one was not held accountable

---

material and to claim that this law prohibits socializing (with Jews) on the Sabbath ignores the fact that the Karaite sources he quotes refer to mingling with *gentiles* on the seventh day. If they were relevant to our law, we would be left with a repetition of CDC 11:14f.

[168] As far as I can tell, the only occurrences of the preposition *m* + *raṣon* are in the *Sifraʾ* Ṣaw 17:6, 18:2, ʾEmor 18:9. All other passages use the prepositions *b*, *k*, and *l*. If the origin of the *Sifraʾ* was in the priestly schools, we can understand how it might have linguistic affinities with the Qumran texts. To substantiate such a claim, several other parallels would have to be found.

[169] On the property issue at Qumran, see above, 90.

[170] Schechter, Rabin, Segal, *ad loc.*, and Ginzberg, 436. Cf. Revel, 48 n. 75.

[171] Rabin's translation.

[172] *Teʾezaza Sanbat* prescribes death for fasting on the Sabbath. See W. Leslau, *Falasha Anthology* (1969), xxxiii, 20 (*Teʿezaza Sanbat*) who says that the Falashas permitted fasting if the Day of Atonement fell on the Sabbath. Contrast the report of Ginzberg, 437 and M. Wurmbrand, "*Hilkhot Shabbat ʾeṣel Ha-Falashim*," *Sefer Urbach*, ed. A. Biram (1955), 243. The Samaritans did fast, basing themselves on exegesis of *ʾakh* in Lev. 23:27 (Lowy, 112).

[173] B. Rosh Ha-Shanah 19a, B. Taʿanit 17b. Cf. *Megillat Taʿanit*, ed. Lichtenstein, 351. The Rabbis permitted fasting on the Sabbath under certain circumstances (an amoraic tradition in B. Shabbat 11a, B. Taʿanit 12b). Cf. Tchernowitz IV, 367f. For a later period, see D. Kaufmann, "Was the Custom of Fasting on Sabbath Afternoon Part of the Early Anglo-Jewish Ritual?" *JQR* O.S. 6 (1894), 754-6 and *Tosafot* to B. Pesaḥim 105a.

[174] P. Taʿanit 3:11 (ed. Krot. 3:13, 67a), P. Nedarim 8:1 (ed. Krot. 8:2 (although *halakhah* 2 is unmarked), 40d). Rabin's mistaken reference to P. Taʿanit 3:2 is apparently based on a misreading of Charles's note in *APOT* II, 827 who, however, refers to "Jer. Taan. iii. II." References must be checked. Cf. Albeck, *Jubiläen*, 44 n. 58.

if forced to fast for lack of food. Further, the Day of Atonement could not fall on the Sabbath according to the sectarian calendar.[175]

The view of the Karaites [176] was to commend (or at least allow) fasting on the Sabbath. The widespread references to Sabbath fasting in the Latin classical writers [177] may indicate that it was an old practice.

It may be that the order of the regulations favors this second interpretation. According to the first, it would be difficult to explain why this law did not follow CDC 10:17-19.

It is still necessary to ask how a prohibition against fasting on the Sabbath may be derived from Scripture. The Talmudic discussion [178] gives no source.[179] It is probable that the law is derived by the Rabbis and the sect (if the second interpretation is accepted) from an exegesis of the words *we-qara'ta le-shabbat ʿoneg* (Is. 58:13).[180]

In a passage which seems to have been influenced by *we-khibadeto* of Is. 58:13, Jub. 50:9-10 emphasizes that the Sabbath is a feast day. The tannaim also made the eating of three (or four) meals obligatory on the Sabbath, and some amoraim connected this with Is. 58:13.[181] If the second interpretation of this law is accepted, one can assume that the Isaiah passage did serve as the source of this law. The sect, unlike the book of Jubilees and Rabbinic literature, would have only stated this prescription in its negative formulation—the prohibition against fasting.

11. *CDC 11:5-7: Pasturing Animals*

אל ילך איש אחר הבהמה לרעותה חוץ מעירו כי אם אלפים באמה אל ירם את ידו להכותה באגרוף אם סוררת היא אל יוציאה מביתו

No one shall walk after an animal to pasture it outside his city more than (lit. "except for") two thousand cubits. Let him not raise his hand

[175] S. Talmon, "Calendar Reckoning," 176. Cf. A. Jaubert, "*Le Calendrier des Jubilés et de la secte de Qumran*," *VT* 3 (1953), 250-264, J. Morgenstern, "The Calendar of the Book of Jubilees, its Origins and its Character," *VT* 5 (1955), 34-76, and Jaubert's answer, "*Le Calendrier des Jubilés et les jours liturgiques de la semaine*," *VT* 7 (1957), 35-61.

[176] J. Hadassi, *'Eshkol Ha-Kofer*, 56d, other sources in Revel, 48.

[177] J. Hugh Michael, "The Jewish Sabbath in the Latin Classical Writers," *AJSLL* 40 (1924), 122-4. The widespread nature of this conception leads one to wonder if many Hellenistic Jews did not practice such a custom against which halakhic texts from this period are protesting.

[178] See note 173.

[179] The words *dibre torah* in B. Rosh Ha-Shanah 19a and B. Taʿanit 17b refer to the Sabbath and festivals themselves, not to the prohibition of fasting.

[180] See Kimchi to Is. 58:13.

[181] B. Shabbat 117b-119a.

to strike it with a fist.[182] If it is stubborn, let him not take it out of his house.

This set of regulations must be taken as a group since all three parts deal with the problem of pasturing animals on the Sabbath. The two thousand cubit limit has already been discussed at length.[183] Apparently, the normal Sabbath limit for a man at Qumran was one thousand cubits. In pasturing his animals, the sect allowed a man to walk an additional one thousand cubits. The tannaim have a two thousand cubit limit for people and do not allow it to be extended, even if an animal has escaped beyond the boundary.[184] The reason for this difference is easily understood. In interpreting Num. 35:4 and 5 the sect chose to take the "one thousand" as referring to people while the Rabbis understood the "two thousand" in the same way. The sect then had the additional one thousand available and used it to extend the limit for a man pasturing animals. The Rabbis, having already gone to the full limit in regard to people, could find no exegetical means for the extension of that limit.

But was it permitted to drive animals? This law makes it clear that animals can only be pastured if they can be relied upon to remain within the limit. If not, animals were to be kept in the house, since the driving of animals is prohibited by the second clause of this law.[185] Such a proscription would no doubt be the result of an exegesis of Ex. 20:10 and Deut. 5:14 which prohibit the working of animals on the seventh day.

Under normal circumstances, the tannaim prohibited the handling of animals on the Sabbath since one was not allowed to hunt, trap, or kill them (*muqṣeh*).[186] However, in cases where the animal had fled into the public domain, the tannaim allowed pushing it toward the private domain or pulling it by reins or ropes.[187]

---

[182] See Rabin's note, *ad loc.*, for support of this translation. Presumably nothing but the hand might be used as carrying on the Sabbath was forbidden in the public domain.

[183] Above, 91-98.

[184] T. Shabbat 17(18):12. If CDC 10:21 is read *ʾalpayim*, Ginzberg (437f.) would be correct in seeing complete agreement between the sectarian practice and tannaitic law (M. Beṣah 5:3, cited in Ginzberg as II, 3).

[185] So Ginzberg, 438. Cf. T. Shabbat 4(5), *TK* III, 56ff.

[186] See M. Shabbat 18:2, T. Shabbat 15(16):1 (and *TK* III, 242), and the discussion in B. Shabbat 128b, as well as M. Shabbat 5 (Ginzberg, 438).

[187] Note Lieberman's statement that according to the Palestinian Talmud it was even forbidden to touch (not only to move) *muqṣeh* (*Yerushalmi Ki-Fshuto*, 93f.). This view must represent the older Palestinian *halakhah*.

Possibly, the sect accepted the law of *muqṣeh* [188] as it applied to animals but went further than the Rabbis in its application. The sectarians did not permit its relaxation in the case of escaped animals. As a rule, it may be assumed that the older *halakhah* must have been more demanding in regard to Sabbath observance. Perhaps this sectarian law represents the Palestinian *halakhah* at a stage earlier than that recorded in the tannaitic literature.[189]

The Ethiopic Apocalypse of Baruch (Fifth Baruch), highly regarded by the Falashas, contains a passage which may be in agreement with this Qumran law.[190] This section tells of priests and teachers being punished (after death) because "They taught not the glory of the Sabbath, saying 'Honor (it), and introduce not into the dwellings donkeys, mules, oxen, sheep, goats, or even hens.'"[191] This practice may refer to the bringing of animals from domain to domain and indicate that this was forbidden. Leslau [192] has seen the material in this part of the Apocalypse of Baruch as going back to second and third century Christian sources. It should be said, though, that this passage may simply indicate a prohibition of having animals in the house on the seventh day.[193]

Further, Jub. 50:12 can be seen as containing a similar prohibition to that of CDC.[194] But, as Ginzberg notes,[195] this interpretation is probably based on an inferior reading of the text.

12. *CDC 11:7-9: Carrying from Domain to Domain*

אל יוציא איש מן הבית לחוץ ומן החוץ אל בית ואם בסוכה יהיה אל יוצא ממנה ואל יבא אליה

> No one shall carry (anything) from the house to the outside, or from the outside into (the) house.[196] And if he is in the *sukkah*,[197] let him not carry (anything) out from it or bring (anything) into it.

---

[188] This will be discussed at the end of the chapter.

[189] The prohibition of striking animals found in Jub. 50:12 cannot be cited as a parallel to our law as its context reveals that it deals with actions directed toward killing the animal.

[190] Ginzberg, 438.

[191] Trans. Leslau, *Falasha Anthology*, 70. See his introduction to the text, 57-64.

[192] Pp. 63f.

[193] I do not know of such a prohibition, however, in any of the sources.

[194] Cf. Tchernowitz IV, 364.

[195] Pp. 438 n. 4 and 439 (erroneously numbered 339). Cf. above, n. 189.

[196] Ginzberg (439 and n.) observes that the use of the verb *yṣ*ʾ for taking out and bringing in is representative of the oldest halakhic terminology (Cf. M. Shabbat 1:1). Later terminology used *hakhnasah* for bringing in. The second clause of our law uses the *hifʿil* of *bw*ʾ in the same way. He suggests that the second part

(Note 197 p.t.o.)

The first clause of this law is the prohibition of carrying from the private into the public domain or vice versa. From the wording, it is clear that this law is a rephrasing of Jer. 17:21 and 22.

M. Shabbat 1:1 seems to be similarly based.[198] Although this *mishnah* is linguistically tied to the Jeremiah passage, the Palestinian Talmud [199] contains an argument about its derivation. Some amoraim persist in saying that the law stems from Ex. 36:6. This may reflect the general Rabbinic tendency to avoid deriving *halakhot* from the prophets, even where so explicitly stated. The sect had no such compunctions and must have derived its law from Jeremiah. In addition, the wording of Jub. 2:29 and 30 seems to indicate that this author also derived his law from Jeremiah, as he also mentions carrying in or bringing out. Jub. 50:8, however, shows no such influences.

The Sadducees disagreed with this prohibition [200] (or with some of its details [201]). Anan ben David only forbade carrying on the shoulder, proving his interpretation by citing Num. 7:9. Hadassi proscribed carrying from domain to domain. Some Karaites followed him, and

---

of M. Shabbat 1:1 (after *keṣad*) is to be assigned to a later date than the first clause. The same may be true of the clause in our law relating to the *sukkah*. It may be a later addition dealing with a practical problem that had arisen for the sectarians. On the relation of Qumran to Rabbinic terminology, cf. Rabin, *QS*, 108f. Further evidence of the antiquity of our regulation may lie in the absence of domains similar to the Rabbinic *karmelit* and *maqom paṭur*. The absence of these last two terms in T. Shabbat 1:1 MS. Vienna (accepted as the correct reading by Lieberman, *TK* III, 1) is not a parallel in that the Tosefta recognizes the existence of these domains, although not using the usual terms.

[197] Reading with Rabin. Schechter reads *mwbh* which he emends to *mbwy* (followed by Albeck, *Seder Moʿed*, 79). Actually the first character does look like a *mem*, but the third is certainly a *kaf*. Note the similarity of *mem* and *samekh* in the MS. The only difference is the opening in the lower left corner of the *mem*.

Our translation assumes that the text refers to the *sukkah* built for the festival of Sukkot. It is equally possible that the text refers to a booth used as a temporary shelter for watchmen or for the harvest. In either case, the law would be the same. (Cf. Job Targum, Col. 11:9 (to Job 27:18), pp. 32f., 111, S. Kaufman, "Job Targum," 320). On this entire passage, cf. Rabin, *QS*, 109f.

[198] See Albeck's "*HWT*," 405. Our interpretation is in disagreement with *Tosafot* to B. Shabbat 2a, *s.v. yeṣiʾot*, who suggests dependence on Ex. 16:29.

[199] P. Shebuʿot 1:1 (32a) (not "c" as cited by Rabin). I do not know the source of Rabin's statement that the Jeremiah derivation was that of the school of Caesarea while that of Ex. the majority. It is true that R. Ḥizkiah lived in Caesarea (M. Margaliot, *Encyclopedia Le-Ḥakhme Ha-Talmud We-Ha-Geonim* I, 285) but this alone does not warrant Rabin's assertion. Cf. B. Shabbat 96b, *Tosafot*, *s.v. u-mi-mai*, and *Torah Temimah* to Ex. 36:6.

[200] B. Horayot 4a.

[201] If we accept the amoraic rationalization further down the page. Cf. Ginzberg, 439. According to Revel, 39f., the Sadducees did not accept the prohibition of carrying in the courtyard (*ḥaṣer*).

others, Anan.[202] It is certain from Anan's use of the word *masa'* that he also is dependent on Jeremiah.[203] The Falashas, on penalty of death, prohibit all carrying from domain to domain.[204]

Rabin assumes that the sect, with Josephus (Ant. 3, 10:4), required "that each family must have its own private booth for Tabernacles."[205] This was probably the case as Neh. 8:16 indicates that each man built his own family booth. However, such booths could be constructed on public property. This was probably the usual practice in the sect's communal settlements. It could be claimed, though, that the sect would not have allowed carrying even from communal dwellings in an enclosed domain; in other words, that the sect did not accept (if they existed by this time) the Rabbinic enactments regarding the *'erub ḥaṣerot*.[206] Even on private property,[207] the sectarian law may have regarded the *sukkah* as a separate domain and hence prohibited carrying into it or from it.

13. *CDC 11:9: Opening a Sealed Vessel*

אל פתח כלי טוח בשבת

Let him not open [208] a plastered vessel [209] on the Sabbath.

It was apparently the practice in ancient times to seal pottery vessels with clay after filling. The clay would then harden, forming an airtight seal. When the jar was to be opened, the clay seal had to be broken. [210] The breaking of such seals on the Sabbath was forbidden by

202 Aescoly, 34f., citing *'Eshkol Ha-Kofer*, 74b. Cf. Revel, 40f.

203 Harkavy, *Mi-Sifre Ha-Miṣwot*, 69 and trans. in L. Nemoy, *Karaite Anthology*, 17.

204 Aescoly, 32f.

205 Commentary, *ad loc.*

206 See above, 103.

207 We must remember that CDC gives the impression that members of the sect lived outside of the Qumran center. Cf. A. Rubinstein, "Urban Halakhah and Camp Rules in the 'Cairo Fragments of a Damascus Covenant,' " *Sefarad* 12 (1952), 283-96.

208 Reading *yftḥ* with Schechter. A *yod* could not have stood in our MS. as there is no space. In fact, the space between the *lamed* and *pe* is smaller than usual between words. We must assume that this error arose from the misreading of a previous copy. Kimbrough (493) takes this as a passive, probably because of the absence of *'ish*.

209 Num. 19:15 is the source for the use of *ptḥ* with *keli*. An opened vessel is defined there as *'asher 'en ṣamid patil 'alaw*, "with no lid fastened down" (new JPS). Targ. Onkelos and Jon. here refer to the absence of a *megufah*, confirming the explanation we give below. The Fragmentary Jerusalem Targ. refers to the lack of a *puryeta'*, a "lid with rims, close fitting cover" (Jastrow). Cf. *Sifre* Num. 126 and the note of Horovitz, *ad loc.*

210 T. Kelim, Baba' Qamma' 4:20 (ed. Zuckermandel, 574) connects *keli* with

the sect. The tannaim [211] permitted the breaking of the entire jar (as destruction does not violate the Sabbath),[212] and the majority view also allowed the breaking of this clay seal.[213] The view of R. Judah [214] however, agreed with that of the sect. The formulation of this law in the Mishnah ("'We do not pierce the clay seal of a jar,' the words of R. Judah, but the Sages permitted (it).") leads one to believe that R. Judah is here reflecting an older and stricter *halakhah* which is still preserved as normative in the sectarian document. This same stringency is evident in the Karaite law of J. Hadassi.[215] There is no way of knowing whether this Karaite tradition goes back to the older *halakhah* or if it was taken from the Mishnah in an attempt to adopt stringencies long rejected by Rabbinic tradition.

14. *CDC 11:9f.: Wearing of Perfume Bottles*

אל ישא איש עליו סמנים לצאת ולבוא בשבת

No one shall carry spices on himself (whether) to go out or to come in [216] on the Sabbath.

---

the root *ṭwḥ*. CDC seems then to be using the normal terminology current in Palestine. See J. Brand, *Keli Ha-Ḥeres Be-Sifrut Ha-Talmud*, (1952/3), 111-173 (especially 136), 265-270. Brand notes that M. Kelim 12:5 mentions a special tool used to open these sealed vessels. Apparently the entire seal (*megufah*) was not removed unless all the contents were to be used immediately.

[211] M. Shabbat 22:3. Cf. (Pseudo-)Ran, *Ḥiddushim, ad loc.* Ginzberg (440 n. 1) cites the view of R. Ashi (B. Beṣah 33b according to Rashi and *Tosafot*. Cf. *ʿArukh Ha-Shalem* 5, 198, *s.v. mstqy.*) that this *mishnah* allows only the opening of previously broken vessels that have been temporarily stuck together with clay. Even though R. Ashi is a late amora (d. 427, Strack, 132f.), Ginzberg considers his interpretation unquestionable. P. ʿErubin 3:3 (21a) makes it clear that this *mishnah* does mean to include whole vessels. See Lieberman, *TK* III, 274. Nevertheless, B. Beṣah 33b leads Ginzberg to see the law of CDC as referring to making an opening in the vessel itself, and he says that the sect shared this prohibition with the Mishnah.

[212] Rashi to B. Shabbat 146a.

[213] T. Shabbat 16(17):13 permits with no disagreement the tearing of skin coverings on wine jars. It is possible to assume that this is in complete agreement with the majority view of the Mishnah and that the view of R. Judah is simply not reflected, or that even R. Judah admitted the permissibility of opening the skin covers. The difference would then lie with the material of which the cover was made. R. Judah forbade the opening of clay covers as the clay so closely resembled (or was identical to) the material of which the jar was made that it appeared as a case of "completing a vessel" (*metaqqen keli*). The skin, however, was clearly a covering put on after the completion of the vessel and could give no such impression. Cf. Lieberman, *TK* III, 274f.

[214] This is Judah b. ʾIlʿai, flourished about 130-160, a pupil of Akiba (Strack, 115).

[215] *ʾEshkol Ha-Kofer*, 148, p. 56a.

[216] Reading with Schechter even though, as he points out, the *waw* of *lbwʾ* is quite short for a MS. of this late date. On this expression, see BDB, p. 424a, and

Although formulated in the masculine, this law probably refers to the practice by women of wearing small ornamental perfume bottles around their necks.[217] The tannaim also forbade the wearing of these on the Sabbath, whether empty or full. If worn empty, thus serving only as ornaments, the Rabbis did not require a sin offering, while the wearing of such bottles with their perfume or spices necessitated the sin offering. There was some disagreement as to empty bottles, but everyone agreed that *a priori* (*le-khatḥilah*) it was forbidden to wear them on the seventh day.[218]

Rabin's translation of *sammanim* as "medicament" makes the sect stricter than the Rabbis. The tannaim permit going out on the Sabbath with bandages [219] or medicines in the mouth. Nevertheless, it seems more logical to assume that the Sabbath code of the sect is here dealing with the *realia* of Second Temple times.

15. *CDC 11:10f.: Handling Rocks and Earth*

אל יטול בבית מושבת סלע ועפר

Let him not handle [220] rock or earth in a dwelling [221] house.

It is clear that the handling of rock or earth in the public domain was forbidden as this would constitute carrying. But in the house the

CDC 11:11. This phrase shows that the problem here is of carrying from domain to domain.

[217] Cf. Is. 3:20 (*bate nefesh*) and Song 1:13. A picture of a perfume bottle appears in Y. Yadin, *Masada* (1966), 149.

[218] M. Shabbat 6:3, T. Shabbat 4(5):11 (cf. Lieberman, *TK* III, 67f.). See also Gilat, *Mishnato*, 133f.

[219] M. Shabbat 6:5, T. Shabbat 5(6):3-5 (Rabin).

[220] Standard tannaitic language in discussing the law of *muqṣeh*. See M. Shabbat 17 (Rabin).

[221] Translating with new JPS and RSV to Lev. 25:29, *bet moshab*. Rabin's assumption that *moshebet* should be read *moshab* is not necessary. The pl. forms of *moshab*, *e.g. moshebotam*, Ex. 10:23 etc., are all built on a putative *moshebet*. It may have been an alternate form in ancient times which was not preserved in biblical tradition. Schechter (LX) and Ginzberg (440) note the phrase used by the Karaites *meqom moshebet*, a place populated by Jews who observe the Sabbath according to the law, as opposed to the *maqom meḥullal*, populated by non-Jews who do not observe the Sabbath (J. Hadassi, *ʾEshkol Ha-Kofer*, 54c, Aaron ben Elijah of Nicomedia, *Gan ʿEden*, 30d, Ginzberg, n. 3). CDC 11:14f. can be related to our law and taken as referring to such a *meqom moshebet*. Ginzberg gives several reasons for rejecting this possibility. First, our text reads *bet*, while in 11:14 the author uses *maqom*. Second is the use of *yiṭṭol*. Third, given the law of CDC 11:14f., why specify *bet moshebet* in regard to this particular regulation? Instead Ginzberg (441) suggests reading *magbeshet* and taking it as a form of *gabshushit* (cf. T. ʾOhalot 17:9, *gabush* and B. Shabbat 73b (cited as "a" by Ginzberg)). The text would accordingly be translated, "Let him not handle in the house a pile of rock or earth." However, the evidence for the noun *magbeshet* is not sufficient.

sect forbade the handling of certain objects in a way similar to the Rabbinic law of *muqṣeh* (lit. "set apart").[222] This law specified that whatever was not expected to be used on the Sabbath or holy day could not be handled thereon. Its purpose was to prevent violations of the Sabbath laws.

The Qumranites went on record as considering the unusable earth and stones forbidden. It was only several hundred years later that the Rabbis incorporated this ruling into their system. Even then it is never expressly stated, rather assumed in discussion. An amoraic source in B. Shabbat 46a indicates that the handling of pebbles was forbidden, and another in B. Beṣah 12a similarly forbids the handling of rocks.[223] Dust on the floor of the house is also considered *muqṣeh* in B. Beṣah 8a.[224]

Josephus reports (Wars 2, 8:9) that the Essenes adhered to an even stricter regulation. They did not handle any vessels or tools,[225] even those which could be used legitimately on the Sabbath.

Philo, in his discussion of the exact violation committed by the *meqoshesh ʿeṣim* ("gatherer of sticks," Num. 15:32-5), indicates that he also accepted the law of *muqṣeh*. Referring to the law against kindling fires on the Sabbath, Philo states that this regulation "applies equally, I presume, to collecting the means for kindling fire."[226] The main principle of his argument, says Belkin, is that "anything which a person is not allowed to use on the Sabbath, he may not collect or move from its place."[227] Since it is forbidden to make a fire (using wood) on the Sabbath, it is also forbidden to gather the sticks.

T. Shabbat 14(15):1 is cognizant of a period [228] in which all tools or instruments were considered *muqṣeh*. By tannaitic times this restriction was limited to those which could only be used in violation of the Sabbath. Stones and earth may originally have been forbidden because of their possible use in construction or (in regard to rocks) as tools.

The general Talmudic view considered *muqṣeh* to be a Rabbinical

---

[222] On the derivation of this term see Gilat, *Mishnato*, 123 n. 85.

[223] Cf. B. ʿErubin 35a where Rashi considers this *shebut de-rabbanan* and Cohen, 154.

[224] Also quoted in B. Shabbat 50a.

[225] The equivalent of Heb. *kelim* often used in conjuction with the verbs *nṭl* and *ṭlṭl* in tannaitic literature.

[226] *Spec. Laws* II, 251, trans. Colson. Cf. *Life of Moses* II, 220.

[227] Belkin, 198.

[228] The time of Nehemiah according to B. Shabbat 123b.

ordinance, yet one amoraic view [229] held that it was derived from Ex. 16:5 ("You shall prepare what you will bring"). This verse commands that anything to be used on the Sabbath must be prepared beforehand. Anyone who used anything not so prepared (*muqṣeh*) violated this positive injunction and performed forbidden labor.[230] In the Talmud, it can be seen from the context in which it appears that *muqṣeh* is declared a biblical ordinance only to avoid a contradiction that would necessitate reformulating a position on another question.[231] Philo must have accepted the biblical derivation.[232] Perhaps the origin of the sect's equivalent of *muqṣeh* was Ex. 16:5. Although this source cannot be ascertained with certainty, the sect must have had some Scriptural basis for this law.

16. *CDC 11:11: Carrying Infants*

אל ישא האומן את היונק לצאת ולבוא בשבת

> Let the parent [233] not carry the infant [234] to go out or to come in [235] on the Sabbath.

Tannaitic law also prohibited the carrying of children who could not walk. Once a child was able, the Rabbis permitted the parents to "walk" him in the public domain by moving his feet, one in front of the other.[236] Once able to walk, if carried (from domain to domain)

---

[229] B. Pesaḥim 47b.

[230] *Torah Temimah* to Ex. 16:5.

[231] On the next page the Talmud shows that *muqṣeh* cannot be a biblical ordinance.

[232] Belkin, 199, comparing 1 Macc. 2:32-38.

[233] Patterned on Num. 11:12. *ʾOmen* can be a "father," "foster father," or a "pedagogue." See Targumim and commentaries, *ad loc.* All versions take *ʾomen* as masc. except Vulgate which translates *nutrix*, a fem. noun ("nurse, foster mother"). The unpublished Palest. Targ. MS. Neofiti 1, Targ. Jon. and Fragmentary Pal. Targ. translate *pedagogaʾ* (Gk. παιδαγωγός), a slave who took children to and from school (Liddell and Scott, *s.v.*). See *Bereshit Rabbah* 1:1 and the note in Theodor-Albeck, *ad loc.* For the significance of the masc. in Num. 11:12, see Abravanel, *ad loc.* Cf. Is. 49:23. Slomovic, 11-13 suggests that Num. 11:11f. served as a mnemonic for the entire series of regulations in CDC 11:9-13. Some of the "key words," however, are rather far from those which they are supposed to suggest. It is hard to see how this mnemonic could have been used.

[234] The use of "to go out or to come in" shows that this law refers to carrying from domain to domain (Rab. *hoṣaʾah*) as opposed to handling (Rab. *ṭilṭul* and *muqṣeh*).

[235] See CDC 11:9f. and our n. 216.

[236] M. Shabbat 18:2. M. Shabbat 21:1 is cited erroneously by Rabin as it deals with the problem of *muqṣeh* as is clear from the use of the verb *noṭel*.

no punishment was incurred to the bearer [237] because of the rule that "a living being carries himself."[238] There is no way of knowing the sect's position regarding aiding children to walk or carrying those able to walk.

Belkin,[239] assuming *'omen* could be translated as "nurse," sees this law in a different light. He connects this law with the following regulation which concerns the encouragement of servants to perform work. He interprets this law, in agreement with Philo, to mean that although the parents might carry the child, a servant must not do so because servants could not be asked to do even permitted labors on the Sabbath. Belkin fails to notice that the parallel use of the phrase *la-ṣet we-labo'* in CDC 11:7-9 shows that it refers to carrying from domain to domain. This would be forbidden to master as well as servant.

CDC 11:14f. prohibits spending the Sabbath in a place where there are non-Jews. At first glance, this would seem immediately to dispose of Belkin's interpretation. It must be remembered, though, that the institution of non-Israelite servitude was regarded as a mechanism for conversion in post-biblical Judaism.[240] Therefore, these non-Jewish servants may not have been regarded as gentiles to be avoided on the Sabbath.

17. *CDC 11:12: Encouraging a Servant to Labor*

אל ימרא איש את עבדו ואת אמתו ואת שוכרו בשבת

> No one shall urge on [241] his servant, his maidservant, or his hireling [242] on the Sabbath.

[237] T. Shabbat 8(9):18.

[238] A minority view in B. Shabbat 141b, B. Yoma' 66b, etc. but used by Rashi in B. Shabbat 142a to explain T. Shabbat 8(9):18.

[239] P. 203 (Rabin).

[240] Cf. CDC 12:10f.

[241] Cf. Ex. 1:14. See T. Sanhedrin 5:2, quoted in B. Sanh. 25b (cf. Rashi, *ad loc.*), Kohut, *'Arukh Ha-Shalem*, *s.v. mr* (4). Rabin notes that Arab. *mry* means "to urge on" while Syr. *ethmarri* means "to race." As to the spelling with *'alef*, Ginzberg refers to a similar spelling in CDC 12:5, but this text is subject to two interpretations. Many cases of the interchange of final *'alef* and *he'* are attested in Qumran Hebrew (Licht, *MH*, 47, Kutscher, 122f.). See Ges. 74k. Ginzberg also suggests that *mr'* might be a denominative from Aramaic *mara'*, "master," but this is unlikely as it is nowhere attested. Schechter's translation "provoke," even supported by Ginzberg's reference to *Te'ezaza Sanbat* which prohibits swearing or cursing, cannot be correct. Why would the servants be singled out? Is not this prohibition of the Falasha *halakhah* universally applicable?

[242] The Dead Sea Scrolls may have obviated the emendation to *skyrw* proposed by Schechter. The scrolls attest to the interchangeability of forms such as *qoṣer* and *qeṣor* (Licht, *MH*, 45f.). Here we may have the substantive use of biblical passive *sakhur* ("hired"), "a hireling."

Rabin states that this law refers to Jewish servants. He reasons that in CDC 11:2 it has already been commanded that non-Jews not be sent to do work on the Sabbath, and that the servant and maidservant mentioned in 12:11 are described as having "entered with him the covenant of Abraham." Neither of these passages in reality supports Rabin's view.

The first (CDC 11:2) refers to forbidden labors which the Jew may not have done for him on the Sabbath by a *free* non-Jew. The second passage Rabin cites (CDC 12:11) does not mean that the servants are Jews, rather that they are indentured through the institution of *ʿebed kenaʿani*, an instrument for religious conversion.[243] The *ʿebed kenaʿani* was forbidden to perform any labor whatever on the Sabbath for an Israelite even if that labor was permissible for the Jew.

As Rabin observes, the sectarian law here agrees with Philo's proscription of a slave's doing any work at all for the master, even if it did not violate the Sabbath.[244] Since the slave was permitted to do such work for himself, it would appear that the objection was to the Israelite's instructing him or urging him to do the labor. Tannaitic law prohibits a Jew's instructing a non-Jew to work on the Sabbath but permits an Israelite to benefit from work performed voluntarily.[245] The Essenes did not own slaves.[246]

18. *CDC 11:13f.: Caring for Domesticated Animals*

אל יילד איש בהמה ביום השבת ואם תפיל אל בור ואל פחת אל יקימה בשבת

> No one shall deliver an animal on the Sabbath day. And if it fall[247] into a cistern or pit, let him not lift it out[248] on the Sabbath.

Here are presented two laws dealing with help that one might desire to give to domesticated animals on the Sabbath. Tannaitic law forbade delivering (*i.e.* removing the fetus from the uterus) animals

---

243 On this institution see L. N. Dembitz, "Slaves and Slavery," *JE* 11, 405-7, Tchernowitz III, 314-318. Indeed, such servants were probably circumcised (the "covenant of Abraham") immediately after purchase. Cf. Gen. 17:27, Ex. 12:44.

244 *Spec. Laws* II, 66-68. See Belkin, 203, Ginzberg, 442.

245 See M. Shabbat 16:6.

246 *Every Good Man* 79.

247 Reading *tpwl* with Schechter. Rabin's attempt to connect the two laws we cite here (whose relation is discussed below) can only lead to a preposterous *Sitz im Leben*.

248 Cf. Deut. 22:4 and especially Eccl. 4:10.

on Sabbaths or festivals.[249] It was, however, permissible to aid in the delivery on festivals by holding the newborn to prevent its falling, breathing air into its nostrils to start respiration, or putting the udder in the animal's mouth to encourage nursing.[250] A later opinion considered it permissible to manipulate the flesh of the mother in such a way as to make the delivery easier.[251]

From the sectarian formulation it appears that the Qumranites also forbade aiding in the actual delivery. It is logical to assume that they also, like the Rabbis, forbade giving aid on the Sabbath. As to the sect's ruling relative to holidays, there is no way of being sure. One cannot presume the sect stricter than tannaitic Judaism and claim that no help whatever was allowed on festivals. Unfortunately, the sectarian literature available does not clarify this question.

The second regulation deals with the problem of an animal trapped in a cistern or pit on the Sabbath. T. Shabbat 14(15):3 records the ruling that in case an animal should fall into a cistern (or well), it should be provided with food (*parnasah*) to keep it alive. (Only after the Sabbath was it to be removed from the pit.) The amoraim [252] were more lenient, permitting the placing of pillows or cushions to allow the animal to come up. Here the sect is in agreement with the tannaitic *halakhah* which does not permit the removal of an animal from a cistern. It is clear from the citation of the Tosefta in the Babylonian Talmud that the tannaim are discussing a situation in which the water level in the pit is endangering the animal's life.[253] Even so, the animal cannot be removed from the pit. No doubt the sectarian law deals with the same problem.

Mt. 12:11 and Lk. 14:5 also react to this same situation. The New Testament records a general tendency in Palestine toward leniency. The owners of such animals, perhaps with no legal mandate, simply removed their animals from the pits to save their lives.[254]

---

249 M. Shabbat 18:3 and Albeck's comment, *ad loc.* Cf. Albeck's "*HWT*," *ad loc.*

250 T. Shabbat 15(16):2. I have listed the measures in order of B. Shabbat 128b where this Tosefta is quoted. The Babylonian Talmud preserves the logical order of actions, for which reason the Tosefta text is probably more authentic.

251 B. Shabbat 128b. The view is that of the amora R. Naḥman.

252 B. Shabbat 128b. Cf. P. Beṣah 3:4 (62a), Cohen, 154.

253 See B. Shabbat 128b, M. T. Shabbat 25:2 (Lieberman, *TK* III, 230).

254 In the latter passage the Gk. has φρέαρ clearly indicating that the pit or well was full of water and, hence, constituted a danger to the animal's life.

19. *CDC 11:14f.: Spending the Sabbath among Gentiles*

אל ישבית [א]יש ב]מקום קרוב לגוים בשבת

No [o]ne shall rest [255] [in] a place close to the gentiles on the Sabbath.[256]

This translation is in accord with either of two possible explanations. First, at face value, the sect would require that the Sabbath not be spent in the company of gentiles. It has already been proposed [257] that servants of the type of *ʿebed kenaʿani* may be exceptions to this rule. A guess may be hazarded that this law also excepted those freemen in the process of conversion to Judaism.

A similar restriction, based on the word *moshebotekhem* ("your dwelling places") in Lev. 23:3 was in force among the Samaritans [258] and Karaites. The Karaite Sahl ben Maṣliaḥ castigates the Rabbinites for fraternizing with non-Jews on the Sabbath.[259] It is certainly possible that the Qumran sect derived a similar regulation from the same Scriptural passage.[260]

Ginzberg, however, has rejected this interpretation because *qarob le-* would be superfluous.[261] He suggests a second interpretation in which this law is related to a requirement that the Sabbath be spent in ritual purity. Among non-Jews there would always be the risk of impurity.[262] Ginzberg sees M. Shabbat 1:7 as evidence that gentiles were not tolerated among Jews on the Sabbath. This tannaitic discussion does not concern such a prohibition. Rather, it discusses the extent to which an Israelite may help a non-Israelite to prepare for a journey which might extend into the Sabbath. Anan's prohibition of living with non-Jews [263] cannot be relevant here, since it is not specifically related to Sabbath law. Ginzberg himself cites Talmudic

---

[255] Reading *yšbwt* with Schechter and Ginzberg (442 n. 1).

[256] Ginzberg (n. 2) omits *ba-shabbat* as a redundancy after *yishbot*.

[257] Above 120.

[258] L. Wreschner, *Die samaritanische Tradition* (1888), 13-15.

[259] Pinsker II, 32. Translated in Nemoy, 115. Cf. above, 117 n. 221.

[260] It is noted in both Talmudim (P. Pesaḥim 4:1 (30d), B. Pesaḥim 51a) that in Acre it was the custom not to sit on a gentile's chair on the Sabbath. If the interpretation proposed in the Babylonian Talmud is correct, the reference was to chairs used for commercial purposes. The residents of Acre were apparently extremely careful to avoid this situation which might look as though they were making transactions. This stringency was not observed in the rest of the country. It is doubtful if this passage ought then to be compared (as Rabin has done) to the sectarian restriction here under discussion.

[261] P. 422.

[262] This was the Samaritan view. See Lowy, 113.

[263] *Sefer Ha-Miṣwot*, 6.

evidence [264] that prominent sages spent the Sabbath among gentiles, but dismisses this material as an exception to the rule.

A third sense would require the following translation: No [o]ne shall make a Sabbath camp [265] [in] a place near gentiles on the Sabbath. The intention is to describe the establishment of a technical residence for the Sabbath, allowing a traveller to carry within it and to walk the distance of the Sabbath limit in any direction. The regulation might also describe the setting up of a permanent residence and the application of the Sabbath laws to it. Such residence could not be set up "close to," *i.e.* "in partnership with" a non-Jew. This would accord well with the Rabbinic laws which similarly prevent the establishment of such a partnership of domain (allowing the carrying of objects on the Sabbath) with a non-Israelite unless the property be rented from him.[266]

20. *CDC 11:15: Violation of the Sabbath for the sake of Wealth*

אל יחל איש את השבת על הון ובצע בשבת

> No one shall violate [267] the Sabbath for the sake of wealth or profit [268] on the Sabbath.[269]

Rabin and Ginzberg [270] interpret this law as proscribing Sabbath violation to save property from destruction. They contrast this restriction with the permissibility of saving a human life, described according to them, in the next law (CDC 11:16f.). It will be shown that actually the sect's legislation is susceptible to two interpretations. Either the sect did allow *piqquaḥ nefesh* (violating the Sabbath to save a life) or possibly, in a shocking stringency, it diverged from this cornerstone of Rabbinic *halakhah*.[271] Indeed, a contrast such as that

[264] B. ʿErubin 65b. Cf. M. Shabbat 16:6, 8.

[265] Reading as in n. 255. For this usage of *šbt*, see, *e.g.*, M. Pesaḥim 3:7, B. ʿErubin 51a (Jastrow, *s.v.*).

[266] B. ʿErubin 62a.

[267] Cf. Num. 30:3 and Rashi, *ad loc.*

[268] Same phrase "wealth or profit" in CDC 10:18. See 87f. nn. 23 and 24.

[269] *Ba-shabbat* here may be the result of analogy with the other laws which end with *ba-shabbat* or *ba-yom ha-shabbat*. It may also be misplaced from the line below (assuming that the scribe was holding to the line division in the MS. before him). It would then belong after the corrupted *maqom* X. In any case, the phrase is superfluous here.

[270] Ginzberg, 443.

[271] Its importance is such that Maimonides (M.T. Shabbat 2) prefaces his discussion of the forbidden categories of work with a discussion of *piqquaḥ nefesh*. In contrast, CDC 11:16f., which can be taken as an equivalent regulation, is the last provision of the Sabbath code.

Rabin and Ginzberg see here does exist in T. ʿErubin 3(4):5 which allows the violation of the Sabbath to fend off an attack in the case of mortal danger. If the enemy wants property only, however, it is not permissible to profane the Sabbath.[272]

The regulation is also subject to a second interpretation. It may be that the sect is simply reiterating the prophetic law developed through *midrash halakhah* in the time of Nehemiah which prohibits commercial transactions on the Sabbath.[273] Such a law is also contained in Jubilees 50:8 and is echoed in the Falasha literature.[274] The relative newness of this law would make it especially important to remind the sectarians of it.

The first interpretation proposed here is dependent on a particular exposition of the next law, namely that which assumes that the sect adhered to the principle of *piqquaḥ nefesh*. The second interpretation, however, presupposes no particular understanding of the next regulation.

21. *CDC 11:16f.: Saving of Life*

וכל נפש אדם אשר תפול אל מקום מים ואל מקום אל יעלה איש בסולם וחבל וכלי

> And as to [275] any human being who falls [276] into a place [277] of water or into a reservoir, [278] no one shall bring (him) [279] up with a ladder, rope, or instrument.

---

[272] Cf. Josephus, Ant. 12, 1:1, Wars 2, 16:4, and Apion 1:22 (end), A. Z. Aescoly, *Sefer Ha-Falashim* (1943), 30, 37f. See also M. D. Herr, "*Li-Beʿayot Hilkhot Milḥamah Be-Shabbat Bi-Yeme Bayit Sheni U-Be-Tequfat Ha-Mishnah*," *Tarbiẓ* 30 (1961), 242-256, 341-356, especially 243-249. Ginzberg (443) observes that if the author of CDC adhered to the principle of *piqquaḥ nefesh*, he had to write after the Maccabean revolt. This point must be well taken.

[273] For the background of this law, see Kaufmann, *Toledot* IV, 332 and Tchernowitz III, 112-117.

[274] Wurmbrand, 238.

[275] Rabin's explanation necessitates "But."

[276] Fem. to agree with *nefesh*.

[277] Schechter emends to *mqwh* in accordance with Lev. 11:36. We reserve this reading for the second occurrence of *maqom*.

[278] According to Schechter and Rabin, there must originally have stood here the description of another place in which a man's life was endangered. We however, emend to *mqwh*. Cf. Is. 22:11. Perhaps one should translate "ritual bath" but it is questionable if *mqwh* had as yet become a technical term. It is not used in CDC 10:10-13 which deals with purification in water (on which see S. Lieberman, *Greek*, 135 n. 151). The vocalization *miqweh*, persistent in Rabbinic literature (as opposed to *miqwah* of Is. 22:11) is dependent on an exegesis of Lev. 11:36. The pls. *miqwot* and *miqwaʾot* cannot be used to substantiate vocalization as *miqwah* because it is not unusual for masc. nouns derived from III-*he*ʾ roots to form pls. with the fem. termination, *e.g. sadeh*, pl. *sadot*. (For the addition of the *ʾalef* in *miqwaʾot* see Segal, *Diqduq*, 93. See also *ʿArukh Ha-Shalem* 5, *s.v. mqwh*.)

[279] *Yaʿaleha*, agreeing with *nefesh*. Ginzberg's emendation to *ʾal yaʿalehu* is considered below. See his explanation, 442.

As mentioned above, this law is susceptible to several interpretations. Ginzberg, believing it inconceivable that any Jewish group could have rejected the concept of *piqquaḥ nefesh*, emended accordingly. In his reading the passage is translated: "And every human being who falls into a place of water or into a place from which one cannot come up, let any man bring him up with a ladder, rope, or instrument."[280] Ginzberg's interpretation may be supported by context. First, CDC 11:13f. does not allow violation of the Sabbath for the sake of an animal. If the same were the case for a human being, this law concerning a person who falls into a reservoir would be superfluous. Second, if one accepts Ginzberg's exegesis of the preceding law, our law would be set in contradistinction to it. While the Sabbath may not be violated for the sake of property alone, it may be set aside to save human life.

However, Ginzberg missed a point essential to the interpretation which will be proposed here. It is possible that the sect accepted the doctrine of *piqquaḥ nefesh* but required that it be accomplished (where possible?) without the use of equipment which would fall under the category of *muqṣeh*. It is also possible that in its extreme stringency the sect rejected the notion of *piqquaḥ nefesh*.[281]

Maimonides (M.T. Shabbat 2:3) mentions *ʾapiqorsim* who opposed this doctrine. Rabin is probably correct in his identification of the *ʾapiqorsim* with some group of Karaites.[282] It is well-known that many of the Karaite teachings may have lain dormant for many years prior to the spread of Karaism.[283] It is even possible that there was literary contact between the Karaites and ancient Jewish sects (including the Qumran group).[284] So it may be that these *ʾapiqorsim* preserved an ancient opposition to the violation of the Sabbath even to save a life. Yet the Karaite halakhic sources [285] agree with the Rabbinic tradition [286] in allowing violation of the Sabbath to preserve human

---

[280] P. 443f.

[281] Kimbrough's statement (497) that he has "accepted the proposal of Rabin, Ginzberg, and Dupont-Sommer in order to get around the inhumanity of the rule..." betrays a lack of objectivity. He does, at least, admit that it is "only surmise."

[282] So also Aescoly, 36, 38 who also includes the Sadducees.

[283] Baron, *History* V, 215f.

[284] But see J. Heller, L. Nemoy, "Karaites," *EJ* 10 (1971), 762f.

[285] See Revel, 48 who cites Hadassi, Aaron ben Elijah, Bashyatchi, etc. There were some who disagreed in doubtful cases. See Revel's n. 74.

[286] For a survey, see "Pikkuʾaḥ Nefesh," *EJ* 13 (1971), 509f.

life. The rejection of the doctrine of *piqquaḥ nefesh* is also attributed to the Falashas.[287]

Rabbinic Judaism emphasizes that it is proper to violate one Sabbath for the purpose of insuring the continued observance of many more. Lev. 18:5 ("that thou shalt live by them") was interpreted to mean that the commandments were to insure life and not bring death.[288] Ex. 31:16, because of its apparent redundancy, was pressed into service to provide the source of a law calling for the violation of the Sabbath to save another's life.[289]

This principle of *piqquaḥ nefesh* was the creation of the Hasmoneans.[290] Early in the Maccabean rebellion, a group of strict constructionists allowed themselves to be killed rather than defend themselves. They even refused to block up the entrances to their hiding places, indicating that they took the law of *muqṣeh* to be a biblical injunction.[291] Tannaitic law allowed the use of equipment (otherwise *muqṣeh*) for *piqquaḥ nefesh*. Philo seems to have accepted the permissibility of *piqquaḥ nefesh*.[293]

Of all the possible explanations of this sectarian regulation it would seem most probable that the sect did accept the doctrine of *piqquaḥ nefesh* but required that the laws of *muqṣeh* be strictly adhered to as well. From this it follows that the sect probably had a distinction similar to Rabbinic *le-khatḥillah* (*a priori*) and *be-di-ʿabad* (*a posteriori*).[294] In Rabbinic law this distinction allows the setting of optimum (*le-khatḥillah*) standards of performance as well as minimum (*be-di-ʿabad*) standards based on lenient interpretations and doubtful cases. One can fall back on these minima if it is not possible to meet the higher standards called for by the law. Once it is granted that the sect allowed certain Sabbath violations for the saving of life,[295] a regulation

287 Aescoly, 32, 37f., cf. Lowy, 113.

288 B. Yoma' 85b, B. Sanhedrin 74a, M. Shabbat 18:3, *Mekhilta' De-Rabbi Ishmael* Ki Tisa' (to Ex. 31:14).

289 B. Yoma' 85b.

290 1 Macc. 2:29-41. Cf. 2 Macc. 5:25ff. and above, 125 n. 272.

291 Cf. Gilat, *Mishnato*, 127.

292 B. Yoma' 84b.

293 *On Dreams* II, 123-128, trans. Colson and Whitaker, 497-9, cf. Heinemann, *Bildung*, 101.

294 Termed *le-miṣwah* and *le-ʿakeb* in regard to sacrificial law. Perhaps this is the older terminology. Hebrew equivalents are *ba-teḥillah* and *le-she-ʿabar*.

295 Since the sect regarded water sources as separate domains, this action, even with no equipment, involved the removal of the person into another domain. Although the tannaim would not have regarded this a violation (M. Shabbat 10:5) because of the rule that a living being carries itself, the sect would probably not

limiting the means of saving lives must be *le-khathḥillah*. It must be assumed, in other words, that if impossible to save a man without the use of articles in the category of *muqṣeh*, one could use these articles. This conclusion is extremely important in that it sheds light on another point of contact between sectarian and Rabbinic legal methodology.

22. *CDC 11:17f.: Sacrifices*

אל יעל איש למזבח בשבת כי אם עולת השבת כי כן כתוב מלבד שבתותיכם

> No one shall offer (anything) [296] upon the altar on the Sabbath except the burnt-offering of the Sabbath, for thus is it written, "except your Sabbaths (approx. Lev. 23:38 [297])."

This law echoes one of the points of disagreement between the sect and the Jerusalem priesthood. Basing itself on an out-of-context exegesis of Lev. 23:38, the sect concludes that only the burnt-offering (*ʿolah*) may be offered on the Sabbath day.[298] This decision flies in the face of Num. 28:10 which indicates that this offering was to be brought in addition to the regular daily offerings (*tamid*).[299] One can only assume that the sect interpreted the word *ʿal* ("in addition to")[300] in Num. 28:10 to mean "instead of." Hence, there was no contradiction according to their interpretation. If the sect actually perceived this problem and worked it out as set forth above, this is a clear example of *midrash halakhah*. It may be, however, that the two explanations were developed independently, that of Num. 28:10 coming first, so that no one asked about the apparent contradiction. Possibly, this exegesis is an attempt to rationalize an existing belief.

The controversy about offerings on the Sabbath has a long history,

---

have allowed the carrying of adults from domain to domain. They may have agreed with the Rabbis in case the entire affair occurred in the public domain, but there is no way of knowing. See above, 119f. and notes.

[296] Jussive of *ʿlh* (Ges. rule 75k). For the verb, cognate accusative and *mizbeaḥ* proceded by *la-*, see 2 Chron. 29:27, which is, no doubt, the source of our phrase.

[297] MT *shabbetot ʾadonai* ("the Sabbaths of the Lord"). The same variant reading is found in the Vulgate and Quinta (Rabin). Possibly this variant should be considered in light of the sectarian tendency to omit the tetragrammaton (and make the necessary textual adjustments) when quoting Scripture (Ginzberg, 444). Cf. S. Lieberman, "Light on the Cave Scrolls from Rabbinic Sources," *PAAJR* 20 (1951), 400-402.

[298] Cf. Ginzberg, 444. Note that the sect read vv. 37 and 38 as one sentence.

[299] On the *tamid*, see DSW 2:1 and 2 (and above, 65) and 4Q Sl 39 I i (*Serekh Shirot ʿOlat Ha-Shabbat*):22.

[300] The use of *ʿal* for "in addition to" is characteristic of P (BDB, p. 755b). I cannot find any usage like "instead of" in biblical or Rabbinic literature unless it is the meaning "against," which would usually follow a verb.

particularly in regard to the paschal sacrifice if the fourteenth of Nisan should fall on a Saturday. The paschal sacrifice was not a problem for the sect as their calendar fixed Passover on a Wednesday.[301]

The story about Hillel the Elder found in Pesaḥim [302] in which he proves the legality of offering the paschal sacrifice on the Sabbath, has little relevance to the sect's law. In Pesaḥim the problem is a different one from that of this sectarian enactment. None of the tannaim disagrees with the notion that the *tamid* and other sacrifices may be made on the Sabbath. The only question is whether or not the paschal lamb may be offered. Anyhow, in all versions, the claim is that the Bene Bathyra forgot the law, not that they held that the sacrifice could not be offered.[303] So this case cannot be cited as evidence of other groups holding the same view as the sect.[304]

Contrary to Rabin's assertion, Jubilees 50:10 is not ambiguous. It speaks of "burning frankincense and bringing oblations and sacrifices before the Lord for days and for Sabbaths." The first hint that Jubilees does not limit sacrifices on the Sabbath to the *ʿolah* is its use of plural forms. Much more important is the mention of sacrifices "for days." These are clearly the daily *tamid* offerings which Jubilees ordains should be offered on the Sabbath. This is further emphasized in v. 11. Thus Jubilees is not in agreement with the sect on this point.

Josephus (Ant. 18, 1:5) relates that the Essenes did not offer sacrifices in the Jerusalem Temple because they differed with the priests in regard to ritual purity. This practice has no particular revelance to the Sabbath, but may be compared with CDC 6:11-14 which provides that abstention from the Jerusalem cult was a condition for sectarian membership. If so, our law is ideal in nature, looking forward to the restored Jerusalem cult of which the sectarian leaders would take charge.[305]

The citation of a proof-text is rare in Qumran halakhic literature. It may be that because of the uniqueness of this law in the Second

---

[301] Talmon, "Calendar Reckoning," 176.

[302] T. Pesaḥim 4:13, 14, P. Pesaḥim 6:1 (33a), B. Pesaḥim 66a. Cf. Neusner, *Rabbinic Traditions* I, 231-5, 246-251, 254-7, *From Politics to Piety*, 23-35.

[303] The style of the text is that of the older *midrash halakhah*. Ginzberg (445 n. 1) says that it is certain that the Bene Bathyra were not Sadducees.

[304] Cf. Ginzberg, 444f. On Geiger's view that the Sadducees did not permit the paschal sacrifice on the Sabbath, see Revel, 41. Geiger's view seems to be nothing more than a retrojection based on his understanding of the Karaites. On the festival offering, see *Sifra*ʾ ʾEmor 15:5, Neusner, *Rabbinic Traditions* II, 25f.

[305] See above, 78. This rule would be an exception to the generalization of Yadin cited there.

Temple period, the author of the fragments wished to give it special emphasis.

Having disposed of these alleged contemporary parallels, there are a number of medieval cases to be discussed. Again, it is always necessary to consider the possibility that medieval traditions preserve more ancient views. This is especially true in regard to the sacrificial ritual. The history of Jewish codification shows that laws pertaining to sacrifices were practically ignored once no longer applicable.[306]

Among the Karaites a variation of opinion exists. Anan taught that the paschal sacrifice might not be offered on the Sabbath.[307] Benjamin al-Nahawandi, Aaron ben Joseph, and Samuel al-Magribi [308] agreed with the Rabbinic view. Daniel al-Qumisi and Jepeth ben Ali thought that one lamb should be sacrificed and burnt but not eaten—clearly a compromise stand.[309] Qirqisani reports that some Karaites postponed the sacrifice, though not the eating of unleavened bread, for one month to the fourteenth of Iyyar.[310] The Samaritans did not sacrifice on the Sabbath, choosing instead to sacrifice on Friday. If the festival fell on Sunday, they waited until after nightfall Saturday to make the offering.[311]

None of these views corresponds exactly to that found in the Qumran literature. Although each attempts to deal with the problem of the paschal sacrifices, none reflects a controversy regarding other sacrifices on the Sabbath.

It is also possible that this problem is analogous to that of circumcision on the Sabbath. Rabbinic sources apply the rule of a positive commandment superceding a negative. Hence, the commandment of circumcision supercedes the prohibition of labor on the Sabbath.[312] Aescoly [313] claims that the Samaritans prohibited circumcision on the Sabbath, exhibiting a tendency to reject the Rabbinic principle described above.[314]

---

306 The Mishnah and Maimonides' Code are the notable exceptions to this rule.

307 Harkavy, 72f., cf. Ginzberg, *Ginze Schechter* II, 446f., 453-5.

308 Nemoy, 203f.

309 Revel, 41f., Harkavy, 153.

310 Nemoy, 367. This was no doubt in imitation of the "Second Passover" described in Num. 9:6-12 (celebrated in 2 Chron. 30:1-27 where the delay was for reasons not included in the Numbers text).

311 Lowy, 112.

312 A *baraita'* in B. Shabbat 134b-135a, cf. 132a (amoraic). Preparatory acts were permitted by some tannaim (Gilat, *Mishnato*, 130-133).

313 P. 39.

314 But see Lowy, 111f. and 146 n. 112 who cites literary evidence to the contrary.

Anan, in prohibiting circumcision on the Sabbath, has made reference to the view that only the Sabbath sacrifice (*ʿolah*) could be offered on the Sabbath.[315] This opinion seems to be in accord with that of the Qumranites.[316]

Since for the sect a positive commandment would not supercede a negative one, how could sacrifices be allowed on the Sabbath as they involved prohibited labors? On the other hand, if the Torah ordained a Sabbath sacrifice, how could the sect, bound by the Law as it was, reject the sacrifice out of hand? The conclusion could only be that the Sabbath sacrifice is to be the sole exception because of its explicit mention. All other sacrifices (*e.g. tamid*) are to be prohibited.

There is one further opinion to be considered, that of Mishawayh al-ʿUkbari. He did not have the problem of the paschal sacrifice as the solar calendar which he advocated fixed Passover on a Thursday.[317] His view, however, as reported by Hadassi,[318] was that no sacrifice whatsoever was permitted on the Sabbath. He explained the commandments as requiring that Sabbath offerings be prepared before the Sabbath.

The survey of these opinions indicates that some degree of discomfort with the practice of paschal offerings and even with other offerings on the Sabbath persisted into the medieval period. Perhaps some of these views are survivals of ancient traditions not recorded in Rabbinic literature.

Summary: Qumran Sabbath Law

In this chapter a thorough study was made of the Qumran Sabbath *halakhah*. It is important to review some of the main characteristics of this body of law.[319] First, there can be no doubt the sect began its Sabbath on Friday night. Further, the Qumranites began their Sabbath a short time before sunset in order to be sure that they would do no work on the holy day.

---

315 *Sefer Ha-Miṣwot,* 76 (Ginzberg, 444 n. 2). Cf. Lowy, 111f. Nevertheless, Anan commands the reading of a section describing the *tamid* every day, including Saturday. (J. Mann, " ʿAnan's Liturgy and his Half-yearly Cycle of the Reading of the Law," *Journal of Jewish Lore and Philosophy* 1 (1919), 330f., 334f.).

316 If the sect accepted the addition of the Samaritan and LXX, "on the eighth day," to Gen. 17:14, it may also have allowed circumcision on the Sabbath (See Lowy, 111).

317 Z. Ankori, *Karaites in Byzantium* (1959), 377. See above, 85.

318 *ʾEshkol Ha-Kofer*, 98, p. 42a. See also Ginzberg, 444 n. 1, and Segal, *ad loc.*

319 Cf. Ginzberg, *MGWJ* 57 (1913), 157-168, 305f.

All discussion of business was forbidden, including all financial matters or work to be done after the Sabbath. For this reason, it was forbidden to walk in the field on the Sabbath to plan future work. It was probably likewise forbidden to enter into a partnership on the Sabbath.

The sect had two Sabbath limits. It allowed a man to walk one thousand cubits beyond his city limits and two thousand if pasturing his animals. It is unquestionable that the sect accepted the *teḥum shabbat* ("Sabbath limit").

All food had to be prepared before the Sabbath. This included not only cooking but preparation of all kinds. Containers had to be opened in advance. Food could only be consumed or drink taken within the camp. This is probably because otherwise the food or drink was not regarded as prepared before the Sabbath.

For fear of carrying, a person on a journey had to drink directly from the water source. Water could not be drawn. Even within the camp it was forbidden to carry from domain to domain. Children, likewise, could not be carried on the Sabbath. Nor could women wear ornamental perfume bottles.

It was forbidden to have a non-Jew do labor on the Sabbath. A servant might not be instructed to do even permitted work.

It was expected that members of the sect would wear clean, deodorized clothes on the Sabbath. It may have been forbidden to fast on the seventh day.

It was mentioned already that the Sabbath limit was extended for the benefit of animals. Nevertheless, delivering an animal in birth was forbidden as was helping an animal up which had fallen into a pit. In fact, the Sabbath could never be profaned for the saving of material possessions. It is most likely that the sect allowed the violation of the Sabbath to save a human life, but required that, where possible, this be accomplished without the use of instruments or tools which were *muqṣeh*. The sect had a full set of *muqṣeh* prohibitions, for which reason rocks and earth could not be handled.

A strange prohibition is that against spending the Sabbath among gentiles, perhaps because of the danger of impurity or the temptation to violate the holy day. Finally, the sect did not allow (an ideal provision) the offering of any sacrifices on the Sabbath except the burnt-offering.

An interesting question is whether the sect had the legal fictions which the tannaim called *ʿerubin*. Several times, in analyzing individual laws, it was noted that the existence of these legal fictions might answer a question or solve a problem which the observant sectarian must have faced. Yet nowhere is there explicit mention of such a device. It would be folly to conclude by casuistic means that the *ʿerubin* were in existence in this period. Only with the later developments in Pharisaism and the expansion of the traditions of the fathers would such legal fictions have come into wide use. The Qumran sect is apparently earlier than these devices. The Sabbath limit, however, must have developed much earlier than the *ʿerubin* as it is part of the Qumran halakhic system.

CONCLUSION

HALAKHAH AND THE IDENTITY OF THE SECT

When this study was first planned, it was expected that after comparisons of the laws of the Sabbath were made, a table and numerical data could be compiled which would show affinities between the Qumran *halakhah* and the other legal systems which we have compared. Now that the study has been completed, a different picture emerges. Comparative evidence is often oblique. In other words, the various halakhic systems may not refer to the same problem but to a similar one. At other times, the laws are similar but not quite the same. For these reasons, generalized conclusions are difficult to make. Often different groups arrive at the same conclusion by different techniques. This fact brings us to the problem of the method used to derive the legal codes of the various sects, a problem which must be considered apart from the content of these laws.

Both the Dead Sea sect and the Karaites lack an oral Law concept. Scripture, then, becomes the sole source of *halakhah*. In fact, the similarities between the Qumran and Karaite methods are so great that they lead to suspicion that historical connections might exist.

Such connections might be of two types. First, several medieval accounts indicate that some scrolls may have been found in Jericho at the same time that Karaism was developing.[1] These may have been Qumran texts. Moreover, the presence of the *Zadokite Fragments* in the Cairo *genizah* indicates that this text circulated in the early medieval period. Perhaps the early Karaites read texts from the Qumran sect and were influenced by them. Second, it is possible that remnants of various ancient sects survived underground throughout the Talmudic period and that these sects were somehow absorbed into the Karaite movement. Neither of these suggested historical links has been proven, however.

It is also possible to understand the affinities of the Qumran and Karaite sects in a different way. Karaism was to a large extent an attempt to turn the clock back on the development of Rabbinic law and to eliminate those elements which allowed for laws not rooted in

---

[1] See P. Kahle, "The Age of the Scrolls," *VT* 1 (1951), 45ff. and S. Lieberman, "Light on the Cave Scrolls from Rabbinic Sources," *PAAJR* 20 (1951), 402f.

Scripture. This means that the thought processes of Karaite exegesis had to be similar to those of the Dead Sea sect. Are the similarities, therefore, of no historical significance? In light of the many parallels in non-halakhic material collected in N. Wieder's study, *The Judean Scrolls and Karaism*, it would seem that historical connections may have existed.

While to the Dead Sea sect the law is derived through techniques similar to those of the literalist Karaites, it is more often closer in content to the tannaitic *halakhah*. Because the tannaim also used exegesis as a method for the derivation of law, the sectarian and Rabbinic traditions often share the same *midrash halakhah*. Also parallels to the sectarian *halakhah* can be found in minority views or old *halakhot* mentioned by the tannaim.

The Qumran sect is usually identified with the Essenes.[2] Recognizing the differences between the literature of the sect and Josephus's description of the Essenes,[3] scholars have noted that Josephus was trying to explain the Palestinian "parties" to the Greek world. It may also be that the reports of Josephus and of Philo [4] are generalizations including many smaller sects grouped under the heading "Essenes." Indeed, many sects are known from this period.[5] While little is known of the Essene *halakhah*, this group was known for strict Sabbath observance.[6] Philo and Josephus would naturally comment upon those aspects of Sabbath law in which the Essenes differed from the other Jews. This means that the vast majority of Sabbath regulations in which they may have agreed with the Pharisees (Little is known about the Sadducees.) would not be mentioned. It stands to reason, then, that all the sects grouped under the heading "Essenes" in the accounts of Philo and Josephus adhered in the main to similar Sabbath regulations. One such code is represented in the *Zadokite Fragments*, another in Jubilees. Yet once again, no facile identification can be made.

Was the Qumran sect, as Rabin suggested, a group of proto-Pharisees? [7] After all, the many similarities with tannaitic *halakhah* seem to point in this direction. The differences may be accounted for by saying

---

[2] This is followed by Cross, *Ancient Library*. See our Introduction, 1 n. 6.

[3] The most glaring is that the sectarians of Qumran do not seem to have been celibate.

[4] References conveniently gathered in K. Kohler, "Essenes," *JE* 5, 227-30.

[5] *Ibid.*,, 225-7.

[6] Wars 2, 8:9.

[7] *QS*, vii-ix.

that this "proto-Pharisaic" legal system developed at a time when the doctrine of an oral Law and the laws dependent on this doctrine had not yet entered Judaism. However, the employment of a solar calendar at Qumran makes it highly unlikely that the sect was a forerunner of the Pharisees.

After twenty-five years of research in Qumran studies, the sect still cannot be identified with any previously known group. The Qumran sect had affinities with the Pharisaic and Essene traditions, yet its separate identity must be recognized. Qumran texts must be read and evaluated as the literature of what L. Ginzberg called, "an unknown Jewish sect."

BIBLIOGRAPHY

Aaron ben Elijah (of Nicomedia), *Gan ʿEden*, Eupatoria, 1864.

Aboth de Rabbi Nathan, ed. S. Schechter, corrected and reprinted, New York, 1967.

Abraham ben (Ibn) Ezra, *The Commentary of Ibn Ezra on Isaiah*, ed. M. Friedländer, London, 1873.

Abravanel, I., *Perush ʿal Ha-Torah*, 5 pts., 3 vols., Jerusalem, 1963/4.

Abulafia, M., *Yad Ramah (Sefer Ḥiddushe Ha-Ramah ʿal Masekhet Sanhedrin)*, New York, 1970/1.

Aescoly, A. Z., *Sefer Ha-Falashim*, Jerusalem, 1943.

Akavyah, A. A., "*Ha-Emet ʿal Ha-Luaḥ shel Kat Midbar Yehudah*," *Sinai* 47 (1960), 24-48.

Albeck, Ch., *Das Buch der Jubiläen und die Halacha*, Berlin, 1930.

——, *Mabo' La-Mishnah*, Jerusalem and Tel-Aviv, 1959.

——, *Meḥkarim Be-Baraita' We-Tosefta'*, Jerusalem, 1969.

——, ed., *Shishah Sidre Mishnah*, Jerusalem and Tel-Aviv, 1957-9.

Albright, W.F., "The Phoenician Inscriptions of the Tenth Century B.C. from Byblus," *JAOS* 67 (1947), 153-160.

Allegro, J. M., "Further Messianic References in Qumran Literature," *JBL* 75 (1956), 174-87.

——, "Fragments of a Qumran Scroll of Eschatological Midrašim," *JBL* 77 (1958), 350-354.

Allon, G., *Meḥqarim Be-Toledot Yisrael*, 2 vols., Tel-Aviv, 1970.

——, "*Shebut, Reshut, Miṣwah*," *Tarbiẓ* 7 (1935/6), 135-42.

Alt, A., "The Origins of Israelite Law," *Essays on Old Testament History and Religion*, Garden City, New York, 1968, 103-171.

Altmann, A., ed., *Between East and West*, Oxford, 1958.

——, ed., *Biblical Motifs*, Cambridge, Mass., 1966.

Andreasen, N. A., *The Old Testament Sabbath*, SBL Dissertation Series 7, Missoula, Montana, 1972.

[Ankori, Z.,] "Bashyazi," *EJ* 4 (1971), 297f.

——, *Karaites in Byzantium*, New York and Jerusalem, 1959.

Babylonian Talmud, ed. Vilna (with commentaries and Alfasi), reprinted New York, 1964.

Bacher, W., "*Die Ausdrücke, mit denen die Tradition bezeichnet wird*," *JQR* O.S. 20 (1908), 572-596.

——, *ʿErkhe Midrash*, trans. A. Rabinowitz, Tel-Aviv, 1922/3.

Baer, S., *Siddur ʿAbodat Yisrael*, reprinted, Tel-Aviv, 1956/7.

Baillet, M., "*Fragments du Document de Damas. Qumrân, Grotte* 6," *RB* 63 (1956), 513-23 and Pl. II.

Baillet, M., Milik, J.T., Vaux, R. de, *Discoveries in the Judaean Desert* III, Oxford, 1962.

Bardke, H., *Qumran-Probleme*, Deutsche Akademie der Wissenschaften zu Berlin, Schriften der Sektion für Alterumswissenschaft 42, Berlin, 1963.

Baron, S., *A Social and Religious History of the Jews*, 14 vols. and index to vols. 1-8 have appeared, New York, Philadelphia, 1952-69.

Barthélemy, D., Milik, J.T., *et. al.*, *Discoveries in the Judaean Desert* I, Oxford, 1955.

Bartholomae, C., *Altiranisches Wörterbuch*, Strassburg, 1904.

Bashyatchi, E., *Sefer Ha-Miṣwot Ha-Niqra' 'Aderet 'Eliyahu*, Eupatoria, 1835.

Bauer, H., Leander, P., *Kurzgefasste Biblisch-Aramäische Grammatik*, Hildesheim, 1965.

Baumgarten, J. M., "The Beginning of the Day in the Calendar of Jubilees," *JBL* 77 (1958), 355-60.

——, "The Counting of the Sabbath in Ancient Sources," *VT* 16 (1966), 277-86.

——, "Does *tlh* in the Temple Scroll Refer to Crucifiction?" *JBL* 71 (1972), 472-81.

——, "The Exclusion of '*Netinim*' and Proselytes in 4Q Florilegium," *RQ* 8 (1972), 87-96.

——, "Reply," *JBL* 78 (1959), 157.

——, "The Unwritten Law in the Pre-Rabbinic Period," *Journal for the Study of Judaism* 3 (1972), 7-29.

Beegel, D.M., "Ligatures with Waw and Yodh in the Dead Sea Scrolls," *BASOR* 129 (1953), 11-14.

Belkin, S., *The Alexandrian Halakah in Apologetic Literature of the First Century C.E.*, Philadelphia, 1936.

——, *Philo and the Oral Law*, Cambridge, Mass., 1940.

Bemidbar Rabbah, ed. Vilna, reprinted, New York, 1952 (part of edition of *Midrash Rabbah*).

Bietenhardt, H., "*Sabbatvorschriften von Qumran im Lichte des rabbinischen Rechts und der Evangelien*," *Qumran-Probleme*, ed. H. Bardke, Deutsche Akademie der Wissenschaften zu Berlin, Schriften der Sektion für Alterumswissenschaft 42, Berlin, 1963, 53-74.

Biram, A., ed., *Sefer Urbach*, Jerusalem, 1955.

Blank, S.H., "The LXX Rendering of Old Testament Terms for Law," *HUCA* 7 (1930), 259-283.

The Book of Isaiah, (New Translation by the Jewish Publication Society) Philadelphia, 1973.

Bowman, R., *Aramaic Ritual Texts from Persepolis*, The University of Chicago Oriental Institute Publications 31, Chicago, 1970.

Brand, J., *Keli Ha-Ḥeres Be-Sifrut Ha-Talmud*, Jerusalem, 1953.

——, "*Megillat Berit Dameseq U-Zemanah*," *Tarbiz* 28 (1958/9), 18-39.

Bright, J., "The Apodictic Prohibition: Some Observations," *JBL* 92 (1973), 185-204.

Brown, F., Driver, S., Briggs, C., *A Hebrew and English Lexicon of the Old Testament*, Oxford, 1966.

Brown, S., " 'The Secret of the Kingdom of God' (Mark 4:11)," *JBL* 92 (1973), 60-74.

Brownlee, W.H., "Biblical Interpretation among the Sectaries of the Dead Sea Scrolls," *BA* 14 (1951), 54-76.

——, "A Comparison of the Covenanters of the Dead Sea Scrolls with Pre-Christian Jewish Sects," *BA* 13 (1950), 50-72.

——, *The Dead Sea Manual of Discipline*, *BASOR* Supplementary Studies 10-12, New Haven, 1951.

Bruce, F.F., "Dead Sea Scrolls, Description," *EJ* 5 (1971), 1398f.

——, *The Teacher of Righteousness in the Qumran Texts*, London, 1956.

Büchler, A., *Ha-Kohanim We-ʿAbodatam*, trans. N. Ginton, Jerusalem, 1966.

——, "Schechter's 'Jewish Sectaries,' " *JQR* N. S. 3 (1912/3), 429-485.

Burney, C., *The Book of Judges and Notes on the Hebrew Text of the Book of Kings*, reprinted, New York, 1970 (with "Prolegomenon" by W. F. Albright).

Burrows, M., with Trever, J., Brownlee, W.H., *The Dead Sea Scrolls of St. Mark's Monastery, Vol. II, Fascicle 2; Plates and Transcription of the Manual of Discipline*, New Haven, 1951.

Buttrick, G.A., *The Interpreter's Dictionary of the Bible*, 4 vols., New York, 1962.
Cassuto, U., *Perush ʿal Sefer Bereshit*, Jerusalem, 1969.
——, *Perush ʿal Sefer Shemot*, Jerusalem, 1969.
Charles, R.H., *The Apocrypha and Pseudepigrapha of the Old Testament*, 2 vols., Oxford, 1913.
Chomsky, W., "The Ambiguity of the Prefixed Prepositions *bet, lamed, mem* in the Bible," *JQR* N. S. 61 (1970), 87-89.
Cohen, B., *Law and Tradition in Judaism*, New York, 1959.
——, "Sabbath Prohibitions Known as Shebut," *Proceedings of the Rabbinical Assembly* 9 (1949), 123-161.
Cooke, G.A., *A Critical and Exegetical Commentary on the Book of Ezekiel*, Edinburgh, 1960.
——, *A Text-Book of North-Semitic Inscriptions*, Oxford, 1903.
Cross, F.M., *The Ancient Library of Qumran*, Garden City, N. Y., 1961.
Dahood, M., *Ugaritic-Hebrew Philology*, Rome, 1965.
Davidson, I., ed., *Essays and Studies in Memory of Linda R. Miller*, New York, 1938.
Delcor, M., "*Contribution à l'étude de la législation des sectaries de Damas et de Qumran*," *RB* 61 (1954), 533-553, 62 (1955), 62-75.
Dembitz, L. N., "Slaves and Slavery," *JE* 11, 403-407.
De-Vries, B., "Baraita, Beraitot," *EJ* 4 (1971), 189-193.
Donaldson, J., Roberts, A., eds., *Ante-Nicene Fathers*, 10 vols., New York, 1907.
Donner, H., Röllig, W., *Kanaanäische und Aramäische Inschriften*, 3 vols., Wiesbaden, 1968.
Driver, G.R., *Aramaic Documents of the Fifth Century B. C.*, Oxford, 1957.
——, *The Judaean Scrolls: The Problem and a Solution*, Oxford, 1964.
Driver, S.R., *An Introduction to the Literature of the Old Testament*, Cleveland, 1956.
Edels, Samuel (Maharsha), *Ḥiddushe Halakhot We-ʾAggadot*, in *Babylonian Talmud*, ed. Vilna.
Ehrlich, A., *Mikra ki-Pheschuto*, 3 vols., Berlin, 1899-1901.
Encyclopaedia Biblica, Vols. 1-6, Jerusalem, 1965-71.
Encylopaedia Judaica, 16 vols., Jerusalem, 1971-2.
Encyclopedia Talmudit, Vols. 1-14, Jerusalem, 1951-1973.
Epstein, A., "*Le Livre des Jubilés*," *REJ* 21 (1890), 80-97, 22 (1891), 1-25.
Epstein, B., *Torah Temimah*, 5 vols., reprinted, Jerusalem, 1968/9.
Epstein, J.N., *Maboʾ Le-Nusaḥ Ha-Mishnah*, 2 vols., Jerusalem and Tel-Aviv, 1964.
——, *Meboʾot Le-Sifrut Ha-Tannaim*, ed. E. Z. Melamed, Jerusalem and Tel-Aviv, 1957.
Even-Shoshan, A., *Ha-Millon He-Ḥadash*, 7 vols., Jerusalem, 1971.
Feigin, S., "Etymological Notes," *AJSLL* 43 (1926), 53-60.
Feldblum, M., *Diqduqe Soferim, Masekhet Giṭṭin*, New York, 1966.
Fensham, F.C., " 'Camp' in the New Testament and Milḥamah," *RQ* 4 (1963-4), 557-562.
Ferguson, E., "Qumran and Codex 'D', " *RQ* 8 (1972), 75-80.
Finkelstein, L., "The Book of Jubilees and the Rabbinic Halaka," *HTR* 16 (1923), 39-61.
——, "The Development of the Amidah," in *Contributions to the Scientific Study of Jewish Liturgy*, ed. J. Petuchowski, New York, 1970, 91-177.
——, *The Pharisees*, 2 vols., Philadelphia, 1966.
Frankel, Z., *Darkhe Ha-Mishnah*, Tel-Aviv, n.d.
——, *Meboʾ Ha-Yerushalmi*, Breslau, 1869/70.
Frankl, P.F., "*ʾAḥare Reshef Le-Baqqer Be-Sifrut Ha-Qaraim*," *Ha-Shaḥar* 7 (1875/6), 646-50, 701-13, 8 (1876/7), 29-31, 119-27, 177-84.

Freedman, D.N., Greenfield, J., eds., *New Directions in Biblical Archaeology*, Garden City, New York, 1971.
Friedrich, J., Röllig, W., *Phönizisch-Punische Grammatik*, Rome, 1970.
Gilat, Y., "*Le-Qadmutam shel ʾIssure Shabbat*," *Bar-ʾIlan, Sefer Ha-Shanah Le-Madaʿe Ha-Yahadut We-Ha-Ruaḥ*, Ramat Gan and Jerusalem, 1963, 106-119.
——, *Mishnato shel Rabbi ʾEliʿezer ben Hyrcanus U-Meqomah Be-Toledot Ha-Halakhah*, Tel Aviv, 1968.
Ginzberg, L., "*Eine unbekannte jüdische Sekte*," *MGWJ* 55 (1911), 666-98, 56 (1912), 33-48, 285-307, 417-48, 546-66, 664-89, 57 (1913), 153-67, 284-308, 394-418, 666-96, 58 (1914), 16-48, 143-77, 395-429.
——, *Eine unbekannte jüdische Sekte*, New York, 1922.
——, *Ginze Schechter* I-II (*Genizah Studies in Memory of Doctor Solomon Schechter*, Vols. 1, 2), New York, 1928-9.
——, *The Legends of the Jews*, 7 vols., Philadelphia, 1968.
——, *Perushim We-Ḥiddushim Ba-Yerushalmi*, 4 vols., New York 1941-61.
——, *Seride Ha-Yerushalmi*, New York, 1909.
——,"Tamid, the Oldest Treatise of the Mishnah," *Journal of Jewish Lore and Philosophy* 1 (1919), 33-44, 197-209, 265-295.
Glueck, N., *Hesed in the Bible*, trans. A. Gottschalk, New York, 1967.
Golb, N., "The Dietary Laws of the Damascus Covenant in Relation to those of the Karaites," *JJS* 8 (1957), 51-69.
——, "Literary and Doctrinal Aspects of the Damascus Covenant in Relation to those of the Karaites," *JQR* N. S. 47 (1957), 354-74.
Goldschmidt, D., ed., *Maḥazor La-Yamim Ha-Nora'im*, 2 vols., Jerusalem, 1970.
Goodenough, E.R., *The Jurisprudence of the Jewish Courts in Egypt*, New Haven, 1929.
Gordon, C.H., *Ugaritic Textbook*, Rome, 1965.
Goshen-Gottstein, M.H., "Linguistic Structure and Tradition in the Qumran Documents," *Aspects of the Dead Sea Scrolls*, ed. Y. Yadin, C. Rabin, Scripta Hierosolymitana, Vol. 4, Jerusalem, 1958.
——, " 'Sefer-Hagu'—The End of a Puzzle," *VT* 8 (1958), 286-8.
Gray, G.B., *A Critical and Exegetical Commentary on Numbers*, New York, 1903.
Greenberg, M., "Idealism and Practicality in Numbers 35:4-5 and Ezekiel 48," *Essays in Memory of E. A. Speiser*, ed. W. Hallo, New Haven, 1968, 59-66.
Greenberg, S., "*Le-Berurah shel Mishnah*," *Sinai* 10 (1941/2), 158f.
Grintz, J., "Jubilees, Book of," *EJ* 10 (1971), 324-6.
Guttmann, A., "The Problem of the Anonymous Mishnah," *HUCA* 16 (1941), 137-155.
Hadassi, J., *Sefer ʾEshkol Ha-Kofer*, Gozlow, 1836.
Hallo, W., ed., *Essays in Memory of E. A. Speiser*, American Oriental Series 53, New Haven, 1968.
Haran, M., "Priests and Priesthood,"*EJ* 13 (1971), 1069-1086, and biblio., 1090.
Harkavy, A., *Mi-Sifre Ha-Miṣwot Ha-Rishonim Li-Bene Miqraʾ*, *Zikaron La-Rishonim* 8, reprinted, Jerusalem, 1968/9.
Harris, Z., *A Grammar of the Phoenician Language*, American Oriental Series 8, New Haven, 1936.
Heinemann, I., *Darkhe Ha-Aggadah*, Jerusalem, 1970.
——, "*Die Lehre vom Heiligen Geist im Judentum und in den Evangelien*," *MGWJ* 66 (1922), 169-180.
——, "*Hitpatḥut Ha-Munaḥim Ha-Miqsoʿiyim Le-Ferush Ha-Miqraʾ*," *Leshonenu* 14 (1945/6), 182-9, 15 (1946/7), 108-115, 16 (1947/8), 20-28.
——, "*Midrash*," *Enc. Bib.* 4, 695-701.
——, "*Miṣwah*," *Enc. Bib.* 5, 229-235.
——, *Philons griechische und jüdische Bildung*, Hildesheim, 1962.

Heller, J., Nemoy, L., "Karaites," *EJ* 10 (1971), 761-782, Biblio., 785.
Herr, M.D., "*Li-Be'ayat Hilkhot Milḥamah Be-Shabbat Bi-Yeme Bayit Sheni U-Bi-Tequfat Ha-Mishnah*," *Tarbiẓ* 30 (1961), 242-256, 341-356.
——, "Midrash," *EJ* 11 (1971), 1507-1514.
Herschler, M., *Massekhet Ketubot 'im Shinuye Nusḥa'ot*, Jerusalem, 1971/2.
Higger, M., *'Oṣar Ha-Baraitot*, 10 vols., New York, 1930-50.
Higgins, A., "Priest and Messiah," *VT* 3 (1953), 321-36.
Hoenig, S., "An Interdict against Socializing on the Sabbath," *JQR* N. S. 62 (1971), 77-83.
Honeyman, A.M., "Note on a Teacher and a Book," *JJS* 4 (1953), 131f.
Hunzinger, C.H. "*Fragmente einer älteren Fassung des Buches Milḥamā aus Höhle 4 von Qumrān*," *ZAW* 69 (1957), 131-51.
Jacobs, L., "Are there Fictitious Baraitot in the Babylonian Talmud?" *HUCA* 42 (1971), 185-196.
Jastrow, M., *Dictionary of Talmud Bavli, Yerushalmi, Midrashic Literature and Targumim*, 2 vols., reprinted, New York, 1950.
Jaubert, A., "*Le Calendrier des Jubilés et les jours liturgiques de la semaine*," *VT* 7 (1957), 35-61.
——, "*Le Calendrier des Jubilés et de la secte de Qumran*," *VT* 3 (1953), 250-264.
Jellin, A. L., *Yefeh 'Enayim*, in *Babylonian Talmud*, ed. Vilna.
Jonah ben (Ibn) Janaḥ, *Sefer Ha-Shorashim*, ed. W. Bacher, Berlin, 1896.
Josephus, *Works*, trans. H. St. J. Thackeray, R. Marcus, A. Wikgren, L. Feldman, 9 vols., Cambridge, Mass. , 1926-65.
Kahana, A., ed., *Ha-Sefarim Ha-Ḥiṣonim*, 2 vols., Jerusalem, 1969/70.
——, *Sifrut Ha-Historiyah Ha-Yisraelit*, 2 vols., reprinted, Jerusalem, 1968/9.
Kahle, P., "The Age of the Scrolls," *VT* 1 (1951), 45ff.
Katzenstein, H.J., "Some Remarks on the Lists of the Chief Priests in the Temple of Solomon," *JBL* 81 (1962), 377-384.
Kaufman, S., "The Job Targum from Qumran," *JAOS* 93 (1973), 317-327.
Kaufmann, D., "Was the Custom of Fasting on Sabbath Afternoon Part of the Early Anglo-Jewish Ritual?" *JQR* O. S. 6 (1894), 754-6.
Kaufmann, Y., *Toledot Ha-'Emunah Ha-Yisraelit*, 4 vols., Jerusalem and Tel-Aviv, 1966/7.
Kautzsch, E., ed., *Gesenius, Hebrew Grammar*' trans. A.E. Cowley, Oxford, 1910.
Kepler, T.S., "Sabbath Day's Journey," *IDB* 4, 141.
Kimbrough, S.T., "The Concept of Sabbath at Qumran," *RQ* 5 (1964-6), 483-502.
Kimchi, D., *Sefer Ha-Shorashim*, ed. J. Biesenthal, F. Lebrecht, Berlin, 1847.
Kimron, A., "*Ha-Habḥanah ben Waw Le-Yod Bi-Te'udot Midbar Yehudah*," *Bet Miqra'* 52 (1972/3), 102-112.
Kohler, K., "Essenes," *JE* 5, 224-232.
Kohut, A., *'Arukh Ha-Shalem*, 9 vols., reprinted, Israel, 1970.
Kosmala, H., "Maskil," *The Journal of the Ancient Near Eastern Society of Columbia University* 5 (1973, The Gaster Festschrift), 235-241.
Kutscher, E.Y., *Ha-Lashon We-Ha-Reqa' Ha-Leshoni shel Megillat Yisha'yahu Ha-Shelemah Mi-Megillot Yam Ha-Melaḥ*, Jerusalem, 1959.
Lagrange, M.-J., "*La secte juive de la Nouvelle Alliance au pays de Damas*," *RB* 9 (1912), 213-240, 321-360.
La Sor, W.S., "The Messiah of Aaron and Israel," *VT* 6 (1956), 425-9.
Laurin, R., "The Problem of the Two Messiahs in the Qumran Scrolls," *RQ* 4 (1963), 39-52.
Lauterbach, J.Z., "Philo Judaeus, his Relation to the Halakah," *JE* 10, 15-18.
——, *Rabbinic Essays*, Cincinnati, 1951.
Leaney, A.R.C., *The Rule of Qumran and its Meaning*, Philadelphia, 1966.

Lehmann, M.R., "Midrashic Parallels to Selected Qumran Texts," *RQ* 3 (1961-2), 545-551.
Leibel, D., "*Shabbatah shel Kat Midbar Yehudah*," *Tarbiz* 29 (1960), 296.
Leslau, W., *Falasha Anthology*, New York, 1969.
Levine, B., "Aramaic Texts from Persepolis," *JAOS* 92 (1972), 70-79.
——, "Damascus Document IX, 17-22. A New Translation and Comments," *RQ* 8 (1973), 195f.
——, "*Mulūgu/Melûg*: The Origins of a Talmudic Legal Institution," *JAOS* 88 (1968), 271-285.
Lewin, B.M., "*Le-Toledot Ner shel Shabbat*," *Essays and Studies in Memory of Linda R. Miller*, ed. I. Davidson, New York, 1938.
——, *ʾOṣar Ha-Geonim*, 13 vols., Haifa, 1928-62.
Levy, J., *Wörterbuch über die Talmudim und Midraschim*, 4 vols., Leipzig, 1883.
Lexicon Biblicum, 2 vols., Tel-Aviv, 1964/5.
Licht, J., *Megillat Ha-Hodayot*, Jerusalem, 1957.
——, *Megillat Ha-Serakhim*, Jerusalem, 1965.
——, "*Ṣadoq, Bene Ṣadoq Bi-Yeme Bayit Sheni*," *Enc. Bib.* 6, 677f., Jerusalem, 1971.
——, "*Sefarim Ḥiṣonim U-Genuzim*," *Enc. Bib.* 5, 1103-1121.
Licht, J., Sperber, D., "Mishmarot and Ma'amadot," *EJ* 12 (1971), 89-93.
Lichtenstein, H., "*Die Fastenrolle: Eine Untersuchung zur jüdisch-hellenistischen Gerichte*," *HUCA* 8-9 (1931-2), 257-351.
Liddell, H., Scott, R., *A Greek-English Lexicon*, revised and augmented by H. Stuart Jones, R. McKenzie, with a Supplement, Oxford, 1968.
Lieberman, S., *Greek in Jewish Palestine*, New York, 1965.
——, *Ha-Yerushalmi Ki-Fshuto*, Jerusalem, 1934.
——, *Hellenism in Jewish Palestine*, New York, 1962.
——, "Light on the Cave Scrolls from Rabbinic Sources," *PAAJR* 20 (1951), 395-404.
——, *Tosefet Rishonim*, 4 vols., Jerusalem, 1937-9.
——, *Toseftaʾ Ki-Fshutah*, 8 vols. have appeared, New York, 1955-73.
Liver, J., "*Bene Ṣadoq She-Be-Kat Midbar Yehudah*," *Eretz Yisrael* 8 (1967), 71-81.
——, "The Doctrine of the Two Messiahs in Sectarian Literature in the Time of the Second Commonwealth," *HTR* 52 (1959), 149-85.
——, "*Ha-Mashiaḥ Mi-Bet Dawid Bi-Megillot Midbar Yehudah*," *ʿIyyunim Bi-Megillot Midbar Yehudah*, ed. J. Liver, Jerusalem, 1964.
——, ed., *ʿIyyunim Bi-Megillot Midbar Yehudah*, Jerusalem, 1964.
——, *Toledot Bet Dawid Me-Ḥurban Mamlekhet Yehudah we-ʿad le-ʾaḥar Ḥurban Ha-Bayit Ha-Sheni*, Jerusalem, 1959.
Loewenstamm, S., "*Karet*," *Enc. Bib.* 4, 330-332.
——, "*Mishpaṭ, Mishpaṭ Ha-Miqraʾ*," *Enc. Bib.* 5, 614-37.
Lowy, S., "Some Aspects of Normative and Sectarian Interpretation of the Scriptures," *Annual of Leeds University Oriental Society* 6 (1969), 98-163.
Luzzatto, S.D., *Perush Shadal ʿal Ḥamishah Ḥumshe Torah*, ed. P. Schlesinger, Tel-Aviv, 1965.
——, *Perush Shadal ʿal Sefer Yeshaʿyah*, Tel-Aviv, 1970.
Macalister, S., *The Excavation of Gezer*, 3 vols., London, 1912.
MacKenzie, D.N., *A Concise Pahlavi Dictionary*, London, 1971.
Maharsha. See Edels, Samuel.
Maimon, J.L., ed., *Sefer Ha-Yobel Mugash Li-Khbod Ha-Rab Shimʿon Federbush*, Jerusalem, 1960.
Maimonides, M., *Mishneh Torah*, ed. Vilna, reprinted (with additions), 5 vols., Jerusalem, 1955.

Malter, H., *Massekhet Ta'anit min Talmud Babli*, New York, 1930.
Mandelkern, S., *Veteris Testamenti Concordantiae*, reprinted, Jerusalem and Tel-Aviv, 1967.
Mann, J., " 'Anan's Liturgy and His Half-yearly Cycle of the Reading of the Law," *Journal of Jewish Lore and Philosophy* 1 (1919), 329-353.
——, *Texts and Studies in Jewish History and Literature*, 2 vols., intro. by Gerson Cohen, New York, 1970.
Marcus, R., *Law in the Apocrypha*, Columbia University Oriental Studies 26, New York, 1927.
——, "*Mebaqqer* and *Rabbim* in the *Manual of Discipline* VI, 11-13," *JBL* 75 (1956), 398-402.
Margaliot, M., *Encyclopedia Le-Ḥakme Ha-Talmud We-Ha-Geonim*, 2 vols., Tel-Aviv, 1946.
——, "*Mi-Berit Dameseq 'ad Serekh Ha-Yaḥad*," *Sinai* 30 (1951/2), 9-21.
Margoliouth, G., "The Two Zadokite Messiahs," *JTS* 12 (1910-11), 446-50.
Marmorstein, A., "*Eine unbekannte jüdische Sekte*," *Theologisch tijdschrift* 52 (1918), 92-122.
Massekhet Soferim, ed. M. Higger, New York, 1936/7.
Mekhilta' De-Rabbi Shim'on ben Yoḥai, ed. J.N. Epstein, E.Z. Melamed, Jerusalem, 1955.
Mekhilta' De-Rabbi Shim'on ben Yoḥai, ed. D. Hoffmann, Frankfurt, 1905.
Mekhilta' De-Rabbi Ishmael, ed. M. Friedmann (Ish Shalom), Vienna, 1869/70.
Mekhilta' De-Rabbi Ishmael, ed. H.S. Horovitz, I.A. Rabin, Jerusalem, 1960.
Mekhilta' De-Rabbi Ishmael with *Birkat Ha-Neṣib* by N.Z.J. Berlin, Jerusalem, 1970.
Metzger, B.M., ed., *The Oxford Annotated Apocrypha*, New York, 1965.
Michael, J. Hugh, "The Jewish Sabbath in the Latin Classical Writers," *AJSLL* 40 (1924), 117-124.
Midrash Bereshit Rabba', ed. J. Theodor, Ch. Albeck, Jerusalem, 1965.
Midrash Ha-Gadol, Sefer Shemot, ed. M. Margaliot, Jerusalem, 1966/7.
Midrash Rabbah, ed. Vilna, 2 vols., reprinted, New York, 1952.
Midrash Tanḥuma', ed. S. Buber, Vilna, reprinted Jerusalem, 1963-4.
Midrash Tanḥuma', with comm. by Ḥanokh Zundel ben Joseph, Vilna, 1833.
Midrash Tannaim, ed. D. Hoffmann, 2 vols., Berlin, 1900, 1909.
Midrash Wa-Yiqra' Rabbah, ed. M. Margaliot, 5 vols. (in 3), Jerusalem, 1971/2.
Milik, J.T., "*Fragment d'une source du Psautier* (*4QPs 89*) *et fragments des Jubilés, du Document du Damas, etc.*," *RB* 73 (1966), 94-106.
——, "*Texte des variantes des dix manuscrits de la Régle de Communauté trouvés dans la grotte 4*," *RB* 67 (1960), 411-16.
——, "*Le travail d'édition des fragments manuscrits de Qumran*," *RB* 63 (1956), 49-67.
Mishnah, ed. Ch. Albeck, with vocalization by H. Yalon, 6 vols., Tel-Aviv, 1957-9.
Mishnah, ed. Vilna, reprinted, 12 vols., New York 1952/3.
Mishnat Rabbi 'Eliezer, ed. H. Enelow, New York, 1933.
Moore, G.F., *Judaism*, 2 vols., New York, 1971.
Morgenstern, J., "The Calendar of the Book of Jubilees, its Origin and its Character," *VT* 5 (1955), 34-76.
Mowinckel, S., "The Hebrew Equivalent of Taxo in Ass. Mos. ix," *Supplements to VT* 1 (1953), 88-96.
——, *The Psalms in Israel's Worship*, trans. D.R. Ap-Thomas, 2 vols., New York and Nashville, 1962.
Naḥmanides, M., *Ḥiddushe Ha-Ramban*, 2 vols., New York, 1966/7.
——, *Perushe Ha-Torah Le-Rabbenu Mosheh ben Naḥman*, ed. C. Chavel, 2 vols., Jerusalem, 1959-60.

Nebe, G.W., "*Der Gebrauch der sogennanten nota accusativi ʾet in Damaskusschrift XV, 5.9 und 12,*" *RQ* 8 (1973), 257-264.

Nemoy, L., *Karaite Anthology*, New Haven, 1952.

Nemoy, L., Schwartz, J., "*Pirqe Shabbat Me-ʾAl-Qirqisani,*" *Horeb* 1 (1934), 200-206.

Neufeld, E., "Hygiene Conditions in Ancient Israel (Iron Age)," *BA* 34 (1971), 42-66, reprinted from *Journal of the History of Medicine and Applied Sciences* 25 (1970).

Neusner, J., " 'By the Testimony of Two Witnesses' in the Damascus Document IX, 17-22 and in Pharisaic-Rabbinic Law," *RQ* 8 (1973), 197-218.

——, *From Politics to Piety*, Englewood Cliffs, New Jersey, 1973.

——, *A History of the Mishnaic Law of Purities* III, Leiden, 1974.

——, "Rabbinic Traditions about the Pharisees before A.D. 70: The Problem of Oral Transmission," *JJS* 22 (1971), 1-18.

——, *The Rabbinic Traditions about the Pharisees before 70*, 3 vols., Leiden, 1971.

——, "Types and Forms in Ancient Jewish Literature: Some Comparisons," *History of Religions* 11 (1972), 354-390.

Nissim ben Reuben Gerondi, *Ḥiddushe Ha-Ran*, reprinted, n.d., n.p. Some of the commentaries in this collection are not his (*EJ* 12 (1971), 1186).

North, R., "Maccabean Sabbath Years," *Biblica* 34 (1953), 501-515.

Noth, M., *Numbers*, trans. J. D. Martin, Philadelphia, 1968.

Nyberg, H. S., *A Manual of Pahlavi*, reprinted, Wiesbaden, 1964.

Odeberg, H., *3 Enoch or the Hebrew Book of Enoch*, with "Prolegomenon" by Jonas C. Greenfield, New York, 1973.

Olmstead, A. T., *A History of the Persian Empire*, Chicago, 1959.

Orlinsky, H., ed., *Notes on the New Translation of the Torah*, Philadelphia, 1969.

Palestinian Talmud, ed. Krotoschin, reprinted, Jerusalem, 1960.

Palestinian Talmud, ed. Zhitomir (with commentaries), reprinted, New York, 1968.

Pardo, D., *Ḥasde Dawid*, 5 vols., I, Leghorn, 1776, II, Leghorn, 1789/90, III, Jerusalem, 1889/90, IV, Jerusalem, 1970, V, Jerusalem, 1971.

Patrick, D., "Casuistic Law Governing Primary Rights and Duties," *JBL* 92 (1973), 180-184.

Pesiqtaʾ [*De-Rab Kahanaʾ*], ed. S. Buber, Lyck, 1868, reprinted, New York, 1949.

Pesiqtaʾ De-Rab Kahanaʾ, ed. B. Mandelbaum, 2 vols., New York, 1962.

Pesiqtaʾ Rabbati, ed. M. Friedmann (Ish Shalom), Vienna, 1880.

Petuchowski, J., ed., *Contributions to the Scientific Study of Jewish Liturgy*, New York, 1970.

Philo, [*Works*], ed., trans., F. H. Colson, G. H. Whitaker, R. Marcus, 10 vols. + 2 supplementary vols., Cambridge, Mass., 1929-1953.

Pinsker, S., *Liqqute Qadmoniot*, 2 vols., Vienna, 1860.

Ploeg, J. van der, "Studies in Hebrew Law," *CBQ* 12 (1950), 248-59, 416-27, 13 (1951), 28-43, 164-71, 296-307.

Ploeg, J. van der, Woude, A. S. van der, *Le Targum de Job de la grotte XI de Qumran*, Leiden, 1971.

Priest, J. F., "*Mebaqqer, Paqid* and the Messiah," *JBL* 81 (1962), 55-61.

Pritchard, J., ed., *Ancient Near Eastern Texts*, Princeton, 1969.

Rabbinovicz, R., *Diqduqe Soferim*, 15 vols., reprinted, New York, Jerusalem and Montreal, 1959/60.

Rabin, C., *Qumran Studies*, Oxford, 1957.

——, "Semitic Languages," *EJ* 14 (1971), 1149-1157.

——, "The 'Teacher of Righteousness' in the Testaments of the Twelve Patriarchs ?" *JJS* 3 (1952), 127f.

Rabin, C., *The Zadokite Documents*, Oxford, 1954.
——, Yadin, Y., eds., *Aspects of the Dead Sea Scrolls*, Scripta Hierosolymitana 4, Jerusalem, 1958.
Rabinowitz, I., "*Pēsher/Pittārōn*. Its Biblical Meaning and its Significance in Qumran Literature," *RQ* 8 (1973), 219-232.
——, "The Qumran Author's *spr hhgw/y*," *JNES* 20 (1961), 109-14.
Rabinowitz, L. I., "Talmud, Jerusalem," *EJ* 15 (1971), 997-9.
Ran. See Nissim ben Reuben Gerondi.
Rashi. See Solomon ben Isaac.
Ratner, B., *ʾAhabat Ṣiyyon Wi-Yerushalayim*, 7 vols. (12 pts.), reprinted, Jerusalem, 1966/7.
Ratzaby, Y., "Remarks Concerning the Distinction between *Waw* and *Yodh* in the Habakkuk Scroll," *JQR* N.S. 41 (1950/1), 155-7.
Revel, B., *The Karaite Halakhah*, Philadelphia, 1913, first published in *JQR* N.S. 2 (1911-12), 517-44, 3 (1912-13), 337-96.
Richardson, H.N., "*Skt* (Amos 9:11): 'Booth' or 'Succoth'?" *JBL* 92 (1973), 375-81.
Ringgren, H., *The Faith of Qumran*, trans. E. T. Sander, Philadelphia, 1963.
Ritba. See Yom Tob ben Abraham.
Ritter, B., *Philo und die Halacha*, Leipzig, 1879.
Rosenthal, F., *A Grammar of Biblical Aramaic*, Wiesbaden, 1963.
Rosenthal, J., "*ʿAl Hishtalshelut Halakhah Be-Sefer Berit Dameseq*," *Sefer Ha-Yobel Mugash Li-Khbod Ha-Rab Shimʿon Federbush*, ed. J.L. Maimon, Jerusalem, 1960, 293-303.
Roth, C., *The Historical Background of the Dead Sea Scrolls*, Oxford, 1958.
Rowley, H.H., "The Teacher of Righteousness in the Dead Sea Scrolls," *BJRL* 40 (1957), 114-146.
Rubinstein, A., "Urban Halakhah and Camp Rules in the 'Cairo Fragments of a Damascus Covenant,'" *Sefarad* 12 (1952), 283-96.
Sachs, N., *Mishnah Zeraʿim ʿim Shinuye Nusḥaʾot*, Jerusalem, 1971.
Samuel ben Meir, *Perush Ha-Torah*, ed. D. Rosin, Breslau, 1881.
Sarna, N.M., "Bible, the Canon, Text," *EJ* 4 (1971), 816-36.
——, "The Interchange of the Prepositions *Beth* and *Min* in Biblical Hebrew," *JBL* 78 (1959), 310-316.
——, "The Order of the Books," *Studies in Jewish Bibliography, History and Literature in Honor of I. Edward Kiev*, ed. C. Berlin, New York, 1971, 407-13.
Schalit, A., "Josephus Flavius," *EJ* 10 (1971), 251-263, and biblio., 265.
Schechter, S., *Documents of Jewish Sectaries*, 2 vols. in 1, with "Prolegomenon" by J.A. Fitzmyer, New York, 1970.
Schechter, S., Taylor, C., *The Wisdom of Ben Sira*, Cambridge, 1899.
Schiffman, L.H., "The Qumran Law of Testimony," to appear in *RQ* 8:32.
Scholem, G., *Jewish Gnosticism, Merkabah Mysticism, and Talmudic Tradition*, New York, 1965.
Schürer, E., *A History of the Jewish People in the Time of Jesus Christ*, trans. S. Taylor and P. Christie, 5 vols., New York, 1891.
Segal, M.H. (M.Ṣ.), *Diqduq Leshon Ha-Mishnah*, Tel-Aviv, 1935/6.
——, "*Drš*, *Midrash, Bet Midrash*," *Tarbiẕ* 17 (1945/6), 194-6.
——, *Sefer Ben Siraʾ Ha-Shalem*, Jerusalem, 1971/2.
——, "*Sefer Berit Dameseq*," *Ha-Shiloaḥ* 26 (1912), 390-406, 483-506.
Sellers, O.R., "A Possible Old Testament Reference to the Teacher of Righteousness," *IEJ* 5 (1955), 93-95.
Shemot Rabbah, ed. Vilna, reprinted, New York, 1952 (part of edition of *Midrash Rabbah*).

Shir Ha-Shirim Rabbah, ed. Vilna, reprinted, New York, 1952 (part of edition of *Midrash Rabbah*).

Siegal, J.P., "The Employment of Palaeo-Hebrew Characters for the Divine Names at Qumran in the light of Tannaitic Sources," *HUCA* 42 (1971), 159-172.

——, *The Scribes of Qumran, Studies in the Early History of Jewish Scribal Customs, with Special Reference to the Qumran Biblical Scrolls and to the Tannaitic Traditions of MASSEKHETH SOFERIM*, Brandeis University Doctoral Dissertation, Waltham, Mass., 1972.

Sifra' De-Be Rab, ed. I.H. Weiss, Vienna, 1862.

Sifra' De-Be Rab (Torat Kohanim), with commentaries, Jerusalem, 1958/9.

Sifra or Torat Kohanim, According to Codex Assemani LXVI, with a Hebrew Introduction by L. Finkelstein, New York, 1956.

Sifre De-Be Rab, ed. M. Friedmann (Ish-Shalom), Vienna, 1863/4.

Sifre De-Be Rab (Numbers), ed. H.S. Horovitz, Jerusalem, 1966.

Sifre on Deuteronomy, ed. L. Finkelstein, reprinted, New York, 1969.

Sifre Zuta', in *Sifre De-Be Rab* (Numbers), ed. H.S. Horovitz, Jerusalem, 1966, 227-336.

Silberman, L., "The Two Messiahs of the Manual of Discipline," *VT* 5 (1955), 77-82.

Slomovic, E., "Toward an Understanding of the Exegesis in the Dead Sea Scrolls," *RQ* 7 (1969), 3-15.

Solomon Ben Isaac, *Rashi ʿal Ha-Torah*, ed. A. Berliner, reprinted, Jerusalem and New York, 1969.

Sonne, I., "Remarks on the 'Manual of Discipline' (1QS) Column VI, 6-7," *VT* 7 (1957), 405-8.

Steinglass, F., *Persian-English Dictionary*, Beirut, 1892.

Strack, H., *Introduction to the Talmud and Midrash*, New York, 1965.

Strugnell, J., "The Angelic Liturgy at Qumran—4Q *Serek Šîrôt ʿÔlat Haššabāt*," *Suppl. to VT* 7 (1960), 318-345.

Sukenik, E.L., *Megillot Genuzot*, 2 vols., Jerusalem, 1950.

——, *'Oṣar Ha-Megillot Ha-Genuzot She-Bi-Yede Ha-'Unibersiṭah Ha-ʿIbrit*, Jerusalem, 1956.

Sutcliffe, E.F., "The General Council of the Qumran Community," *Biblica* 40 (1959), 971-983.

Talmon, S., "Aspects of the Textual Transmission of the Bible in the Light of Qumran Manuscripts," *Textus* 4 (1964), 95-132.

——, "The Calendar Reckoning of the Sect from the Judaean Desert," *Aspects of the Dead Sea Scrolls*, ed. C. Rabin, Y. Yadin, Scripta Hierosolymitana 4, Jerusalem, 1958.

——, "The 'Desert Motif' in the Bible and in Qumran Literature," *Biblical Motifs*, ed. A. Altmann, Cambridge, Mass., 1966, 31-63.

——, "*Le-ʿInyan Ha-Luaḥ shel Kat Midbar Yehudah*," *Tarbiẓ* 29 (1960), 394f.

——, "*Maḥazor Ha-Berakhot shel Kat Midbar Yehudah*," *Tarbiẓ* 28 (1958/9), 1-20.

——, "The New Covenanters of Qumran," *Scientific American* 225, no. 5 (Nov., 1971), 73-81.

——, "A Note on the Dead Sea Manual of Discipline, (1QS) VI, 11-13," *JJS* 8 (1957), 113-115.

——, "The Sectarian *yḥd*—a Biblical Noun," *VT* 3 (1953), 133-40.

——, "The Three Scrolls of the Law that were Found in the Temple Court," *Textus* 2 (1962), 14-27.

Ta-Shma, I.M., "Rishonim," *EJ* 14 (1971), 192f.

Tchernowitz, Ch., *Toledot Ha-Halakhah*, 4 vols., New York, 1945-53.
Teicher, J.L., "The Dead Sea Scrolls: Documents of a Jewish Christian Sect of Ebionites," *JJS* 2 (1951), 67-99.
The Torah, (New translation by Jewish Publication Society) Philadelphia, 1962.
*Tosefta*ʾ, ed. S. Lieberman, 4 vols. have appeared, New York, 1955-73.
*Tosefta*ʾ, ed. M. Zuckermandel, reprinted, Jerusalem, 1962/3.
Tur-Sinai, N.H., *Peshuṭo shel Miqra*ʾ, 4 vols. (6 pts.), Jerusalem, 1962-7.
Urbach, E.E., *Baʿale Ha-Tosafot*, Jerusalem, 1968.
——, "*Ha-Derashah Ki-Yesod Ha-Halakhah U-Beʿayat Ha-Soferim*," *Tarbiẓ* 27 (1957/8), 166-182.
——, "Mishnah," *EJ* 12 (1971), 93-109.
Vliet, H. van, *No Single Testimony, A Study on the Adoption of the Law of Deut. 19:15 par. into the New Testament*, *Studia Theologica Rheno-Traiectina* IV, Utrecht, 1958.
Weinfield, M., "*'Ha-Berit We-Ha-Ḥesed—' Ha-Munaḥim We-Gilgule Hitpatḥutam Be-Yisrael U-Ba-ʿOlam Ha-ʿAtiq*," *Leshonenu* 36 (1972), 85-105.
——, "*Nekhar, Nokhri, Nokhriyah*," *Enc. Bib.* 5, 866f.
——, "The Origin of the Apodictic Law," *VT* 23 (1973), 63-75.
Weingreen, J., "The Title Moreh Sedek," *JSS* 6 (1961), 162-74.
Weis, P.R., "The Date of the Habakkuk Scroll," *JQR* N.S. 41 (1950/1), 125-154.
Wellhausen, J., *Prolegomena to the History of Ancient Israel*, Cleveland and New York, 1965.
Wernberg-Møller, P., *The Manual of Discipline*, Leiden, 1957.
——, "Observations on the Interchange of ʿ and *ḥ* in the Manual of Discipline (DSD)," *VT* 3 (1953), 104-5.
——, "*Ṣedeq, Ṣadiq and Ṣedaqah* in the Zadokite Fragments, the Manual of Discipline and the Habakkuk Commentary," *VT* 3 (1953), 310-15.
——, "Some Passages in the Zadokite Fragments and their Parallels in the Manual of Discipline," *JSS* 1 (1956), 110-28.
——, "*Waw* and *Yod* in the 'Rule of the Community,' " *RQ* 2 (1959-60), 223-36.
Wieder, N., "The Dead Sea Scrolls Type of Biblical Exegesis among the Karaites," *Between East and West*, ed. A. Altmann, Oxford, 1958, 75-106.
——, *Hashpaʿot ʾIslamiot ʿal Ha-Pulḥan Ha-Yehudi*, Oxford, 1957.
——, "The Idea of a Second Coming of Moses," *JQR* N.S. 46 (1955-6), 356-64 (with a postscript by S. Zeitlin, 364-6).
——, *The Judean Scrolls and Karaism*, London, 1962.
——, "The Law-Interpreter of the Sect of the Dead Sea Scrolls: The Second Moses," *JJS* 4 (1953), 158-75.
——, "Notes on the New Documents from the Fourth Cave of Qumran (4QpNah., Bless., 4QTestim.)," *JSS* 7 (1956), 71-6.
——, "The Qumran Sectaries and the Karaites," *JQR* N.S. 48 (1956/7), 97-113, 269-92.
——, "Sanctuary as a Metaphor for Scripture," *JJS* 8 (1957), 165-175.
Winter, P., "Notes on Wieder's Observations on the *Doresh Ha-Torah* in the Book of the New Covenanters of Damascus," *JQR* N.S. 45 (1954-5), 39-47.
Wolfson, H.A., *Philo*, 2 vols., Cambridge, Mass., 1968.
Wreschner, L., *Die samaritanische Tradition*, Halle, 1888.
Wurmbrand, M., "*Hilkhot Shabbat ʾeṣel Ha-Falashim*," *Sefer Urbach*, ed. A. Biram, Jerusalem, 1955, 236-243.
Yadin, Y., *Bar-Kokhba*, New York, 1971.
——, *The Ben Sira Scroll from Masada*, Jerusalem, 1965.
——, *Masada*, New York, 1966.
——, *Masada, First Season of Excavations, 1963-64*, Jerusalem, 1965.

——, *Megillat Milḥemet Bene ʾOr Bi-Bene Ḥoshekh*, Jerusalem, 1955.
——, "A Midrash on 2 Sam. vii and Ps. i-ii (4Q Florilegium)," *IEJ* 9 (1959), 95-7.
——, "Pesher Nahum (4QpNahum) Reconsidered," *IEJ* 21 (1971), 1-12.
——, *The Scroll of the War of the Sons of Light against the Sons of Darkness*, trans. B. and C. Rabin, Oxford, 1962.
——, "The Temple Scroll," *New Directions in Biblical Archaeology*, ed. D.N. Freedman, J. Greenfield, Garden City, New York, 1971, 156-166.
——, "Three Notes on the Dead Sea Scrolls," *IEJ* 6 (1956), 158-62.
Yalon, H., "*ʾAsimiliẓaṣiah shel Taw Be-ʿIbrit U-Be-ʾAramit*," *Tarbiẓ* 3 (1931/2), 99-106.
——, "*Megillat Sirkhe Ha-Yaḥad*," *Qiryat Sefer* 28 (1951/2), 65-74.
——, "*Megillat Yishaʿyahu ʾA*," *Qiryat Sefer* 27 (1950/1), 163-72.
——, *Megillot Midbar Yehudah*, Jerusalem, 1967.
——, "*Pesher Ḥabaqquq*," *Qiryat Sefer* 27 (1950/1), 172-5.
Yom Tob ben Abraham, *Ḥiddushe Ha-Ritbaʾ*, 2 vols., New York, 1961.
Zeitlin, S., "The Beginning of the Day in the Calendar of Jubilees," *JBL* 78 (1959), 153-6.
——, "History, Historians and the Dead Sea Scrolls," *JQR* N.S. 55 (1964/5), 97-116.
——, (Postscript to N. Wieder, "The Idea of a Second Coming of Moses,") *JQR* N.S. 46 (1955-6), 364-6.
——, "The Takkanot of Erubin, a Study in the Development of the Halaka," *JQR* N.S. 41 (1950/1), 351-362.
——, *The Zadokite Fragments*, *JQR* Monograph Series 1, Philadelphia, 1952.

INDEX OF CITATIONS

I. HEBREW SCRIPTURES

Genesis

1:4 84 n. 5
15:4 101 n. 115
17:14 131 n. 316
21:28f. 36 n. 92

Exodus

1:14 120 n. 241
2:5 102 n. 116
10:23 117 n. 221
12:16 106
16:5 98-99, 119, n. 230
16:23 84 n. 2, 98-99
16:25 85 n. 8
16:29 82, 91, 94-8, 101, 114 n. 198
20:8 109
20:10 106, 112
27:7 106 n. 146
31:14 88 n. 29
31:16 127
33:7 97
36:6 114
36:6 114 n. 199
40:12-15 74

Leviticus

4:3 23 n. 10
5:26 23 n. 10
10:6 82 n. 36
10:9 82 n. 36
11:32 106 n. 146
11:36 125 n. 277-8
11:43 82 n. 36
13:9 39 n. 109
13:29 39 n. 109
13:45 52 n. 206
16:2 82 n. 36
18:5 24 n. 22, 127
18:24 82 n. 36
19:3 86
19:4 82 n. 36
19:29 82 n. 36
19:31 82 n. 36
23:3 97, 123
23:27 110 n. 172
23:38 128
24:12 36
25 79 n. 16
25:4 79
25:14 82 n. 36
25:29 117 n. 221
25:36 82 n. 36

Numbers

4:37 26 n. 35
7:9 114
9:6-12 130 n. 310
11:11f. 119 n. 233
11:12 119 n. 233
11:28 65 n. 282
15:32-5 118
15:34 36
19:15 115 n. 209
21:18 57-8
23:9 22 n. 7
24:1 25 n. 25
28:10 79, 128
30:3 124 n. 267
30:4 63
30:11 22 n. 4
30:15 46 n. 157
30:17 46
31:19 107 n. 156
31:23 108 n. 157
35:2-5 91, n. 47, 94
35:4 92 n. 48, 112
35:5 92 n. 48, 112

Deuteronomy

5:12 86
5:14 106, 112
6:4 94 n. 65
13:15 54
15 79 n. 16
15:2 87 n. 21
17:6 93
17:8-13 70
17:17 30, n. 58
17:18 88 n. 26

19:14 39 n. 105
21:5 70
22:4 121 n. 248
22:19 69 n. 311
23:13 93
24:10 87 n. 21
27:9 31 n. 67
29:28 22 n. 1
31:10 65 n. 283
32:47 88 n. 26
15:2 88 n. 26
32:47 87 n. 20
33:10 70

Joshua

3:4 93, n. 56
11:15 48 n. 176

Judges

2:7-13 30 n. 60
2:13 30 n. 60
14:18 34
16:20 25 n. 25
19:28 106 n. 145
20:30f. 25 n. 25

1 Samuel

2:30 74
3:10 25 n. 25
8:10 25 n. 25
17:7 33 n. 73
19:10 69 n. 307
20:25 25 n. 25

2 Samuel

8:17 73
13:19 106 n. 145
15:24ff. 73
17:5 73
18:19 73
19:12 73
20:25 73
21:19 33 n. 73
23:5 63 n. 274

1 Kings

1:8 73
1:32 73
1:34 73
1:38 73
1:39 73
2:26-7 73
2:35 73 n. 334
4:4 73

2 Kings

12:9 58 n. 242
20:13 33 n. 73
20:14 63
22:8 31 n. 62
22:23 34
23:22 30 n. 60

Isaiah

3:20 117 n. 217
8:11 54 n. 220, 60
9:16 87 n. 20
16:3 27 n. 42
22:11 125 n. 278
28:26 49
30:7 87 n. 20
32:6 87 n. 20
34:16 54
39:2 33 n. 73
40:3 26 n. 31
41:18 24 n. 23
49:23 119 n. 233
54:16 57-8
55:6 35 n. 83
56:3 104
56:6 104
58:13 89, 90 n. 39, n. 41, 91, n. 45, 109-110, 111, n. 180

Jeremiah

2:35 89 n. 31
5:1 23 n. 8
17:13 49
17:21-22 114, n. 199, 115
32:11 30 n. 59
35:4 87 n. 18
35:14 47-8
45:3 35 n. 82
20:37 53
22:30 35 n. 83
37:23 60
43:19 74
44:6-16 73
44:10 60
44:15 75

Hosea

4:14 46 n. 155
7:15 50

Joel

1:11f. 98 n. 91

Amos

5:26-7 31
9:11 31, n. 66, 32

Micah

1:11 33 n. 73

Zephaniah

1:6 23 n. 8

Malachi

1:10 38 n. 104

Psalms

1:1 60
2:1ff. 60
8:7 26 n. 32
10:15 35 n. 83
15:2 26 n. 30
19:13 22 n. 1
45:9 108
73:7 32 n. 68
78:23 84 n. 1
89:29 50 n. 195
111:2 54
118:27 63
119:138 24 n. 21
119:144 24 n. 21

Proverbs

3:4 35 n. 84
27:5 27 n. 42

Job

2:10 87 n. 20
4:3 50
25:2 26 n. 32
27:18 114 n. 197
41:12 109 n. 162

Song of Songs

1:13 117 n. 217
3:6 108, n. 161, 109 n. 164
4:6 109 n. 164
4:14 109 n. 164

Ecclesiastes

4:10 121 n. 248

Esther

4:7 36, n. 91
6:2 34
10:2 36 n. 91

Daniel

6:3-5 61-2
9:2 33 n. 75
11:33 25 n. 24
11:39 26 n. 32
12:1 34
12:3 25 n. 24

Ezra

2:62 34
4:18 36
7:10 54
9 105
10 105

Nehemiah

7:5 34
7:64 34
8:7 25 n. 24
8:8 36-7
8:14 34
8:16 115
8:17 30 n. 60
9:14 24 n. 20
10:31-40 80 n. 25
13:1 34

1 Chronicles

5:38f. 31 n. 62
18:16 73
15:11 73
24:3 73
24:6 73
24:31 73
28:9 35 n. 83
29:22 73-4

2 Chronicles

13:22 54
15:2 35 n. 83
24:27 54
29:11 65 n. 282
29:27 128 n. 296
30:1-27 130 n. 310
33:13 33 n. 73
34 34
34:14 31 n. 62

II. QUMRAN LITERATURE

Zadokite Fragments

1:6 44 n. 140
1:10 39 n. 107
2:13 66 n. 288
3:12-16 77
3:13f. 24 n. 19
3:21ff. 75
4:4f. 66 n. 288
4:4-6 37 n. 97
4:7 66 n. 287
4:7-10 38, 43, 50
4:8 37 n. 96
4:10 39 n. 107
5:1-5 30
5:5-11 47 n. 165
5:6-11 46 n. 159
5:21-6:1 26 n. 39
6:1-11 57
6:7 56
6:11-14 129
6:13-15 38
6:14 25 n. 25, 35 n. 86, 37 n. 96, n. 98, 66 n. 287
6:15 77
6:18-20 35
7:1f. 48 n. 167
7:1-2 47
7:1-3 46
7:5 49 n. 179-81
7:5-6 50
7:6a 60, 66 n. 287
7:6-9 46, 52
7:8 49 n. 180
7:14-16 31
8:2 40 n. 114, 50 n. 193
8:5 46 n. 155
8:11 58 n. 239
9:1-8 47 n. 165
9:8 82 n. 38
9:10-12 98 n. 91
9:15 42 n. 122
9:17-22 92
10:3 48 n. 168, 169, 49 n. 178
10:4-7 52-3, 71
10:10-13 102 n. 119, 125 n. 278
10:14 45, 82
10:14-17 77, 84-87
10:14-11:18 77
10:17 107 n. 155
10:17-19 87, 111
10:18 124 n. 268
10:19-11:6 91 n. 45
10:20f. 90-1
10:21 91, 92 n. 48, 101 n. 111, 106, 112 n. 184
10:22f. 98, 101
10:23 101
11:1f. 102
11:2 104, 121
11:3f. 106
11:4f. 109
11:5 92 n. 48
11:5f. 92, 94
11:7-9 101, 113, 120
11:9 115
11:9-13 119 n. 233
11:9f. 116, 119 n. 235
11:10f. 117
11:11 117 n. 216, 119
11:12 120
11:13f. 121, 126
11:14f. 100, 105-6, 110 n. 167, 117 n. 221, 120, 123
11:15 124
11:16f. 124, n. 271
11:17f. 80 n. 25, 86, 128
11:18-12:1 80 n. 25
11:19 109 n. 165
12:3 42 n. 122, 78 n. 6
12:5 120 n. 241
12:3-6 78
12:10f. 120 n. 240
12:11 121
12:15 42 n. 122
12:19 66 n. 287
12:19-20 43
13:2 44 n. 140, 71 n. 321
13:3 72
13:4-7 42
13:5 42 n. 122
13:7 42 n. 122
14:1 50 n. 195
14:3-6 66
14:6-8 44, 53 n. 211, 71
14:7 66 n. 287
14:12 42 n. 122
14:17-19 38, 42-3
15:9-10 33
15:10-13 29
16:1f. 33
16:1-2 35
16:2-4 40

16:3 33 n. 78
16:12 42 n. 122, 45
16:13 45
19:1f. 50 n. 191
19:2-5 46
19:5 66 n. 287
19:15 60
19:19 42 n. 122
20:1 42 n. 122
20:6 56
20:6-7 58
20:9 42 n. 122
20:10 42 n. 122, 57
20:13 57
20:27-30 42
20:27-33 43 n. 129
20:31f. 43, 50-1
20:34 43 n. 129

Manual of Discipline

1:1 67 n. 295
1:3 26 n. 39
1:9 23 n. 13, 27
1:16 61, 64 n. 278
2:15 42 n. 122
2:20 62 n. 267
3:1 50, n. 188, 52
3:5-6 52
3:17 42 n. 122
3:19 27 n. 44
4:2 42 n. 122
4:4 42 n. 122
4:18 42 n. 122
4:20 42 n. 122
5:1 59, 61 n. 266
5:2 71
5:2-3 70
5:6f. 57
5:7-12 22, 57
5:8f. 70 n. 318
5:12 42 n. 122
5:15f. 71
5:23 62 n. 267, 66
6:3-4 71
6:6-8 32, 45, 47
6:8 61 n. 266
6:8-10 68
6:8-13 68
6:14 44 n. 139
6:15 45 n. 147
6:21-23 67
6:22f. 45 n. 147
6:24 45, 59
6:24-7:25 88 n. 28
6:25 28 n. 48
7:2 67
7:9 88, n. 27
7:10-12 69
7:11 68
8:1-2 28
8:1-16 28
8:11 35
8:11f. 28, 32, 57
8:15 25 n. 25
8:15-16 59
8:17 48 n. 171
8:17f. 48
8:18 45 n. 150
8:19 42 n. 122, 67
8:20 45
8:24 42 n. 125, 45
8:24f. 45
8:25f. 58
9:2 67
9:5 42 n. 122
9:7 70-1
9:10f. 43 n. 131, 51
9:13-14 25
9:13f. 35 n. 84
9:17 27
9:18-20 26, 33 n. 79
9:19f. 35 n. 84
10:10 85
10:14 85
10:22 87 n. 20, 88 n. 27

Habakuk Commentary (*Pesher*)

11:8 79 n. 18

Thanksgiving Scroll (*Hodayot*)

5:11 27 n. 42

War Scroll

2:1 128 n. 299
2:1-2 65
2:2 128 n. 299
2:4 78
2:4f. 78
2:6 65
2:8f. 79
3:3 53 n. 216
3:12 53 n. 216
4:6 65
5:4 62 n. 267

7:1 62 n. 267
7:6f. 93
9:10 61 n. 266
10:10 25 n. 24
15:5 67 n. 295
19:9 79 n. 18

Manual of Benedictions

3:22-5 72

Rule of the Community (*Serekh Ha-ʿEdah*)

1:1 61 n. 266

Liturgies

4Q Sl 39 I i:22 128 n. 299

III. APOCRYPHA AND PSEUDEPIGRAPHA

2 (4) Esdras

14:6 28 n. 45

Judith

8:6 110

Ben Sira

40:29 49
51:23 54-5

1 Maccabees

2:22-28 119 n. 232
2:29-41 127 n. 290
4:46 51 n. 201
6:49 80 n. 22
6:53 80 n. 22
14:41 51 n. 201

2 Maccabees

5:25ff. 127 n. 290
8:25-28 107 n. 156
12:38 107, n. 156

Enoch

72:2ff. 84 n. 1

Jubilees

2:29 98, 103
2:29-30 114
31:1 108 n. 159
45:16 11
50:3ff. 79 n. 20
50:8 89, 98, 103 n. 130, 114, 125
50:9-10 111
50:10 129
50:11 129
50:12 94, 110, 113
50:12f. 79 n. 20

Psalms of Solomon

3:4 50

IV. PHILO AND JOSEPHUS

Every Good Man

79 121 n. 246

Life of Moses II

220 118 n. 226

Special Laws II

66-68 121 n. 244
251 118 n. 226

On Dreams II

123-28 127 n. 293

Antiquities

3, 10:4 115
12, 1:1 125 n. 272
13, 8:1 80 n. 23
13, 8:14 95 n. 71
13, 10:6 51 n. 203
13, 10:12 95 n. 71
16, 6:2 86
18, 1:5 129

Wars

1, 2:4 80 n. 23

2, 8:9	93 n. 58, 95 n. 69, 97 n. 83, 99 n. 98, 118, 135 n. 6
2, 16:4	125 n. 272
2:122	62
2:166	62
4, 9:12	87

Apion

125 n. 272

V. NEW TESTAMENT

Matthew

12:11	122

Luke

1:8	64 n. 277
14:5	122

John

18:28	107 n. 152

Acts

1:12	96
10:28	107 n. 152

Hebrews

5:6, 5:10, 6:20, 7:11, 7:17, 7:21	64 n. 277

VI. RABBINIC LITERATURE

A. *Mishnah*

Berakhot

6:6	109 n. 162

Bikkurim

3:2	88 n. 25

Shabbat

1:1	113-14, n. 196
1:3	81
1:4	69
1:7	123
1:7-9	106 n. 141
3:4	98 n. 94
5	112
6:3	117 n. 218
6:5	117 n. 219
7:2	82, 98 n. 93
10:5	127 n. 295
11:4	103
16:6	105 n. 140, 121 n. 245, 124 n. 264
16:8	124 n. 264
17	117 n. 220
18:2	112 n. 186, 119 n. 236
18:3	122 n. 249, 127 n. 288
21:1	119 n. 236
22:3	116 n. 211
23:1	88
23:1-3	89 n. 36
23:3	90
24:4	98 n. 92

ʿErubin

3:2	97 n. 80
4:8	92 n. 47
5:1	94 n. 61
6:1	97 n. 80
8:6-8	103 n. 128
10:6	103

Pesaḥim

3:7	124 n. 265

Yomaʾ

6:4-5	95

Beṣah

2:2	102
3:4	98 n. 92
5:2	48, 89
5:3	92, 112 n. 184

Rosh Ha-Shanah

2:5	96
2:9	66 n. 288

Taʿanit

4:2 78 n. 11

Megillah

4:3 72 n. 324

Ḥagigah

1:8 24

Nedarim

3:10 97 n. 79
9:6 110

Sotah

3:4 40 n. 111
5:3 91 n. 47, 92

Giṭṭin

3:8 98 n. 91

Sanhedrin

1:3 72 n. 324
3:1 72 n. 325
4:2 66 n. 290
7:5 37 n. 94

ʾAbot

1:1 56
2:14 33 n. 74

Tamid

7:4 79 n. 18

Kelim

12:5 116 n. 210

Negaʿim

3:1 39-40 n. 111

Parah

1:1 37

B. *Tosefta*

Berakhot

6:2 35 n. 82

Shabbat

1:16 69 n. 305
1:21 106 n. 141
1:22 106 n. 141
1:23 109 n. 162
4(5) 112 n. 185
4(5):11 117 n. 218
5(6):3-5 117 n. 219
7(8):5-7 89 n. 36
7(8):10-13 90
8(9):18 120 n. 237-8
14(15):1 118
14(15):3 122
15(16):1 112 n. 186
15(16):2 122 n. 250
16(17):13 116 n. 213
17(18):12 112 n. 184

ʿErubin

3(4):5 125
3(4):11 101 n. 112
4(6):1-8 94 n. 61

Pesaḥim

4:13 129 n. 302
4:14 129 n. 302

Kippurim

3(4):13 96

Sukkah

4:11 86
4:12 87

Rosh Ha-Shanah

1:18(2:3) 66 n. 288

Taʿanit

3(4):3 78 n. 11

Sanhedrin

5:2 120 n. 241

Makkot

5(4):15 32 n. 73

Kelim, Babaʾ Qammaʾ

4:20 115 n. 210

ʾOhalot

17:9 117 n. 221

Zabim

2:1 107 n. 152

C. *Palestinian Talmud*

Berakhot

4:1(7c) 84 n. 1
9:2(13c) 35 n. 82

Shebiʿit

1:1(33a) 84, n. 4
8:4(38a) 89
9:1(38d) 98 n. 91

Shabbat

1:5(3d) 109 n. 162

ʿErubin

3:3(21a) 116 n. 211
4:1(21d) 94 n. 64, 101 n. 112

Pesaḥim

4:1(30d) 123 n. 260
6:1(33a) 129 n. 302

Sheqalim

4:2(48a) 29 n. 51

Yomaʾ

8:1(40d) 104

Beṣah

2:2(61b) 102 n. 122
3:4(62a) 122 n. 252

Taʿanit

3:2 110 n. 174
3:11(67a) 110 n. 174
4:2(68a) 34, n. 81

Nedarim

8:1(40d) 110 n. 174

Sotah

3:4(19a) 40 n. 111

Giṭṭin

3:8(45a) 98 n. 91

Qiddushin

4:5(66a) 72 n. 325

Shebuʿot

1:1(32a) 114 n. 199
1:5(33b) 31 n. 67

D. *Babylonian Talmud*

Berakhot

26b 86 n. 15
58a 35 n. 82

Shabbat

2a 114 n. 198
11a 110 n. 173
18a 109 n. 162
38a 98 n. 94
46a 118
50a 118 n. 224
50b 106 n. 150
73b 117 n. 221
74b 98 n. 93
96b 114 n. 199
114b 99 n. 96
117b-119a 111 n. 181
119a 108 n. 159, 109
123b 118 n. 228
128b 112 n. 186, 122 n. 250-3
132a 130 n. 312
134b-135a 130 n. 312
141b 120 n. 238
142a 120 n. 238
146a 116 n. 212
150a 105 n. 140
150a, b 89 n. 36

ʿErubin

30a 96
31b 97 n. 80
35a 118 n. 223

38b 91
38b, 39a 91 n. 44
48a 101 n. 112
51a 94, 124 n. 265
65a 29
65b 124 n. 264

Pesaḥim

47b 119 n. 229
50b 86, n. 15
51a 123 n. 260
56b 98 n. 92
66a 129 n. 302
105a 110 n. 173

Yoma'

30a 61
66b 120 n. 238
81a, b 84 n. 3
84b 127 n. 292
85b 127 n. 288-9

Beṣah

6b 98 n. 92
8a 118
12a 118
18a, b 102
32a 33 n. 73
33b 116 n. 211

Rosh Ha-Shanah

9a 84 n. 4
12b 65 n. 283
16b 102 n. 121, 107 n. 156
19a 110 n. 173, 111 n. 179

Ta'anit

12b 110 n. 173
17b 110 n. 173, 111 n. 179

Megillah

6b 35 n. 82

Ketubot

60a 36 n. 93
106a 29 n. 51

Sotah

21b 40 n. 111
36b 26 n. 32

Giṭṭin

60b 30 n. 59

Baba' Qamma'

82a 108 n. 159

Sanhedrin

25b 120 n. 241
30a 78 n. 7
74a 127 n. 288
87a 37 n. 98
103a 33 n. 73

Horayot

4a 114 n. 200

Ḥullin

14a 98 n. 92
106b 63

Niddah

34a 107 n. 152
57a 97 n. 80
67b 63

E. *Minor Tractates*

Mas. Soferim

6:4 34 n. 81

F. *Targumim*

Jonathan

Gen. 17:1 39 n. 107
Ex. 16:5 99 n. 95
16:23 99 n. 95
16:29 94 n. 64, 101 n. 112
Lev. 18:5 24 n. 22
25:27 40 n. 115

25:50 40 n. 115
25:52 40 n. 115
27:18 40 n. 115
27:23 40 n. 115
Num. 2:3 66 n. 288
11:12 119 n. 233
19:15 115 n. 209
31:23 108
Deut. 1:15 64 n. 279
20:5 64 n. 279
31:10 65 n. 283

Onkelos

Gen. 17:1 39 n. 107
33:18 39 n. 107
Ex. 12:5 39 n. 107
Num. 19:15 115 n. 209
Deut. 1:15 64 n. 279
8:5 49 n. 187
20:5 64 n. 279

Fragmentary Palestinian

Num. 11:12 119 n. 233
19:15 115 n. 209

Neofiti

Gen. 6:4 66 n. 288

Targum

Is. 9:16 87 n. 20
32:6 87 n. 20
58:9 90
Ezek. 4:12 108 n. 158
4:15 108 n. 158
Pr. 6:7 64 n. 279
Ruth 1:16 96 n. 78

G. *Midrashim*

Mekhilta' De-Rabbi Ishmael

Pisḥa' 9 105 n. 140, 108 n. 159
Yitro 7 86 n. 11
Ki Tisa' 127 n. 288

Mekhilta De-Rabbi Shim'on b. Yoḥai

12:16 108 n. 159
20:8 86 n. 11, 108 n. 159, 109

Sifra'

Ṣaw 17:6 110 n. 168
18:2 110 n. 168
Shemini 4:9 107 n. 156
Tazria' 1:9 39-40 n. 111
Zabim 1 to Lev. 15:2 107 n. 152
'Emor (8)12:4 108 n. 159
14:7-9 84 n. 3
15:5 129 n. 304
18:9 110 n. 168

Sifre Numbers

147 108 n. 159

Sifre Deuteronomy

87 28 n. 45

Midrash Tannaim

5:12 86 n. 11
33:27 34 n. 81

Bereshit Rabbah

1:1 119 n. 233
9:5 34 n. 81

Wa-Yiqra' Rabbah

34:16 91 n. 44

Be-Midbar Rabbah

2:9 93 n. 56

Shir Ha-Shirim Rabbah

3:7 29 n. 51

Midrash Tanḥuma

Be-Midbar 9 93 n. 56

Midrash Tanḥuma Ed. S. Buber

Be-Midbar 4bf. 93 n. 56

Pesiqta' Rabbati

14 37 n. 95

INDEX OF HEBREW AND ARAMAIC TERMS EXPLAINED

(NUMBERS IN PARENTHESES INDICATE NOTES)

אבד, 98 (91)
אובד בשדה, 100
אומן, 119 (233), 120
און, ע׳ דבר און.
אין, 81
איש, 81, 115
איש הדורש, 28 (49), 32, 35, 57, 76
אל, 80–82
אלף, 94
אלפים, 94, 112 (184)
אם, 81 (35)
אמר, 46
אסמכתא, 17
אפיקורס(ים), 126
את, 44 (139)
בדיעבד, 127
בוא, 106 (146), 113 (196), 120
בית דין, 69
בית התורה, 57
בית מדרש, 54–57, 69
בית מושב, 117 (221)
בן (ה)נכר, 104 (135), 105 (139), ע׳ נכרי.
בני צדוק, 31 (62), 60, 70–76
בעל קרי, 102
בצע, 87 (24)
בקר, ע׳ מבקר, מבקרי מומין.
בראשונה, 51, ע׳ ראשון.
ברר, 72 (325)
גוי(ם), 105 (139)
גלה, 26 (39), 30 (59), ע׳ נגלה (נגלות).
דבר, 44 (143), 88 (26)
דבר און, 90
דבר דבר, 89–90
דברי תורה, 111 (179)
דרבנן, 102
דורש התורה, 56–57 (235), 58, 72 (326)
דקדק, ע׳ מדוקדק.
דרש, 54–58 (239), ע׳ איש הדורש, דורש התורה, מדרש.
דרש משפט, 33, 45, 47, 56
הון, 87 (23)
הוצאה, 119 (234)
היקש, 18, 79 (21)
הכנה, 99, 103, ע׳ מוכן.
הכנסה, 113 (196)

המשפטים הראשונים, 43 (130), 50–52
זונות, 46 (155)
זכר, 86
זנות, 46 (155)
זקף, 70
חוק, 61, ע׳ מחוקק.
חפצך, 90
חתם, 30 (59)
טהרה, 45 (149)
טוח, ע׳ כלי טוח.
טלטל, 118 (225), 119 (234)
יום השבת, 87 (19)
יחד, 22 (3), 59 (248)
יסור(ים), 46 (160), 49–50, 52–53
יסר, 43, 49–51, 53–54 (220), ע׳ מוסר.
יצא, 113 (196), ע׳ הוצאה, לצאת ולבוא.
ישיבה, 69
כאשר אמר, 46
כון, ע׳ הכנה, מוכן.
כלי(ם), 115 (209, 210), 116 (213), 118 (225)
כלי טוח, 115–116 (209–210)
כנס, ע׳ הכנסה.
כתוב על ספר, 40 (116)
לדרוש משפט, ע׳ דרש משפט.
לכתחילה, 127–128
לצאת ולבוא, 120
לקח על, 106 (145)
לקירויו, 102 (122)
לא, 80–82
מבקר, 29 (51)
מבקרי מומין, 29 (51)
מגופה, 115–116 (209–210)
מגרש, 91 (47), 92
מדוקדק, 33 (78), 35, 40 (116), 41
מדרש, 3, 19, 42, 45 (153), 54–60, 76, 91, ע׳ בית מדרש.
מדרש הלכה, 18–19, 60 (254), 86, 91, 101, 125, 128, 129 (303), 135
מדרש התורה, 24, 56, 58
מוכן, 98–100
מוסר, 49
מועדי תעודותם, 27 (41)
מוקצה, 52 (205), 112 (187), 113, 117

סרך התורה, 66 (287)
סרכא (סרכין), 61, 64, 67
סתר, 27 (42), 28 (45), ע׳ נסתר(ות).
עבד כנעני, 121, 123
עולה, 128–129, 131
עולת שבת בשבתו, 79
על, 128 (300)
עלף (עליפות), 32–33 (73)
עמד, 70
ענש, 69 (311)
עצת רשעים, 60
ערב, 109–110 (167)
ערוב(ין), 103, 109 (167), 132–133
ערוב חצרות, 115
ערוב תחומין, 94, 97
עת בעת, 44
פורייתא, 115 (209)
פטר, 69 (307)
פיקוח נפש, 124–127 (271–272)
פקיד, 44, 71
פרוש, 3, 36–42, 65–66 (287), 76–77, 89, 91
פרוש המשפטים, 43
פרוש התורה, 36–37, 43, 51, 66 (287)
פרוש מעשיהם, 36
פרוש שמותם, 36, 65–66 (288)
פרנסה, 122
פרש, 36–38 (100), 66 (288), ע׳ פרוש.
פרשת הכסף, 36
פשר, 41, 54, 60, 75
פתה, 29 (52)
פתי, 39–40 (111)
פתר, 69 (307)
צוה, 48, ע׳ מצוה.
צורך הבורא, 97
קהל, 78
קלקל, 98 (91)
קץ, 40 (114)
ראשון, 43 (130), 51–52, ע׳ משנה ראשונה.
ראשונים, 16–17
רב חילא, 67
רוב אנשי בריתם, 73
רוח, 47 (162)
רוח הקדש, 26 (38), 27 (41)
רשות הרבים, 101
רבים, 68, ע׳ מושב הרבים, רשות הרבים.
שכל, 25 (24), 26, 35, ע׳ משכיל.
שֵׂכֶל, 25 (24), 26, 35 (84), 41, 47 (163)
שבת מנוח, 79 (18)
שבת שבתון, 79
שוטה, 39–40 (111)

(220), 118–119 (231, 234, 236), 126–128, 132
מושב הרבים, 5, 38 (101), 45 (150, 153), 67–71, 76
מחוקק, 58
מיל, 95
מלאכה, 86 (16), 87, 88 (29), 103, 105 (140), 106
מנוח, 79 (18)
מנחה, 86–87
מנחה קטנה, 86 (15)
מסורות, 53–54
מצא, 34, 35 (82, 84, 87), 58, ע׳ נמצא.
מצא כתוב בספר, 34
מצאת, 36
מצוה, 42, 47–50 (195)
מקוה, 125 (278)
מקום מושבת, 117 (221)
מקום מחולל, 117 (221)
מקמו, 91, 94 (64), 95–97, 101
מקרא קדש, 97
מרא, 120 (241)
משכיל, 6, 25 (24), 43, 47, 59, 72, 76
משנה ראשונה, 52
משפט(ים), 29 (53), 38, 42–47 (147, 156), 49–51, 56, 68, ע׳ המשפטים הראשונים.
משפטי התורה, 44, 53 (211)
מתקן כלי, 116 (213)
נבל, 87 (20), 88 (27), 90
נכרי, 105 (139), ע׳ בן (ה)נכר.
נגלה (נגלות), 22–32 (9, 40), 44, 47, 59, 75–76
נגע, 39
נטל, 118 (225), 119 (236)
נמצא, 26 (32), 33–35, 41, 58 (239)
נסתר(ות), 22–25 (9, 19), 27–29, 32, 41, 45, 47, 57–58, 75–77
נשה, 87 (21)
סוכה, 114 (197), 115
סופר(ים), 55
סורך, 65
סורכי המחנות, 64
סירכא, 62
סכות, 31–32 (67)
סמנים, 116–117
ספק, 100
ספק דאורייתא לחומרא, 100
ספר, 33 (45), 34, 40 (116), 55, 67
ספר ההגו, 25 (26), 44, 53, 72
ספר משה, 34
ספר סרך, 67 (295)
סרך, 5, 41, 43, 53, 59–68 (287), 76–77, 82

תחום גזר, 96
תחום שבת, 91, 95, 98, 132
תחתיו, 91, 94 (64), 97, 101
תעודה, ע׳ מועדי תעודותם.

שופט, 64
שוטר, 64
שמר, 84, 86
שער, 84
תוספת מלאכה, 84-86 (1)
תורה, 39 (109), 70, ע׳ דורש התורה,
מדרש התורה, פרוש התורה.

GENERAL INDEX

Aaron ben Elijah, 126 n. 285
Aaron ben Joseph, 130
Abiathar, 73 n. 334
Ablutions. See "Cleansing, ritual."
Absalom, 73
Absence from the assembly, 69
Accidental transgression, 78
Achaemenid bureaucracy, 67
Acre, 123 n. 260
Adonijah, 73
Agriculture, laws of, 5
Ahimaaz, 73
R. Akiba, 82-3, 116 n. 214
Akkadian, 63
Alexandria, 12
Amoraim, amoraic traditions, 14-17, 37, 65, 69, 94, 99 n. 96, 105 n. 140, 110 n. 173, 111, 114, n. 201, 116 n. 211, 118, 122, n. 251, 130 n. 312
Anan ben David, 18, 97, 99, 114, 115, 123, 130, 131, n. 315
Angelic Liturgy. See: "4Q Serekh."
Anointing, 74.
Apocrypha, 10-11, 19.
Arabic, 63, 97, 120 n. 241.
Aramaic, 39 n. 107, 40 n. 115, 41, 52 n. 207, 53 n. 218, 54, 62, 64, 67, 108 n. 158, 109 n. 167, 120 n. 241
Ark of the covenant, 30
R. Ashi, 116 n. 211
Assyrian, 36, n. 90
Attributes of God, 65
Augustus, 86
Avestan, 62

Babylonians, 108 n. 157
*Baraita*ʾ, *baraitot*, 14-16, 86, 91, n. 44, 94, 96, 99 n. 96, 109 n. 162, 110, 130 n. 312
Baruch, Ethiopic Apocalypse of (Fifth Baruch), 113
Bashyatchi, Eliezer, 86, 126 n. 285
Bath, ritual, 102 n. 116, 125 n. 278
  See also: "Sabbath activities: purity and purification."
Ben Sira, 55-7, 74
Bene Bathyra, 129 n. 303
Benedictions, recitation at Qumran, 33
Bet ha-teqiʿah. See: "Trumpet."
Bible, 9-10
  study of, 32-3, 47, 56, 76
Boethusians, 18
Book of the Divisions of the Times into their Jubilees and Sabbatical Cycles, 40-1
Books, preservation of, 70
Boundary stones, 96
Buildings (at Qumran), 56-7
Burnt-offering. See: "Offering, burnt-."

Caesarea, school of, 114 n. 199
Calendar, Israelite, 84 n. 5
  lunar, 10
  Sadducean, 10
  sectarian, 27, 40 n. 112, 77, 79, 84, 111, 129
  solar, 8, 10, 84-5, 131, 136
Camp, purity of, 94
Canon, sectarian, 40-1
Celibacy, 135 n. 3
Chiasm, 28 n. 46
Christians, 1-2, 107 n. 156, 113
Chronicler, Chronicles, 55-6, 74
Circumcision (for conversion), 104, 105 n. 137, 121 n. 243
Citizen, rights of, 6
City limits, 91, 94, 96, 101
Cleansing, ritual, 102
Clothes, storage of, 109
Codification, Jewish, history of, 130
Communal organization, 5
  use and communal ownership. See: "Property, private."
Confession, 42
Confusion of initial *yod* and *mem* verbs, 36 n. 87, 49, 58
  of *yod* and *ʾalef*, 54 n. 220
Conscription, laws of, 7
Converts, religious conversion, 104, n. 136, 105, n. 137, 120, 121, 123
Council of the Community, 28
Court, sectarian, 69, 71, 76, 89
Courts, Jewish, in Alexandria, 12
  of ten, 72 n. 324
Covenant, 22, 24, 36, 39, 50, 72-3, 77
Cult, description of restored, 78, 129
  Jerusalem, 29, 38, 40, 75, 77-9, 128-9.

See: "Priests and Priesthood, Second Temple."
laws of, 7, 8, 12, 78, 80 n. 25, 128-9, 130-1. See: "Sacrifices," "Offering."

Dagon, 80
Daniel, 34, 74
David, 73-4
Day of Atonement, 79 n. 18, 95, 108 n. 159, 109, 110 n. 172, 111
Death penalty, 78, 89, 110 n. 172, 115
Deodorizing a room, 109
Destruction, period of, 96
Diseases, laws of, 5
See also: "Plague."
Disputes, settlement of, 68
Domain, private, 103, 112, 115
public, 94 n. 64, 101, 103, 112, n. 182, 115, 119, 128 n. 295
Dositheans, 1
Dual-Torah concept, 76

Eighteen decrees, 69, 80 n. 25
Elders, 68
Elect of Israel, 60
Elephantine, 67, 97
Eli, 74
R. Eliezer b. Yose Ha-Gelili, 92
Enoch, 10, 84 n. 1
Equinoxes, 86 n. 14
Eschatology, biblical, 74
sectarian, 5-7, 26 n. 31, 60, 68, 75, 79, 93
See also: "Messiah."
Essenes, 1, 62, 93-4, 95 n. 69, 97, 99, 118, 121, 129, 135-6
Eternal life, 24 n. 22, 50
Ethiopic, 61
Examination of sectarian, 29
Examiner, 39
Excision, 88 n. 29
Exegesis, "aggadic", 31, 41, 57, 60
basis of *halakhah*, 33, 75-6
halakhic, 8, 19, 60, 135
Karaite, 18, 24, 135
midrashic, 55
perush, 89, 91, 99, 106, 109, 110
of Philo and Josephus, 13
sectarian, 9, 17, 24, 31, 33, 35-41, 43, 45, 47-9, 51, 53, 54, 56-9, 71-2, 75, 76, n. 347, 89, 111-12, 128
Ezekiel, 74-5

Ezra, 18, 19, 37, 80 n. 25, 104-5, 108 n. 159

Falashas, Falasha *halakhah*, 19, 78 n. 5, 85-6, 88 n. 27, 95, n. 69, n. 70, 99, 103, 107, 110, n. 172, 113, 115, 120 n. 241, 125, 127
Fast days, 35
Festivals, 24, 35, 77, 98, 106, 108, n. 159, 111, n. 179, 122
aiding in delivering a domesticated animal, 122
delivering a domesticated animal, 121-22
laws of, 8
offerings of, 8
ritual purity, 102 n. 121, 107 n. 156
Fines, 69, 90
First Temple period, 74-5
Fluxes, laws of, 5
Form-criticism, 3
Fornication, 46
4Q Serekh Shirot ʿOlat Ha-Shabbat, 78
Frankincense, 107-9, 129
Fratarak, 67

R. Gamliel I, 96
Genizah, Cairo, 4, 134
Gentiles, city of, 97
Geonim, 16
Gezer, 92 n. 47, 96
Greek, 53, 54, 60-2, 87 n. 18, 122 n. 254
taxis, *tasso*, *tagma*, 60-2, 62 n. 268, 63-4

Hadassi, J. (*ʾEshkol Ha-Kofer*), 18, 98, 99 n. 100, 103, 107 n. 156, 114, 116, 126 n. 285, 131
Hai Gaon, 16 n. 70
Halakhah. See: "Law."
Hasmonean period, 11
Hasmoneans, 75, 127
Hebrew, amoraic, 37
biblical, 27 n. 42, n. 44, 36 n. 87, 40 n. 116, 47, 49, 56, 69 n. 307, 311, 80-1, 87 n. 20, n. 21, 105 n. 139, 117 n. 221, 120 n. 242, 128 n. 300
late, 34
Mishnaic, 35 n. 87, 49, 53 n. 218, 81, 105 n. 139
Qumran, 11 n. 50, 27 n. 42, n. 44, 30 n. 60, 31 n. 61, 32 n. 73, 43, 46 n. 155, 49, 51, 52 n. 207, 54-5, 87 n. 21, n. 23, 105 n. 139, 109 n.

167, 110 n. 168, 116 n. 210, 120 n. 241, n. 242
See also: "Chaism," "Confusion of . . .," "Interchange of . . .," "*Lameds*, chain of," "Pun," "Synonymous variants," "Synonyms in construct," "Vowel assimilation."
Rabbinic, 44 n. 143, 48, 55, 60, 105 n. 139, 114 n. 196, 125 n. 278, 128 n. 300
Talmudic, 61-2
tannaitic, 37, n. 98, 51, 55, 57, 69, n. 307, 98, 117 n. 220, 118 n. 225
Hekhalot literature, 79
Hellenistic period, 104, 111 n. 177
Hermeneutics, 92
Herodian period, 96
Temple, 8, 14 n. 64, 87 n. 18
Herodotus, 108 n. 157
Hilkiah the Zadokite, 31, n. 62
Hillel, Hillelites, 20, 34, 96, 102, 103 n. 124, 106, 129
Hippolytus, 97
R. Ḥizkiah, 114 n. 199
Holy and profane, 43
Homer, 35
Hours, length of, 86 n. 14
R. Huna, 99 n. 96

Immersion, 104. See: "Sabbath: Activities: Purity and Purification: ritual immersion."
Immortality of soul, 10
Impurity, avoidance of, 132
and diseases, 70
Incense, burning of, 109 n. 162
Interchange of *bet* and *mem* (as prepositions), 27 n. 44, 32 n. 72, 69 n. 307, 107
of final *ʾalef* and *heʾ*, 120 n. 241
of *qoṣer* and *qeṣor*, 120 n. 242
of *ʿayin* and *ḥet*, 32 n. 73
Islam, 17

J Document, 82
Jepeth ben Ali, 130
Jerusalem, sanctity of, 80 n. 25, 93
John Hyrcanus, 80
Josephus, 12-13, 18, 51, 62, 86, 87, n. 18, 93, 95, 97, 99, 110, 135
Josiah, 31
Jubilees, 8, 10, 11, 19, 40-1, 78, n. 5, 89, 95, 99, 103, 111, 135
found at Qumran, 11 n. 50, 40
Judah, 107 n. 156
R. Judah, 116, n. 213
R. Judah b. ʾIlʿai, 116 n. 214
Judaism, post-biblical, 20, 120
Rabbinic, 2, 17, 20
"Judges of the Congregation", 71-2
Judgment, biblical, 70
sectarian, 51, 58-9, 68, 72
Judith, 10

Karaites, 1, 2, 17, 18, 24, 32, 47, 85, 86, 97, 98, n. 90, 99, 101, 103, 109-10, n. 167, 111, 114, 116, 117 n. 221, 123, 126, 129 n. 304, 130, 134-5
Karet. See: "Excision."
King, statutes of, 8

Lameds, chain of, 46 n. 154, 77
Latin, 64
Latrines, 93-4, 95 n. 69
Law, apodictic, 80-81, 82, n. 36
Babylonian Jewish, 13
biblical, 2, 9, 81, 105 n. 140, 119, 127
books of, 31
casuistic, 80, 81 n. 35
enactment of, 68, 70 n. 318, 72
expounder of, 28, 57
expounding of, 32-3
Hellenistic, 11-12
Jewish, history of, 19-21
Levitical, 75 n. 345
Mesopotamian, 13, n. 61
Mishnaic, 81, 103
older, 116
Palestinian Jewish, 11, 12, 13 n. 61, 112 n. 187, 113
progressive change, 26-7, 44, 75
prophetic derivation, 114
publication of new, 69, 76
Roman, 12
sectarian, to be kept secret, 27, 29, 76
tannaitic. See: "Tannaim."
tannaitic and Philo, 11-12
teaching of, 72 n. 332, 73, 76
See also: "Written Law," "Oral Law."
Leaders, sectarian, 82
Legal fictions, 132-33
Legal methodology, Rabbinic, 128
Levites, 64, 66-7, 72, 75

Levitical cities, boundaries of, 91, 96
Library at Qumran, 40, 83
Lying, 88 n. 27

Maccabean revolt, 75, 107 n. 156, 125 n. 272, 127
Magic, prohibition of, 5
Magribi, Samuel al-, 130
Maimonides, 99 n. 100, 130 n. 306
R. Mana, 99 n. 96
Manasseh, 31
Manna, 96
Manual of Discipline (DSD), 5-7, 25 n. 28, 47-9, 51, 61, 69 n. 307, 85 n. 7, 90
Marriage, laws of, 5, 46-7
Masada, 49
Maskil, *berakhah*, 72
  requirements of, 25, 43, 47
Massoretic text, 11, n. 50, 26 n. 31
Medieval traditions, 130-1
Megillat Ha-Serekhim. See: "*Manual of Discipline*," "*Rule of the Community*," "*Rule Scroll*."
Meir ben Baruch Ha-Levi, 16 n. 70
*Memar Marqa*ʾ, 17
"Men of iniquity", 23-4, 27
"Men of Jericho", 100
Messiah, Messianic era, 51
  of Aaron and Israel, 6
  two-Messiah concept, 51 n. 202
    See also: "Eschatology."
Midrashic order, 82
Midrashim, tannaitic, 14
Military laws, equipment, organization, army, 7, 8, 44 n. 141
  terminology, 61-8
Mishawites, 85
Mishnah, 14, 15, 82, 96, 130 n. 306
Mnemonic, 82, 91 n. 45, 119 n. 233
Monarchy, period of, 54
Mount of Olives, 96
Mustering, 44, n. 141, 66-7

Nabatean, 29 n. 51
Nahawandi, Benjamin al-, 97, 99, 130
R. Naḥman, 122 n. 251
Nehemiah, 19, 37, 118 n. 228, 125
New moon, 108 n. 159
New Testament, 122
Nicanor, 107 n. 156
Ninth of Ab, 104
Nome, 67

Oaths and vows, 5
Offering, burnt-, 128
  for conversion, 104
  daily, 65, 128, n. 299, 129, 131, n. 315
  festival, 129 n. 304
  freewill, 45
  sin, 117
Omer period, date of, 8
Oral Law, 2, 12, 18, 20, 22, 28 n. 45, 32, 40, 41, 48, 55-6, 76, 134, 136
  See also: "Dual-Torah concept."
Oral transmission, 20, 75

Pahlavi, 63
Parapet stone of Herodian Temple, 87, n. 18
Passover, 8, 129-31
  Second, 130 n. 310
P Document. See: "Priests and Priesthood, Writings."
Penalties, 45, 51, 58, 78, 88, n. 27-9
  See: "Death penalty," "Violation of commandments," "Fines."
Perfume bottles, 116-7, n. 217
"Period of evil", 33, 38
  of wickedness", 75, 78
Persepolis texts, 62
Persian, 63, 106 n. 147
Persian period, 67
R. Petaḥiah of Regensburg, 98
Pharisaic-rabbinic tradition, 21
Pharisees, Pharisaism, 1, 10, 14, 21 n. 81, 51, 133, 135-6
Philo Judaeus, 11-12, 89, 118-21, 127, 135
Plague, 39
Pottery vessels, sealing of, 115
Prayers, sequence of daily, 85
  and thanksgivings, laws of, 7
Priests and Priesthood, Aaronides, 70, 75
  biblical, 70, 73-4, 75 n. 345
  chiefs, 65
  courses, 79
  eternal, 74
  Falasha, 95
  high, 75
  Qumran, 22, 38-9, 44, 65, 67, 70-2, n. 332, 76, 82, 107 n. 156, 109
    See: "Priests and Priesthood, Aaronides," "Zadok."
  Second Temple, 75, 78
  Schools, 82, 110 n. 168

Writings (P), 70, 73-5, 82, 83 n. 40, 128 n. 300
See also: "Zadokites."
Prince, 6, 30
Property cases, 68, 70
Property, private, 90, 110, n. 169, 115
Proselyte, semi-proselyte. See: "Convert, religious conversion."
Pseudepigrapha, 10-11, 19
Pun, 31, n. 67, 32, 72 n. 333
Punishment after death, 113
Purity and purification, ritual, 5, 8, 40, 44, 45 n. 149, 102, 107 n. 156, 108 n. 157, 125 n. 278, 129
after sexual intercourse, 108 n. 157
after shedding of blood, 107 n. 156
of the camp, 94
cultic, 5
festivals, 102 n. 121
items touched by a non-Jew, 107
military, 7
pure and impure, 43
See also: "Impurity," "Sabbath-purity and purification."

Qirqisani, 97, 130
Quinta, 128 n. 297
Qumīsī, Daniel al-, 24, n. 17, 130

Rabbis, Rabbinic traditions, law, literature, 11, 13-18, 21 n. 81, 58, 78, 85-6, 88-9, 93-5, 98, 101-2, 105 n. 140, 108, n. 157, 110, n. 173, 111-119, 122-4, 126-7, 130-1, 134
See also: "Tannaim," "Amoraim."
Rank, 47 n. 162, 58
Rations, 69 n. 311
Rekabites, 47, n. 166
Rejection of Jerusalem establishment. See: "Cult, Jerusalem."
of regulations by enemies of the sect, 24, 40, 52
See also: "Men of iniquity."
of views of outsiders, 71
Relations, with pagans, 5
between sexes, 5
sexual, 46
Reproof, 47
Return, period of the, 10, 19, 20, 34, 105 n. 138
Revelation (divinely-inspired exegesis). See: "Exegesis, sectarian."
Revelation, progressive, 25-7, 75, 76, n. 347. See also: "Exegesis, sectarian," "Law, progressive change."
Roster, 66-8, 70
Rule of Benedictions, 6
Rule of the Community, 5-6
Rule Scroll, 5
Ruth, 105

Sabbath, 5, 24, 35
Activities: Aiding in delivery of a domesticated animal, 102
Attending house of study, 97
synagogue, 95, n. 69, 96-7
Baking or cooking, 98-9
Bathing, 102-3
Breaking pottery jars, 116
pottery seals, 115-16, n. 210-11, n. 213
Carrying adults from domain to domain, 127-8 n. 295
a child able to walk, 119-20
from communal dwellings in an enclosed domain, 115
in the courtyard, 114 n. 201
from domain to domain, 94 n. 64, 101, 112 n. 182, 113-15, 117 n. 216, 119 n. 234, 120, 132
infants, children unable to walk, 119-20, 132
in the public domain, 94 n. 64, 101, 103, 112 n. 182, 117, 132
See also: "Domain, public."
on the shoulder, 114
into and from a *sukkah*, 115
Circumcision, 130-1, n. 316
Cleanliness, 107 n. 156
of garments, 106-9, 132
Clothes washing in preparation for the Sabbath on Thursday, 108 n. 159
Commercial transactions, 125, 132
Declaring private property available for communal use, 110
Delivering domesticated animals, 121, 132
Destruction, 116
Discussion of business, 87, n. 24, 88-9, n. 31, 90, 110, 132
Disputing about money, 87, 89
Division of spoils, 107 n. 156
Drawing water, 102-3, 132
Drinking on a journey, 102-4, 132

in public or private domain, 103
Driving animals, 112
Eating and drinking within the camp, 101, 132
food not brought into the camp before the Sabbath, 101
fruits fallen from the tree on the Sabbath, 100-1
lying in the field decaying, 98, n. 91, 100-1
before noon, 110
three or four meals, 111
Encouraging a servant to labor, 120-1
Entering a partnership, 109, 132
Establishment of a partnership of domain (Sabbath camp) with a non-Jew, 124
of technical residence for the Sabbath near gentiles, 124
Fasting, 110, n. 172, n. 173, 111, n. 179, 132
Feeding a domesticated animal trapped in a pit, cistern, or well, 122
Fending off attack in case of mortal danger, 125, 127
Fighting, 79
Going out with bandages or medicines in the mouth, 117
Handling, 119 n. 234
of animals, 112
of dust on the floor of the house, 118
of items not in use on the Sabbath, 118-19.
of pebbles, 118
of rocks and earth, 117-19, 132
of vessels or tools, 118
Helping a child to walk in the public domain, 119
a non-Jew prepare for a journey which might extend into the Sabbath, 123
Hunting, trapping, killing animals, 112, 113 n. 189
Instructing a non-Jew to perform labor, 105-6, 121, 132
Judgment, 89
Keeping animals in house, 112-13
Kindling fires, 99
Leaving one's bed, 97
one's dwelling place, 95
the house, 95, n. 69, 96-8
on a journey, 95
at nightfall, 90
Lending, 87-9
Litigation, 89 n. 31
Offering sacrifices, 128-32
ʿolah, 128-9, 131-2
paschal sacrifice, 129, n. 304, 130
tamid, 129, 131
Opening pottery vessels, 116 n. 211
Pasturing of animals, 91-3, 111-13, 132
Performance of work by a non-Jew (slave, servant), 104-6, 120-1
Placing of cushions so as to aid a domesticated animal trapped in a cistern, pit, or well, 122
Planning work of following day, 87, 89-91, 132
Plucking of fruit to save it from damage, 99
Preparing before the Sabbath, anything used on the Sabbath, 119, 132
food, 98-101, 132
offerings, 131
Purity and purification, ritual, 107, n. 156, 108, 123
ritual immersion, 102-3
Pushing an escaped animal from the public into the private domain, 112-13
Rescuing a domesticated animal trapped in a pit, cistern, or well 122, 132
a human being from a reservoir, 125-8
Riding, 95
Saving human life. See: "Sabbath, violating of Sabbath."
property from destruction. See: "Sabbath, violating Sabbath."
Silence, 89, n. 38
Sitting on a gentile's chair, 123 n. 260
Socializing (with Jews), 109-10 n. 167
with non-Jews, 123
Spending the Sabbath in the vicinity of gentiles, 100, 105-6, 110 n. 167, 120, 123-4, 132
Striking an animal, 111-12, 113 n. 189
Swearing or cursing, 120 n. 241
Tearing of skin coverings on wine jars, 116 n. 213

Touching of *muqṣeh*, 112 n. 187
See: "Sabbath, handling."
Tying up of animals on Friday, 97
Using that which has been brought by a non-Jew from outside the Sabbath limit, 100
Violating of Sabbath, 78, 86, 89, 98, 106, 118
for the sake of an animal, 126
human life, 124-7, 132
wealth, property, 124-6, 132
Walking in the field, 90, 132
Wearing of perfume bottles, 116-17, 132
Work performed by a non-Jew, 121
Working of animals, 112
Sabbath, beginning and ending of, 77, 84, n. 1, 85, n. 6-7, 86, 131
Code, 77-133. See various activities listed under "Sabbath, Activities."
formulation and organization, 3, 80-3, 107 n. 155, 111
laws of, 3, 9, 24, 45, 76 n. 347. See also: "Falashas," "Josephus," "Jubilees," "Philo," "Sabbath, Activities."
limit (*teḥum Shabbat*) (1000, 2000 cubit limits), 90-2, n. 47, 93, 94, n. 64, 95-6, 98, 112, 124, 132-3
liturgy, 78-9, 84 n. 1
Sabbatical year, 79-80, n. 23
Sacrifices, laws of, 127 n. 294, 130 n. 306. See also: "Offerings," "Cult."
Sacrifice, paschal, 129-31
Sadducees, 10, 18, 32, 97, 114, n. 201, 126 n. 282, 129 n. 303, n. 304, 135
Sahl ben Maṣliaḥ, 123
St. Stephen's Gate, 96
Samaritans, 1, 17-18, 96-7, 103, 110 n. 172, 123, n. 262, 130, 131 n. 316
Satrap, 67
Scapegoat, 95
Scribal practices, 30 n. 54-5, 30-1 n. 61, 48 n. 176, 50 n. 192, 66 n. 292, 69 n. 309, 87 n. 22, 91 n. 46, 94 n. 65, 106 n. 148, 114 n. 197, 115 n. 208, 116 n. 216, 124 n. 269
laws of, 9, 13
Sealed Book of the Law, 30
Seating in *moshab*. See: "Voting order."
Second Commonwealth, 10, 18-21, 34, 47, 79, 92 n. 47, 95-6, 105, 117, 129-30
Sect, readmittance to, 58, 67, 78
requirements for joining, 22-3, 27, 35, 69, 129
Sects, Jewish, 13, 17-20, 126, 134
Seminal emission, 102
Servants, servitude, 120, n. 241, 121, n. 243, 123, 132
Session (for exegesis), 76
Shammai, Shammaites, 96, 102, 103 n. 124, 106
Soferim, tractate, 13-14
Solomon, 73, n. 334, 74
Soqotri, 61
Spices, 108, n. 157, 109
Subject organization, 82-3, n. 40
Sukkah, 31
booths for watchmen, harvest, or Day of Atonement, 95-6, 114 n. 197
Philo, 32 n. 69
Tabernacles, 95-6, 113-14 n. 196, n. 197, 115
Susanna, 10
Synonymous variants, 59, n. 248
Synonyms in construct, 52 n. 208, 210, 65 n. 285
Syriac, 44 n. 143, 53, 128 n. 241

Tabernacles, 8, 114 n. 197, 115
Talmud, Babylonian, 15, 88, 102, n. 122, 111, 122, n. 250
Palestinian, 14-16, 102 n. 122, 112 n. 187
Talmudic period, 134
Tamid offering. See: "Offering, daily."
Tannaim, tannaitic law, tannaitic Judaism, 13-16, 21 n. 81, 28 n. 45, 36-7, 52, 66 n. 290, 82, 88-9, 91, 92 n. 47, 94, 98-101, 105, n. 140, 107 n. 156, 108-9, 112, n. 184, 113, 116-19, 121-23, 127, n. 295, 129, 130 n. 312, 132, 134
Targumim, Targum, 64, 89-90, 119 n. 233
Teacher, sect's leader, 42-3
Te'ezaza Sanbat, 19, 89, 95, 103, 110 n. 172, 120 n. 241
Temple, building of, description, 8
Temple Scroll, 8-9, 78, 93
Ten Commandments, 11, 86
Testament of Levi, 60-1, 64
Testimony, law of, 92
Tetragrammaton, 128 n. 297

Tithes, laws of, 5
Theology, sectarian, 7
Tobit, 10
Tosefta, 14, 114 n. 196. 122 n. 250
Traditions of the fathers, 133
Trumpet, sounding of, 86-7, n. 18

Ugaritic, 29 n. 51
ʿUkbari, Mishawayh al-, 131
Ushan period, 21 n. 81

Violation of commandments, 29, 49, 58. Of Sabbath, see: "Sabbath, Activities: violating of Sabbath."
of "ritual" law, 88
Voting, 76
order, 66 n. 290, 67-9
Vowel assimilation, 46, n. 155
Vulgate, 128 n. 297

War Scroll (*War of the Sons of Light against the Sons of Darkness*) (DSW), 6-8, 53, 61-4, 79, 93
Washing before prayer, 102 n. 119
Watercourse, 95 n. 70
Water sources, 127 n. 295. See: "Sabbath, drawing water."
Wisdom literature, 81, 87 n. 23, 90
schools, 55
Worship, non-Israelite, 73, 75
Written Law, 76
transmission, 76

Yavnean period, 20-1, n. 81

Zadok, 73-4
Zadokite Fragments (CDC), 1, 2, 4, 5, 8, 11, 25 n. 28, 30 n. 61, 36, 38, 45-7, 49, 50, n. 192, 58, 60-1, 66, 68-9, 78, 80, 82, 85, n. 7, 88, n. 27, 89 n. 38, 90, 93, 105, 113, 115, 116 n. 210, 125, 134, 135
Zadokites, Zadokite priests, Sons of Zadok, 2, 6, 22, 24 n. 18, 30, 38, 60, 70-73, n. 334, 74-5 n. 345, 76, 82. See also: "Hilkiah the Zadokite."
Zealots, 2